How Shelter Pets are Brokered for Experimentation

How Shelter Pets are Brokered for Experimentation

Understanding Pound Seizure

Allie Phillips

ROWMAN & LITTLEFIELD PUBLISHERS, INC.
Lanham • Boulder • New York • Toronto • Plymouth, UK

Published by Rowman & Littlefield Publishers, Inc.
A wholly owned subsidiary of The Rowman & Littlefield Publishing Group, Inc.
4501 Forbes Boulevard, Suite 200, Lanham, Maryland 20706
http://www.rowmanlittlefield.com

Estover Road, Plymouth PL6 7PY, United Kingdom

British Library Cataloguing in Publication Information Available

Library of Congress Cataloging-in-Publication Data

Phillips, Allie, 1966–
  How shelter pets are brokered for experimentation : understanding pound seizure / Allie Phillips.
      p. cm.
  Includes bibliographical references.
  ISBN 978-1-4422-0211-5 (cloth : alk. paper) — ISBN 978-1-4422-0213-9 (electronic)
  1. Animal welfare—Moral and ethical aspects. 2. Animal shelters. 3. Laboratory animals. I. Title.
  HV4765.M53P45 2010
  179'.4—dc22   2010006261

∞ ™ The paper used in this publication meets the minimum requirements of American National Standard for Information Sciences—Permanence of Paper for Printed Library Materials, ANSI/NISO Z39.48-1992.

Printed in the United States of America

This book is dedicated to Lilac, a tiny pale tortoiseshell cat with large almond-shaped green eyes, who was snatched out of my arms, and away from her three-month-old baby, Linus, on June 10, 2001, by a Class B dealer and transported to an unknown destination and an unknown fate. Regardless of what research experiments were inflicted on Lilac, her life did not end in vain as she inspired in me the passion to dedicate my life to eradicating pound seizure in the United States. This book is dedicated in her memory and her honor, along with the hundreds of other pets that I knew that were sacrificed in the name of research and education. It is also in honor of all the men and women who spend countless hours, tears, and sleepless nights attempting to rescue and re-home cats and dogs from shelters that practice pound seizure. Your efforts are not in vain, and the pets will never be forgotten.

Contents

Part III TAKING ACTION

Acknowledgments

I would like to extend my deepest gratitude to the following individuals and organizations for their help with information, advice, and support during the production of this book:

- Claire Gerus, my literary agent, who believed in me and this book;
- Suzanne Staszak-Silva, my editor, who guided me every step of the way;
- American Humane Association, particularly Tracy Coppola, legislative analyst, for their expertise and supporting me through this process;
- Dr. Robert Willems with the USDA whose expertise and knowledge about the inner workings of Class B dealers were invaluable for this book;
- American Anti-Vivisection Society, particularly Sue Leary and Vicki Katrinak, for their tenaciousness to end pound seizure and animal experimentation;
- Physicians Committee for Responsible Medicine, particularly Dr. John Pippin for his extensive knowledge and advocacy for animals;
- Holly Sauvé, a loyal friend and former volunteer with Friends of Ingham County Animal Shelter, now heading Voiceless-MI to raise awareness and stop pound seizure in Michigan;
- Mike Severino for leading the charge within the Ingham County Commissioners to end pound seizure;
- Judy Dynnik and Jackson County Citizens against Pound Seizure for their successful campaign to stop pound seizure in Jackson County, Michigan;

- Judy Oisten for sharing information from her successful campaign to stop pound seizure in Eaton County, Michigan;
- Sandy Carlton and Frances Schuleit for never giving up on the animals in Montcalm County, Michigan, and successfully being a part of the pound seizure ban;
- Cynthia Armstrong, the Oklahoma state director for the Humane Society of the United States, for her constant advocacy;
- Amy Draeger, Minnesota attorney for spearheading the legislative effort to ban pound seizure in Minnesota;
- Anne Davis, who is still fighting to stop pound seizure in Utah;
- The Oceanside Bed and Breakfast in Scituate, Massachusetts, for graciously hosting me for three days during Thanksgiving 2009 as I wrote a large portion of this book;
- And most important, to my parents, friends, and kitties, Oscar, Lucy, and Sammy, for supporting me as I continue to advocate on a very emotional topic.

"Never doubt that a small group of thoughtfully committed citizens can change the world; indeed, it's the only thing that ever has."

—Margaret Mead.

Part I

DISCOVERING THE SECRET

CHAPTER 1

Introduction

Why am I writing a book exposing the secret world of pound seizure? The reasons are numerous and emotional. I have been an advocate against pound seizure since 2000 and have celebrated numerous successes in protecting thousands of shelter animals from this outdated and barbaric practice. But the success has not been complete. I have suffered years of sleepless nights worrying about the shelter animals in the path of pound seizure, and those already lost. I have been threatened, faced with intimidation tactics, and even had my chosen career forcibly stripped from me all because I was using my voice to speak up for those that could not and to stop a practice that communities do not support.

I grew up in Owosso, a small town in mid-Michigan, surrounded by family and various animals. I always found animals had a keen ability to listen and understand humans, especially when life was difficult or stressful. So it is no surprise to those who know me that I began volunteering at an animal control shelter when I was in the thick of my career as a criminal prosecutor, and that my career steered me toward becoming an animal advocate.

Being a prosecutor was certainly my calling, as was helping animals. After my first year in law school, I knew I was meant to be a prosecutor. I thrived on being in control of my own court docket, caseload, and courtroom. I became an assistant prosecutor in 1995, quickly rose through the ranks of the office to a felony-case assignment, and was given sensitive and difficult cases to handle. The day-to-day toll of handling cases of despicable acts of inhumanity and encountering the worst behavior imaginable started to alter my once trusting personality. After five years, I no longer recognized the person staring back at me in the mirror. My smile was not genuine, my eyes had sadness around the edges, my heart felt dull, and my feelings about the world had turned cynical. Anyone who knew me as a child would not have recognized the person I had become. Progress and success in my career had taken its toll on my spirit. So I decided to get back in touch with my sensitive side and volunteer to help animals. How could anyone be cynical and sad when surrounded by animals, especially homeless animals that simply wanted to be hugged and loved? That happened in January 2000, and I had no idea the life-altering impact such a move would have on my life, or the life of thousands of animals thereafter.

When I started volunteering at the local animal control shelter I was unaware of the concept of pound seizure, or that the shelter I was providing volunteer services to was engaging in this practice. I quickly learned that the shelter had a high euthanasia rate and that a small group of volunteers were dedicated to reducing that rate. Approximately 4,000 animals arrived at the shelter each year, of which only about 400 animals were placed in adoptive homes. The remainder were euthanized or sold for experimentation. The volunteers banded together to form a 501(c)(3) nonprofit organization. We were organized and determined to get as many shelter animals safely into homes, and to make the shelter a better place for animals and humans. We were creative and immediately successful at increasing the adoption rate. Our success, however, was not met with enthusiasm by the staff or shelter director.

I was the volunteer in charge of the shelter cats. I kept a log of all the cats and made a list of the cats that were available for adoption; that is, those that had been at the shelter the longest (and therefore had the least amount of time left). I took photographs of the cats, created a website to showcase both cats and dogs, helped raise money for our advertising efforts and veterinary costs, and even started fostering cats and kittens at my house that needed to be removed from the shelter in order to survive. I would also arrange for other animal groups to rescue cats from the shelter before their time ran out. For me, every animal that made it out of the shelter alive was a miracle. The shelter staff did not make our work easy and often went out of their way to thwart our efforts. I wondered why and soon began to realize why the shelter was not encouraging more rescues and adoptions of the shelter cats and dogs.

When an animal "went missing" the shelter staff was hesitant and often downright resistant to answering our questions. Euthanasia at the shelter occurred daily and during the summer months in high numbers. It was terrible to learn that a pet that I had worked with had been euthanized, primarily due to overcrowding, after I had exerted efforts to find him or her a home. It was terrible to watch the euthanasia technician smirk at the volunteers as he would come into the kennel area and ask, "Who gets to die today?" One time he strolled around the shelter in front of visitors and volunteers with a wheelbarrow of dead animals and all the while whistling. It was ironic that I chose this so-called environment of inhumanity to help me get back in touch with my genuineness. It made me angry and seemed to contradict why I was there. But once you start helping shelter animals, there is no turning back.

It was upsetting to learn that a pet that I and my fellow volunteers had worked to save had been euthanized, but it was even more disturbing when the shelter staff refused to provide us with information on the disposition of the animals so that our records and website would be accurate. The shelter staff's negative reactions to our inquiries seemed odd and suspicious. Once I learned about pound seizure, however, their behavior became understandable since they were attempting to keep the process "under the radar."

Two months into my volunteer service, I adopted my Flame Point Siamese cat, Sammy. He had sat in a cage in a room full of dogs for more than six weeks. He had beautiful crystal blue eyes, was already neutered (which meant he had come from a home), and was friendly and docile. He always "talked" to me when I visited so I was surprised that no one had adopted him. His characteristic meow, which sounded more like the name "Monroe," caught my heart. I was further surprised that the shelter had kept him six weeks since many of the cats and dogs were only kept for the minimum hold period of either four or seven days under Michigan law.

As a shelter worker processed Sammy's adoption paperwork, he commented that Sammy was lucky because "the dealer was eyeing him." I had no idea what he meant and brushed off the comment. When I reflect back on that moment, I now know that the dealer was a U.S. Department of Agriculture (USDA) licensed Class B dealer, an animal broker who took the shelter cats and dogs and resold them for research.

Sammy is now twelve years old and spends his days seeking out a comfortable lap to curl up in and sleep. His nose drips when he is happy, and he has grown a bit deaf, resulting in more boisterous "Monroes." Over the years, I have learned that a docile personality like Sammy is what dealers seek since those animals will be easier to handle in the laboratory. They want former family pets, not feral or vicious animals that cannot be touched. It makes me shudder to think what fate could have awaited Sammy had I not adopted him.

In September 2000, about nine months into my volunteer service, five friendly and adoptable cats disappeared from the shelter's cat room. It was then that I learned of pound seizure. When I went to the shelter office to ask the staff about the whereabouts of the cats, one shelter worker quietly pulled me aside and told me about a Class B dealer who came to the shelter every week to take away the cats and dogs that were slated to be euthanized.

I recall feeling dizzy as I listened to the voice of the shelter staffer tell me about pound seizure—she sounded as if she were talking underwater. She told me of how the shelter allowed the dealer to pay ten dollars to take whatever cats and dogs he wanted that were slated for euthanasia. He would then resell them for a profit to research or training facilities. I could not process if what she was saying was true. It was as if I was hearing something out of a science fiction novel. Like most people, I had never heard of such a thing. I started to become sick to my stomach. Then I got angry.

Having this knowledge put the behavior of the shelter staff and director in context. I became more aware of the goings-on at the shelter. As evasiveness and miscommunication seemed to grow, I learned to put all communication in writing with the shelter director. When I discovered the cats being sold for research on that unforgettable September day, I sent an e-mail to the shelter director questioning why those cats were selected since they had an "adoption hold" placed on them by a volunteer, and all were scheduled to be advertised on the Pet Page in the local newspaper in two days. I requested that the cats be returned immediately. Within thirty minutes, I received an e-mail response from the shelter director claiming no knowledge of the rescue holds and attempting to put the blame back on the volunteers. I found that type of response typical. However, the paperwork procedure at the shelter was hardly the best organized system either. It simply involved a card-file method where shelter staff would staple a "rescue hold" notice to the animal's inventory card. We also had to rely on the shelter staff making these rescue notations on the animal's inventory card.

I could feel the rage rising up within me. I was appalled, in particular, by the dismissive behavior of the shelter director. I said a prayer that evening for all the animals sold for research: Brigette, a tiny black-and-white cat whose loud purr could be heard whenever I approached her cage; Wally, an outgoing brown tabby who liked to head-bonk visitors; Sinatra, the curious blue-eyed tiger with a soft meow; Bootsie, a huggable long-haired black kitty with white boots; and Hershey, a long-haired chocolate Maine Coon who loved to give kisses. For the dealers and researchers to label these as "throwaway cats" was unspeakable to me. I knew them, named them, and loved them.

Learning about the existence of pound seizure was a pivotal moment in my life. But it quickly became apparent that this topic was *verboten* at the shelter. When I asked questions regarding cats and dogs that "went missing," the shelter director's vague answers and stern looks to his staff told me that something was not right. What was the big secret? Why was the shelter staff being silenced? Was the community unaware of this? Why wasn't there a sign at the front counter advising people that the animal they dropped off might be sold for research? I had so many questions, and no one was providing any answers. Instead, the shelter director seemed to be retaliating against the pets if the volunteers, including myself, asked too many questions. Whether he was or not, it was an effective technique to euthanize a shelter pet or sell it for research purposes in an attempt to control or silence us. Those tactics never worked on me; instead, it empowered me to keep talking and keep gathering evidence.

As an attorney sworn to uphold the law and as a person who believed in the First Amendment right to freedom of speech, I was not going to go away or remain silent. When animals disappeared, I asked questions. When shelter staff seemed afraid to talk, I pursued the issue. If I did not receive sufficient answers, I did what any tax-paying citizen is entitled to do—I filed a Freedom of Information Act request with the shelter. Those requests required the shelter to provide documents to me that would answer my questions. Those documents eventually helped to expose the lies and wrongdoing. As we volunteers became increasingly inquisitive, we mobilized to get the animals removed from the shelter. My training as a prosecutor prepared me to stand firm, gather evidence, and speak loudly for these animals. And I did.

The most tragic and memorable incident occurred on June 10, 2001, while I was at the shelter during my lunch hour from work. I was spending time with a tortoiseshell cat named Lilac and her three-month-old black kitten, Linus. I had been working on finding a foster home or animal rescue organization to take Lilac and her son. I already had Winston, Tricks, and Tootsie, three shelter cats, in foster care at my home and simply did not have room for Lilac and Linus. I wrongfully thought they were safe because I had placed a "rescue hold" on both of them knowing I would have a foster home available that weekend.

On that day, I was cradling Lilac in my arms and reassuring her that I would have her and her son safely out of the shelter by that weekend when a man entered the cat room and took her out of my arms. At first I thought he was an adopter. But he had a cold and uncaring look in his eyes and did not handle her with the love and care of an adopter. When I inquired as to whether he was adopting Lilac, he said that she was being taken away to "save human lives." I immediately realized he was a Class B dealer.

I hurried to the shelter office and quickly explained to the staff that I wanted to rescue Lilac and Linus immediately. As I pulled out my wallet to pay the rescue fee (which was three times more than what the dealer had to pay), the shelter director came out of his office with a glib smirk on his face. He informed me that Lilac was not available for rescue. As I attempted to reason with him that he could earn thirty dollars in a rescue fee for Lilac and Linus versus ten dollars from the dealer for Lilac, he simply walked back to his office with a look of satisfaction on his face and shut the door. The shelter staff stood frozen, apparently unwilling to process the paperwork that would have saved them. I was aghast that the shelter was allowing a dealer to take priority over a rescue. I was dismayed that the shelter was turning down thirty dollars when it would only earn ten dollars from the dealer.

When I returned to the cat room a few minutes later, I found Linus alone in his cage. He was meowing insistently and visibly in distress that Lilac was gone. I never saw her again. The dealer must have taken her out the back door. I was sick to my stomach and did not have the energy to walk through the shelter to see what other pets were victims of the dealer. As I cuddled Linus with tears of rage streaming down my cheeks, I vowed to all the cats in that room that I would keep them safe and end pound seizure. I eventually kept both of those promises, including getting Linus safely out of the shelter the next day.

I was not able to save Lilac, and I have never forgotten that. I have dedicated myself since then to raising awareness regarding pound seizure so that other concerned citizens will rise up to ensure that shelters in their community do not engage in this outdated and inhumane practice.

This book is not about the legitimacy of animal research. Although a chapter will be devoted to some progressive research techniques that do not involve animals, the focus instead is on the betrayal of using former family pets as research objects. It will discuss the successful advocacy techniques that we used to stop pound seizure in June 2003 at the shelter where I volunteered. That started a chain reaction of other successful pound seizure campaigns; as of late 2009 only two shelters in the entire state of Michigan practice pound seizure. Subsequent chapters will describe the casualties along the way, including how I sacrificed my career as a prosecutor in order to continue down the path of truth in exposing and stopping pound seizure in my community. Currently as the vice president of public policy for the American Humane Association, I oversaw and initiated legislative initiatives for the organization. In 2009, I drafted a bold and strong anti-pound seizure bill for Michigan. That legislative campaign will be described in detail in chapter 3. In that position, I assisted other states that struggle with pound seizure.

The practice of pound seizure turns a government-funded shelter into a pawn in the highly funded and controversial research industry. A recent undercover investigation shut down one highly profitable Class B dealer in Arkansas that brokered stolen pets for research. In spite of vehement claims from the research and medical communities that "random source animals" obtained from shelters are needed to cure life-threatening diseases, some scientists disagree with those bold and sweeping claims, and more states are passing legislation to prohibit pound seizure. Some states have mandated alternative forms of medical testing without using animals and to encourage universities to progress to advanced techniques of alternative testing methods. But the old-guard research community that fails to progress with advancing technology still believes that squirting shampoo in the eyes of a pet is a way to keep people safe. And too many shelters continue to prefer pound seizure rather than re-home pets.

This book has been painful to write, yet mainstream America needs to know about the practice of pound seizure. It will present the facts so that you, the reader, can decide and, due to the secrecy of this business, it will raise more questions than it can answer. But it is my hope that it will empower you into action.

Allie Phillips

CHAPTER 2

What Is Pound Seizure?

ANIMAL SHELTERS IN THE UNITED STATES

Municipal and government-funded animal shelters (commonly referred to as animal control shelters or "pounds") in the United States have two main duties. The primary duty is to enforce state and local laws regarding animals. The secondary duty is, and should be, to humanely house homeless, abused, neglected, stray, and surrendered pets, usually cats and dogs, and adopt them into appropriate homes. The movement has begun to stop viewing an animal control shelter as a "pound" that simply rounds up unwanted pets and disposes of them, primarily through euthanasia.

Current shelter best practice, as endorsed by the National Animal Control Association, is that shelters should work with the community to locate adoptive homes for the animals, as well as upgrade facilities to provide compassionate housing for pets while providing a high quality of life and reducing disease transmission. Municipal shelters now recognize that the animals in their care are not "just animals," but are sentient beings protected from harm under the laws of all fifty states and, therefore, are entitled to humane and compassionate care while housed at a shelter. The Humane Society of the United States estimates there are between 4,000 and 6,000 animal shelters in the United States.[1]

Animal sheltering in the United States can be broken down into three basic categories: First, open-admission municipal shelters are found in most communities. These are the traditional animal control shelters that must take every animal that arrives on its doorstep, sometimes including wildlife and feral animals. They are referred to as "open admission" because no animal is denied entrance. These shelters are commonly called animal control shelters because the shelter is established by local government and is responsible for controlling the pet population in their community and enforcing local animal control laws. These shelters tend to have high euthanasia rates and few resources. The Michigan shelter where I volunteered for many years is an open-admission municipal shelter.

It is unknown how many open-admission animal shelters exist in the United States since national data on shelters and animals is not maintained. Although many animal control shelters and agencies still use the name—which implies they are duty bound to control animals for the benefit of the human population—there has been a move to reframe the concept toward "animal care and control." Such terminology implies that the shelter must care for the animals, not simply warehouse them until disposal.

The second type of shelter is a limited-admission shelter that is often privately owned and, thus, not government funded. They are frequently called "humane societies" or "SPCAs," even if they are not specifically associated with the Society for the Prevention of Cruelty to Animals. And some are deemed "no-kill" shelters since the shelter can limit the number and type of animals it will admit and, therefore, can ensure that no pet is euthanized due to overcrowding. These shelters are often supported through private donations or grants and have the resources to provide exceptional care and housing for the pets until an adoptive home can be found. One such limited-admission shelter is King Street Cats in Alexandria, Virginia. This shelter rescues approximately 250 cats and kittens each year and accepts cats that often would not fare well in a traditional shelter, such as pregnant and nursing cats, orphaned infant kittens that need bottle feeding, elderly cats, sick and injured cats, and cats with behavior issues or emotional trauma. King Street Cats frequently receives calls from open-admission shelters requesting rescue assistance for a cat or kitten whose time is up or that the shelter is unable to care for. King Street Cats also rescues stray cats and accepts owner-surrendered cats. No cat or kitten is ever euthanized at King Street Cats due to overcrowding or behavioral issues that may make adoption efforts difficult. Cats are allowed to live at King Street Cats as long as it takes to find a suitable adoptable home.

The third type of animal shelter is an animal rescue organization that is frequently formed as a nonprofit charitable organization. These organizations are created because citizens want to help animals in their community. They may rescue animals from the open-admission animal control shelter before the animal is euthanized or sold for research. Animal rescue organizations usually do not have a shelter; instead, they often house pets in foster care situations in volunteer homes or through adopt-a-pet programs at local pet stores. Although there are no statistics on the number of animal rescue organizations in the United States, there are estimated to be more than 10,000. The Petfinder website,[2] which is frequently used by shelters and rescue groups to post animals for adoption, lists more than 14,000 participating shelters and rescue organizations.

Limited-admission shelters, no-kill shelters, and animal rescue organizations have proliferated over the past decade. They often provide relief to overburdened municipal animal control shelters. Citizens who find stray animals or need to surrender their own pet to a shelter often gravitate toward a no-kill shelter or a rescue organization so that they have the peace of mind in knowing that the pet will not be euthanized solely due to lack of space or due to behavioral issues, which is too often the case with a municipal animal shelter. It is these organizations that often are thrust into campaigns to stop pound seizure at shelters.

Progressive shelters, including many open-admission animal control shelters, are now engaging in community outreach efforts to reduce the pet overpopulation problem and increase pet adoptions. It is estimated that at least four million shelter animals per year are euthanized.[3] That is approximately 11,000 shelter animals euthanized each day. These progressive shelters are working to reduce the number by creating volunteer programs where individuals assist the shelter in cleaning cages, feeding the pets, bathing animals, walking dogs, brushing cats, and providing extra care to frightened or ill animals. The shelters are rebuilding facilities to ensure that the housing is sensitive to the various species of animals in their care. There are efforts to maintain appropriate housing for all animals, including the creation of cat-only rooms with spacious cages where cats are free to jump and climb or free-roaming rooms, dog runs with access to a secure outdoor run, bird rooms with plenty of perches, and quiet rooms for potential adopters to meet privately with a pet. Shelters are also creating foster care programs where volunteers can take pets into their home and care for the pet until an adoptive home is found or it is appropriate to be returned to the shelter to be adopted. This is especially popular when dealing with pregnant cats and dogs and their newborn offspring.

Additional efforts made by progressive shelters include increased marketing and public relations, fund-raising events, open houses, and attending other community events to promote the adoption of the shelter pets and to educate the community regarding issues such as spaying and neutering, microchip identification of animals, and proper animal care. These progressive shelters may even establish low-cost spay-neuter and vaccination clinics to assist the community. It is these shelters that overwhelmingly do not engage in pound seizure, unless mandated by law, because they have taken that extra step to understand the importance of caring for homeless and maltreated pets until a new home can be found. They understand the contradiction in selling a pet to research and betraying the community that supports the shelter.

Other shelters are not up to par with the progressive shelters. These shelters are outdated, run-down, and in need of repairs. They refuse the assistance of volunteers, do not photograph the animals for placement on an adoption website, do not engage in fund-raising events, provide minimal, if any, medical treatment to animals, and make it inconvenient for the public to come to the shelter to view animals. The shelters are often insufficiently funded by their local government, yet do not take the step toward raising funds or permitting volunteers to help. The shelters are depressing to enter and, therefore, deter most people from coming in to view the animals. The animals are warehoused in small and dirty cages, provided whatever pet food the shelter has that day, food and water bowls are filthy, and pets are not given any comforts such as a blanket to lie on or a toy to play with. The pets are rarely, if ever, stroked, walked, or shown any form of comfort or kindness. Sometimes these animals lie in their own filth, and their cage is hosed down while they are still in the cage. Some of these shelters euthanize the animals en masse in carbon monoxide or dioxide gas chambers, rather than individualized injection, and some shelters may even shoot animals. The animals are traditionally held for the minimum time period established by law, usually just a few days, and then are disposed of. Yet, it is these animals that most need help. This type of shelter is also the most likely to engage in pound seizure.

In the 1940s, pound seizure became a common practice in taxpayer-funded animal shelters across the country and resulted in numerous state laws requiring the practice. Pound seizure, sometimes called pound release, involves a shelter selling or giving away cats and dogs to Class B dealers, random source animal brokers licensed by the U.S. Department of Agriculture, who then resell the animals for research and experimentation. It also involves shelters providing animals directly to research laboratories or university training programs.

Many pound seizure laws were enacted as a reaction to the expanding pet overpopulation problem and a desire to use unwanted animals for research rather than to breed more animals for research. In essence, why euthanize an animal if that animal could be used in research to help better the lives of humans and animals? Minnesota was the first state to pass a law requiring pound seizure in 1949.

At that time, there were no laws governing the protection of animals in research facilities. However, after a Dalmatian was stolen, sent to a research laboratory, and killed, the Laboratory Animal Welfare Act became federal law in 1966 (it is now known as the Animal Welfare Act [AWA]).

If allowed by state law, research facilities, such as local universities with research departments or private research laboratories, are able to directly obtain cats and dogs from shelters. Class B dealers will also canvass the shelters for cats and dogs that prescribe to orders from research facilities. Some B dealers obtain shelter pets for free, but some shelters charge a nominal fee, if allowed by law. Some B dealers contract with a shelter to obtain animals for free in exchange for the dealer performing other services to the shelter, such as carbon dioxide gas barrel euthanasia.

In Michigan, state law sets the maximum fee at $10 for a Class B dealer or research facility to obtain an animal. In my experience, the fee received by a shelter from a person adopting or rescuing a pet was much higher than that received from a Class B dealer. Thus, it was not in the shelter's financial interest to offer up animals to Class B dealers. Yet, what I encountered and continue to observe in some Michigan shelters is that the B dealers are preferred over rescue organizations.

It is unknown how many shelter animals are sold into the world of experimentation because accurate records are not available from many states. These former family pets are subjected to experimentation that often ends in death. The experimentation can be for cosmetic testing, human or animal drug testing, medical technique or tool testing, biochemical testing, and much more.

POUND SEIZURE PARTICIPANTS

Who are the players in the world of pound seizure? First, there are Class B dealers who are licensed by U.S. Department of Agriculture. Historically, the dealers have had little oversight into their activities due to the agency's restricted resources. They are licensed to buy, sell, or transport any animal that they did not breed or raise themselves. They are only allowed to obtain animals from other dealers, from animal shelters, or from people who breed and raise animals on their property. As described in chapter 5, the procurement of animals often takes place where random source B dealers (RSBDs) are cited for violating the law and where the issue of pet theft has been of concern to legislators.

Currently, there are 1,070 registered B dealers in the United States,[4] but only nine hold the title of "random source" B dealer, individuals who sell cats and dogs to research. Random source dealers broker live animals that are obtained, logically enough, from random sources. A random source animal is one not specifically bred for research and can legally include animals from shelters, from other random source B dealers, or from an individual who bred or raised the animal. Random source animals have also included stray animals, pets obtained from "free to good home" advertisements, and stolen animals; however, none of these latter means of obtaining animals are approved by the Animal Welfare Act.

Random source B dealers are required to keep records of all animals in their possession that show where the animal originated. In September 2008, because of documented concerns regarding the origination of random source animals, the USDA enhanced its policy to tighten its ability to conduct "trace backs" on the animals in the possession of a B dealer. In the 2008 policy, the USDA inspectors are required to conduct a trace back of randomly selected animals on the property of the B dealer at every on-site quarterly visit. Each random source B dealer will further go through a full trace back of all animals in the possession of the B dealer at one time in the first year of the enhanced policy. A trace back requires that the B dealer provide documentation that shows where the animal was obtained, all the way back to its original source. This trace back measure was instituted to prevent B dealers from obtaining stray animals or stolen animals.

"Bunchers" may have a Class B dealer license, but are generally unlicensed by the USDA, and their activities are difficult to trace. They are commonly known to be people who obtain pets from a variety of unapproved random sources, including "free to good home" pet advertisements, pets wandering the streets, and even some accounts of pets being stolen. The buncher either resells the pets to Class B dealers or to research facilities. This is a profit-driven career.

Whether a cat or dog is obtained by a buncher or a B dealer, they are labeled "random source animals" in the research business. These animals are most often family pets who lost their way and arrived, unfortunately, at a shelter that practiced pound seizure. They also include pets given up due to financial reasons or the death of the owner and pets removed from abusive or neglectful homes, puppy mills, dog fighting rings, or hoarding situations.

Additionally, the term "random source" clearly indicates that these animals do not originate from a known source such as a Class A dealer, a person who breeds animals specifically for scientific research. Class A dealers are licensed by the USDA to breed animals for commercial sales, some of which are then sold for research. Class A dealers who breed animals specifically for research provide scientists with animals that have attributes such as known genetic histories or random genes. (Class C dealers are licensed to exhibit animals, such as in circuses, zoos, and rodeos.)

Currently, Class B dealers are under no obligation to inform the public as to where they resell shelter pets. They are required to report their sales and clients to the USDA, but only then can the public file a Freedom of Information Act request and pay the fees associated with the request to obtain the records. The activities of B dealers are cloaked in secrecy and, even when specifically asked, they often refuse to disclose the names of their clients. I have frequently heard the claim that the shelter pets are sold for "life-saving medical research," such as cancer and AIDS research. Yet when asked to provide documentation to support such noble claims, no documentation has been provided.

In a speech before Michigan's Montcalm County Commissioners on January 26, 2009, a Class B dealer provided the following written statement in defense of why he should maintain his pound seizure contract with the county shelter.

Why release animals for research? Animals at the pound must be held for a period of 4 to 7 days. Animals released for research must be held according to Federal law a minimum of 7 days. In addition, R & R Research must hold the animal another 7 days to allow the owner to reclaim the animal. This allows families who have lost an animal an additional 1 day to acquire the animal which would have been euthanized, at no additional cost to the county. Animals used in medical research provide training in surgical techniques, development of new medicines and procedures. Dogs are primarily used for cardiovascular procedures and devices, bone, knee, joint and hip replacement, and older dogs are used for prostate research.

Cats are primarily used in neurological, AIDS, and Sudden Infant Death Syndrome research. Also consider the vaccines, wormers, cancer treatments, and, heartworm medications for your animals. None of these would be available without medical research. Can anyone name just one medical advance which was developed WITHOUT the use of animals? It is a fact that animals are raised exclusively for use in research, however, the cost to raise a dog or cat from birth is prohibitively more expensive than acquiring an animal which would otherwise be euthanized. Given the limited amount of financial resources and the fact that two animals will die instead of one, it simply makes sense to use pound animals. An animal is no longer considered a "pet" once ownership is relinquished, has not been properly cared for, or has failed to be reclaimed, rescued, or adopted.[5]

That dealer lost his contract with Montcalm County on August 1, 2009.

Pound seizure is a profitable business. Although bunchers generally conduct their business under the radar and may not be licensed or document the animals that they obtain and resell for research, Classs B dealers are required by the USDA to maintain records of the number of animals in their care and how much money they earned each year. The B dealer quoted above cited his 2007 gross income as $183,099[6] and his 2006 gross income as $196,272.73.[7]

In recent years, pound seizure has been on the decline. According to the USDA 2007 Fiscal Year Animal Care Annual Report of Activities,[8] the total number of dogs and cats used for research purposes in 2007 was 72,037 dogs and 22,687 cats[9] (these numbers do not differentiate between random source shelter cats and dogs and the cats and dogs bred for research). In 2007, there were a total of 1,027,450 animals used in research;[10] thus only 9 percent of research animals were cats and dogs. By contrast, in 1979, 211,104 dogs and 69,103 cats were used in research, comprising more than 15 percent of research animals.[11]

I believe the decline in pound seizure has occurred for two reasons: First, research and university training facilities are evolving toward non-animal research practices, including the use of computer-simulated and mannequin programs. And second, more shelters have specifically banned the practice of pound seizure, often due to public outcry or a recognition that pound seizure is contrary to the purpose of humanely sheltering animals.

A review of records from the state of Michigan, a state with a law that allows individual shelters to decide whether to engage in pound seizure, shows that pound seizure is on the decline. In 2004, 2,344 shelter cats and dogs were documented as being sold to research[12] whereas only 721 were documented in 2008.[13] In Michigan, I believe the decline is directly related to increasing public awareness and advocacy to end the practice.

The activities surrounding pound seizure are fraught with questionable conduct, and not just on the part of the B dealers. City and county officials, including animal shelter directors and staff, cling to this outdated and unwanted practice as if it were a lifeline. I have often wondered whether there was an incentive for community officials to be involved in pound seizure, but have not been able to obtain documentation to prove my suspicions. Accounts in chapter 11 will detail some of the activities of local government to maintain a grasp on pound seizure at any cost.

CHAPTER 3

Laws and Legislation on Pound Seizure

HISTORY OF PROTECTING RESEARCH ANIMALS

Pepper was a Dalmatian who loved car rides and enjoyed accompanying her "mom," a nurse, to work at a hospital in Allentown, Pennsylvania, and enjoyed mingling with the patients. In 1965, it was unimaginable that Pepper would be instrumental in the passage of the 1966 Laboratory Animal Welfare Act (renamed the Animal Welfare Act [AWA] in 1970) as a means to protect animals in research facilities and to curtail stolen pets from ending up in laboratories. Pepper's life and demise became a tipping point in American history in the protection of animals.

It all began on June 22, 1965. On that day, the lives of the Lakavage family from Slatington, Pennsylvania, changed forever. Pepper had been let out in the backyard that evening and a half hour later, she was gone without a trace. The Lakavages scoured the area searching for Pepper. Someone reported seeing a dog matching Pepper's description being loaded into the back of a truck near the Lakavage farm. That is when they knew she had not run away; instead, she had been stolen.

As detailed in a June 2009 exposé on pet theft on *Slate*,[1] an online website, pet snatching is not a recent phenomenon. Animal auctions, sometimes involving stolen pets, have gone on for decades. One particular auction in Lancaster County, Pennsylvania, took place in an Amish market with hundreds of animals being traded each week. Mrs. Lakavage attended this auction three days after Pepper's disappearance, but left empty-handed and disappointed. Pepper had already ended up with an animal dealer near the Pennsylvania-Maryland border, almost 200 miles from the Lakavages' home.

Five days after her disappearance, Pepper was then sold by the dealer to Bill Miller, who ran Broken Arrow Kennels in McConnellsburg. While transporting Pepper, eighteen other dogs, and a pair of goats, Miller was pulled over by the police. The officers wrote Miller two tickets, one for overloading the vehicle and the other for cruelty in transport, and confiscated the goats and all of the dogs, including Pepper. The animals were taken to a shelter. This should have been Pepper's lucky opportunity to be reunited with her family. However, Miller was allowed to return to the shelter to pay his fine and demonstrate that he had an appropriate transport truck and sales slips for the animals. The shelter reluctantly turned over the animals and later suspected that Miller had forged the sales slips. Fortuitously, Miller commented that the animals were going to a research holding facility in High Falls, New York.

Mr. Lakavage saw a newspaper article on the seizure of the animals, including the two female Dalmatians that were involved. Mrs. Lakavage immediately drove to High Falls, New York, in hopes of finding Pepper at the research holding facility. The owner of the facility was Arthur Nersesian, a retired New York City police officer whose compound was fenced off; alarms would sound when a car entered the driveway. He had even filed a multimillion dollar lawsuit against the New York SPCA for entering his property without permission. Clearly he did not want anyone to see what was taking place there. Knowing not to approach Nersesian alone, Mrs. Lakavage sought the help of the New York State Police. But there was nothing they could do to help her without any evidence that Pepper was on Nersesian's property. Once again, Mrs. Lakavage returned home empty-handed.

Pepper's story quickly made its way to influential people in Washington, D.C., including animal advocates and legislators. Congressman Joe Resnick from New York became involved and made a call to Nersesian, but Nersesian would not let Mrs. Lakavage enter his premises without a search warrant.

In order to obtain evidence that Pepper was on Nersesian's property, the police interviewed Bill Miller who stated that both Dalmatians were sold to Montefiore Hospital in the Bronx and were not taken to Nersesian's property. Desperate phone calls to the hospital were unsuccessful, though it was eventually confirmed that the hospital received two Dalmatians. As detailed in the *Slate* exposé, "On Friday [July 9], while Julia Lakavage was talking to the state troopers in Ulster County, her dog

Pepper was splayed out on an operating table in a large building on Gun Hill Road in the Bronx. Medical researchers had tried to implant her with an experimental cardiac pacemaker, but the procedure went awry, and she died. The dog's body had already been cremated."[2] Although Pepper is anointed with a badge for assisting in the creation of the current-day pacemaker, it is her saga of being stolen and transported across state lines, and in only a matter of days, that fueled a national debate over the theft of pets for medical research. This debate resulted in Congress passing the 1966 Laboratory Animal Welfare Act, now known as the Animal Welfare Act (AWA). The debate, however, still continues today.

The history surrounding the AWA is interesting in that Pepper's Law, HR 9743, resulted in more public discussion than two other socially important bills of the time: the Voting Rights Act and adding Medicare to the Social Security program. President Lyndon Johnson signed Pepper's Law on August 24, 1966. Before the AWA was enacted, pound seizure laws were already being passed in response to a growing shelter pet overpopulation problem and a demand for animals from researchers. The National Institutes of Health (NIH) were consolidated in 1944 and its budget rose from $2.8 million in 1945 to $1 billion in 1965. "That money was feeding a biomedical research establishment with an insatiable need for live animal subjects. To fill the empty cages in Bethesda, Md., and elsewhere, the NSMR [National Society for Medical Research] lobbied for the enactment of 'pound seizure' laws, allowing the forcible appropriation for research of any unclaimed strays that would otherwise be put to death. The first pound seizure laws were passed by the Minnesota state legislature in 1949, and many more followed. New York's Hatch-Metcalf Act allowed the seizure of cats and dogs not only from municipal pounds but from any private shelters holding government contracts."[3]

With the enactment of pound seizure laws in the 1940s, and the AWA still twenty years away from becoming law, the divisiveness and rhetoric between animal welfare and medical researchers grew proportionate to the emotions attached to each side's beliefs. Animal welfare advocates were determined to expose the cruelty and atrocities inflicted on laboratory animals, while medical researchers labeled anyone who opposed animal experimentation as "fanatics" or Communist sympathizers. What is interesting is that six decades later, these same tactics occur.

Dozens of laboratory animal welfare bills were filed in Congress during the 1950s and 1960s, though not one bill was successful, at least not until

Pepper's story reached Joe Resnick. At a legislative hearing for the Laboratory Animal Welfare Act in September 1965, Congressman Resnick made the intent of the bill clear to all who were listening. "This bill," he said, "is concerned entirely with the theft of dogs and cats, . . . and, to a somewhat lesser degrees, the indescribably filthy conditions in which they are kept by the dealer."[4] The steady movement of the medical research community was blocked by the simple intent of the bill, and the ordeal suffered by the Lakavages and Pepper changed the face of animal welfare forever.

The debate over pet theft and animal research continued into 1966 when *Life* magazine ran an eight-page photo essay titled "Concentration Camps for Dogs."[5] The Humane Society of the United States collaborated with *Life* to expose the condition of animals at a Maryland dealer's facility. As a result, the dealer was criminally charged with animal cruelty and eventually pled guilty and relinquished his license to deal animals. When the magazine was distributed to every member of Congress, lawmakers claimed they received more mail regarding Pepper and pet theft than they did on the Vietnam War.

Although subsequent amendments to the AWA extended the reach of protection to animals held in zoos and circuses, or held by pet dealers, and even resulted in a requirement to provide painkillers before and after experiments to animals, there still remains no federal protection for birds, mice, rats, fish, or cold-blooded animals. According to the American Anti-Vivisection Society (AAVS), it is estimated that more than 100 million animals are used in research annually[6] in the United States, and more than 95 percent of those laboratory animals fall into the category that is specifically excluded from the AWA and, therefore, receive no protection from the type and magnitude of experiments that await them.

According to the USDA, "In 2000, the federal government needed to estimate the number of rats, mice, and birds that would be included under a proposed revision to the Animal Welfare Act (AWA). They asked the Library of Congress via the United States Department of Agriculture's Animal Plant Health Inspection Service to make such a report. The report concluded that over 500 million animals would be added to the AWA if mice, rats, and birds were counted."[7]

During the fact finding of the congressionally created Committee on the Scientific and Humane Issues in the Use of Random Source Dogs and Cats in Research, it was confirmed that most research animals are "rodents," not covered by the AWA, and "a relatively small number are dogs and cats, most of which are either 'purposed-bred' specifically for research by licensed commercial breeders (known as Class A dealers), or bred and raised in research colonies."[8]

CURRENT-DAY PROTECTION OF SHELTER AND RESEARCH ANIMALS

The U.S. Department of Agriculture (USDA) is the sole enforcement authority of the AWA. Private citizens or animal welfare organizations do not have authority to bring legal action against offenders under the AWA. The USDA has stated that enforcement of the AWA is difficult due to limited resources to investigate claims. In 2007, USDA was appropriated $17,437,000 by Congress to enforce the AWA, yet that amount is not sufficient.[9] As will be discussed in chapter 5, a documentary from 2005 called *Dealing Dogs* was broadcast on HBO that exposed the practice of C. C. Baird, Class B dealer in Arkansas, who stole dogs and sold them for research. Other investigations, primarily conducted by undercover investigators from nonprofit nongovernmental organizations, have produced similar results. What these private undercover investigators have exposed demonstrates that the USDA has not been given the resources necessary to tackle the suspicious activities surrounding pound seizure.

The AWA and its related regulations are a comprehensive body of laws that currently extend its protection beyond the walls of research facilities. The AWA's original purpose was to protect animals used in research and to prevent stolen animals from arriving at laboratories.

The relevant statutes of the AWA, found in chapter 54 of the United States Code at 7 USC §2131–2159, and the AWA regulations located in the Code of Federal Regulations at 9 CFR Ch. 1 § 2.132 and 2.133, aim to protect shelter animals from pound seizure, as well as protect them after being seized from a shelter by a B dealer. The overall intent of these laws is to allow legal pet owners to reclaim their pet, whether that pet is located at a dealer facility or research facility. However in testing this premise, one Class B dealer did not return phone calls of anyone who had a pet at the facility. Therefore, the AWA is fallible and not fully able to protect pets and reunite them with their owners.

Section 2.132 of the regulations states that Class B dealers may only accept random source animals from other dealers licensed with the USDA, state, county, or city-run animal shelters, or private shelters registered with the state, and from individuals who breed and raise cats or dogs on their property. (See appendix A for complete language.) Class B dealers can also accept nonrandom source animals from breeders. In recent years four B dealers have been cited for accepting animals from improper sources or were unable to show legal documentation regarding the proper procurement of animals.

Section 2158(a)(1) of the AWA requires that an animal must remain at an animal shelter for a minimum of five days before being given to a dealer or research facility. This statute specifically states that the purpose of the law is "to enable such dog or cat to be recovered by its original owner or adopted by other individuals before [the animal shelter] sells such dog or cat to a dealer." (See appendix B for complete language.) As described in chapter 4, this time requirement has been ignored by some animal shelters that are associated with a B dealer. The intent of the law prefers returning pets to the legal owner or allowing an adoption, but it has frequently been thwarted by some shelters.

Section 2135 of the AWA gives animals another five days of holding at the dealer facility before the animal is resold to a laboratory. (See appendix B for complete language.) Section 2.132(c)(3) requires the dealer to hold the cat or dog ten days at the dealer facility, not including the day of acquisition or transportation days. These hold requirements were put in place to allow enough time for families to find their missing or stolen pets.

In addition to the AWA, policies apply to all federally-funded institutions that use animals in research. Since 1985 *The Public Health Service Policy on Humane Care and Use of Laboratory Animals* (PHS Policy) sets forth requirements involving animal research if federal funds are received. Specifically, the PHS Policy requires compliance with the AWA, the AWA regulations, and the National Research Council's *Guide for the Care and Use of Laboratory Animals* (the Guide).[10] The PHS policy also protects all vertebrate animals, whereas the AWA specifically excludes rats, mice and birds.[11] "The *Guide* promotes the humane care of animals used in biomedical research, teaching and testing. It provides guidelines on institutional policies and responsibilities, and performance-based standards for animal environment, housing, management, veterinary care, and physical plant."[12] The PHS policy and the Guide also mandate compliance with the *U.S. Government Principles for Utilization and Care of Vertebrate Animals Used in Testing, Research and Training.* These principles require researchers to justify the use of animals and to treat them humanely. Despite all these laws, regulations, and policies mandated for the treatment of animals in federally-funded laboratories, only the AWA and its related regulations relate to Class B dealers.

On March 10, 2009, I attended a meeting at the USDA where a new standard operating procedure was discussed. The procedure was instituted in September 2008 and established stricter guidelines on conducting trace backs. A trace back on a cat or dog in the possession of a Class B dealer requires that the USDA inspector review documentation that tracks the animal back to its original source of sale, and that the animal was received from a proper source under the Animal Welfare Act. For sellers that are Class B dealers or shelters, all trace backs by USDA inspectors must be conducted in person, not by telephone. We were informed that all nine live animal random source B dealers will endure one 100 percent trace back inspection within a year of the new procedure, and every year thereafter. In addition, every quarterly inspection now requires a trace back of anywhere from four to ten animals in the care at that time. Representatives from USDA commented that finding a trace back violation is like finding a needle in a haystack. Thus, when one is found, it is pretty serious and likely there are significantly more violations.

During a trace back, the USDA inspector reviews the Class B dealers' acquisition and disposition records to determine if all of these requirements are documented: "(1) The name and address of the person from whom a dog or cat was purchased; (2) The USDA license or registration number of the person if s/he is not USDA licensed; (3) The vehicle license number and state, and the driver's license number and state of the person, if s/he is not licensed; (4) The name and address of the person to whom a dog or cat was sold or given and that person's USDA license; (5) The date the dog or cat was acquired or disposed of; (6) The USDA tag number or tattoo assigned to the dog or cat; (7) A description of each dog or cat; (8) The method of transportation, including the name of the initial and intermediate handlers."[13] As outlined in the new standard operating procedure, if a person confirms selling a cat or dog to a dealer and claimed that the cat or dog was bred or raised on the property, the inspectors are required to look for evidence of a kennel on the property, or determine where the animal was raised, rather than simply take the seller's word.

Representatives at the meeting also discussed that the USDA is having problems with dealers changing identification numbers on animals when animals are transferred between dealers and research facilities. Thus, it is difficult to conduct a trace back. The USDA indicated it will be implementing a tracking number for all animals that stays with the animal for life.

Representatives of the USDA also stated that they are encountering situations where suppliers of animals to random source dealers are lying about being the "breeder" of the animal. The AWA requires that a person giving an animal to a B dealer must have bred and raised the animal. The USDA is struggling with closing that loophole. Not surprisingly, the audience at the meeting suggested eliminating the B dealers system altogether. Lastly, when asked how expensive it is for the USDA to oversee just nine dealers, which have the most extensive inspection requirements of any USDA licensee, all that was said was "it is expensive."

Dr. Robert Willems, assistant regional director, Eastern Region, for USDA/APHIS Animal Care, further explains USDA's role in overseeing random source animals:

> The system of supplying random source dogs and cats to research facilities through RSBDs [random source B dealers] is one that developed over the years as a result of the regulations regarding the acquisition of dogs and cats by research institutions contained in the Animal Welfare Act (AWA). Historically, this system of licensed and regulated animal dealers replaced the old system (or, more accurately, the non-system) of unlicensed and unregulated dealers that was in place before the passage of the AWA in 1966. At that time it was found that many of the dogs and cats being supplied for research by these unregulated dealers were in fact stolen pets. Unfortunately, the new system of licensed dealers—or RSBDs, as they came to be known—did not immediately eliminate the practice of stealing pets for resale to the research community. Even with USDA oversight of these RSBDs, the practice continued for some time, though at a diminishing rate.
>
> Individual inspectors trace dogs and cats sold to RSBDs to the persons selling them in an attempt to determine their legitimacy. Such tracebacks, as they came to be called, have resulted in the identification of a number of stolen pets, and aided in the successful prosecutions of the bunchers and dealers involved.
>
> In an attempt to finally put an end to the theft of pets for resale to research, in 1993, Animal Care instituted the formal traceback program currently in place to track dogs and cats sold to RSBDs to their source. In the ensuing years, the number of licensed RSBDs also began to decline. In 1990 there were approximately 150 such dealers licensed throughout the country. Today there are nine.

To my knowledge, no stolen pet has been found to have been sold to a research facility in many years. I believe that the original intent of the AWA—to prevent the sale of stolen pets for use in research—has been achieved, primarily through the efforts of the many individuals in USDA who have worked in this program over the years.[14]

Even with the AWA governing the procurement and sale of random source cats and dogs to research, and clearly prohibiting the brokering of stolen pets, it is well-known that there are too many loopholes in the law, and not enough resources for the USDA to properly administer the AWA.

STATE LAWS ON POUND SEIZURE

In 1983, Massachusetts was the first state to pass a law prohibiting pound seizure as a compromise between the New England Anti-Vivisection Society and research centers in an attempt to avoid the issue being placed on a referendum ballot the following year. The cause for concern was that the ballot language contained a provision that research centers would be regularly inspected by the society. The compromise resulted in a law that banned pound seizure within the state, but also banned the import of shelter animals from other states for research.[15]

As of 2009, a total of seventeen states plus the District of Columbia have passed laws to ban the practice of pound seizure: California, Connecticut, Delaware, Hawaii, Illinois, Maine, Maryland, Massachusetts, New Hampshire, New Jersey, New York, Pennsylvania, Rhode Island, South Carolina, Vermont, Virginia, and West Virginia.

Minnesota and Oklahoma have laws that mandate pound seizure. That means that if a dealer or research facility goes to a shelter looking for cats and dogs for research, the shelter has no legal authority to deny them access. An additional nine states—Arizona, Colorado, Iowa, Michigan, Ohio, South Dakota, Tennessee, Utah, and Wisconsin—have passed laws leaving the decision on pound seizure to the discretion of individual counties or shelters. The remaining twenty-two states have no law on pound seizure and, therefore, the practice is allowed.

Minnesota shelters have not actively practiced pound seizure since 2001, according to Amy Draeger, an attorney with the Minnesota Bar Association's Animal Law Section. Draeger is also spearheading a 2010 legislative bill to change the law to ban pound seizure.[16] According to

Draeger, a 1939 dognapping ring resulted in the creation of Minnesota's pound seizure law. The purpose of creating a pound seizure law is to ensure that only shelter animals be sold to research.

A Minnesota newspaper report from January 30, 1940, confirms that dognapping was at the root of creating a mandatory pound seizure law.

> W. T. Middlebrook, comptroller, yesterday suggested two methods by which the University [of Minnesota] could further protect itself against inadvertent purchase of stolen dogs for research work.
>
> The statement reviewed the recent "dog-napping" furor during which, said Mr. Middlebrook, there were "implications that a St. Paul dog-stealing ring was alleged to have sold hundreds of the animals to the University.
>
> "But since the recent Krueger incident hundreds of people have visited the animal rooms in Millard hall to see nearly 200 dogs and to date only three have been identified as stolen," he said.[17]

The Minnesota Board of Animal Health oversees pound seizure in the state. In 2009, Draeger received written confirmation from the board that only two institutions were registered to obtain random source animals: University of Minnesota and Argosy University.[18] However, the board confirmed that no random source animals have been obtained from Minnesota shelters since 2001. Thus, Minnesota's mandatory pound seizure law is a moot point and, what's more, is poised to be repealed as early as 2010. The City of St. Paul attempted to pass a resolution to ban pound seizure from the city shelter, but the mayor was legally unable to sign it in lieu of the state law. Instead, animals from the shelter sold for research now cost $217, according to Draeger.[19] On the other hand, Minneapolis passed a resolution banning pound seizure from its public animal shelter, and Pine City passed an ordinance against the practice.

Minnesota, like many states, still struggles with the beliefs of the research community that random source animals are needed, while also being home to one of the nine random source Class B dealers. Continuing with pound seizure's theme of secrecy is Draeger's belief that Minnesotans are not aware of the mandatory state law. In August 2009, I was hosting a child protection training course in Winona, Minnesota, and asked numerous attendees whether they knew that Minnesota was a mandatory pound seizure state. Not one person knew what pound seizure was, and all were surprised and concerned to learn of this taint on their state. Draeger says that people are outraged when they learn about this law.

Oklahoma's mandatory pound seizure law was passed in 1951. In speaking with Cynthia Armstrong, the Southwest Region director for the Humane Society of the United States, she shared some history on pound seizure in Oklahoma and efforts to repeal the law. In 1997, animal welfare advocates attempted to repeal the mandatory pound seizure law, without success. However, the law was changed during this time to allow municipalities to pass ordinances to opt out of the mandatory law. Oklahoma City and Tulsa have since passed anti-pound seizure ordinances. However, Armstrong is concerned that "these other cities are sitting ducks for pound seizure because they do not know about it."[20] In 2008, an attempt to expand the current mandatory pound seizure law was heard by the legislature in an effort to allow dead animal carcasses also to be available for research. According to Armstrong, the bill was defeated eleven to five in the Public Health Committee with no one testifying in favor of the bill except the bill sponsors. The driving force behind that bill was a deceased animal random source B dealer from California who had a contract with Oklahoma City. According to Armstrong, although the dealer's contract with Oklahoma City had expired, he had requested that Representative Phil Richardson file the 2008 bill.

In 2009 another attempt was made to expand the existing law and, this time around, the legislative sponsor was better prepared. The bill added the previous animal carcass language and further expanded to include a criminal penalty against shelter staff that refused to turn over live or dead animals for research. The state veterinarian testified in favor of expanding the bill, as did two deans from state veterinary schools. The vote was ten to ten, but did not pass out of the committee.

In early 2009, Madeleine Pickens, the wife of entrepreneur T. Boone Pickens, became aware of Oklahoma State University's (OSU) use of live animals in research through an anonymous student at the university's College of Veterinary Medicine. After being told that the animals underwent multiple invasive and surgical procedures, including breaking bones and removing organs, Mrs. Pickens asked that her $5 million donation to OSU be redirected away from animal research at the Center of Veterinary Health Sciences in Stillwater. Mrs. Pickens did not want the money supporting animal research.[21] In an interview with the *Tulsa World* newspaper, she stated, "I would be embarrassed to be associated with that kind of teaching or research at OSU or anywhere." The Pickenses have donated tens of millions of dollars to OSU and were prepared to pull all funding if the practice continued.

Dr. Michael Lorenz, dean of OSU, defended the practices and denied the allegations made by the anonymous student and Mrs. Pickens. In an article in the *Stillwater News Press* on April 17, 2009,[22] Dr. Lorenz stated, "There is nothing wrong with how we train students. It's about where we get dogs. I've visited people in the vet school and we believe it's ethical and morally permissible to use animals marked to die." At the time of the article, OSU contracted with Class B dealer Schachtele Auction Services from Missouri. Oklahoma State University also had a contract with Henry Lee Cooper of C & C Kennels, whose license was revoked by the USDA in August 2008 for a period of five years due to chronic and numerous violations of the AWA. Oklahoma State University eventually stopped using live animals in the surgery training classes and has since stated that it is working to stop purchasing animals from Class B dealers.[23]

Even though Oklahoma was home to Henry Lee Cooper, a random source Class B dealer whose license was suspended in 2008, Armstrong believes that out-of-state random source B dealers are entering the state to obtain random source cats and dogs from shelters. This is a concern because if a family loses a pet, that pet may be transported across state lines, thus prohibiting the owners from finding their pet. It is the likely scenario for a dog named Blue, who is believed to have been stolen from her backyard in Henrietta, Oklahoma, in February 2008 and has not been seen since. In the end, it is unknown how many Oklahoma shelter animals, or other random source animals, have been brokered to research facilities since the Oklahoma Department of Agriculture does not require the reporting of those statistics. And if animals were brokered to Missouri or other states, those numbers are even more difficult to obtain.

As for the remainder of the states, the laws are either silent on pound seizure, or leave the practice to the discretion of the individual counties and shelters. To better understand the extent to which pound seizure is practiced across the country, in late 2009 my office, the American Humane Association's Office of Public Policy, conducted a survey of the states that have discretionary laws on pound seizure. The results are described in chapter 10. What we found was intriguing.

CURRENT LEGISLATIVE ATTEMPTS TO BAN POUND SEIZURE AND CLASS B DEALERS

I am a registered federal lobbyist through my employment at the American Humane Association. In that position, I worked on the 2007 Pet

Safety and Protection Act (PSP Act) (HR 1280 and S 714) and currently the 2009 PSP Act (HR 3907 and S 1834), both filed by Representative Michael Doyle (PA) and Senator Daniel Akaka (HI). The PSP Act bill would prohibit any research facility, including federally funded research facilities, from accepting cats or dogs from Class B dealers. (See appendix B for bill language.) The bill only allows research facilities to accept cats and dogs from these sources: a dealer who has bred and raised the cat or dog (a Class A dealer); a publicly owned animal shelter so long as the cat or dog came from its legal owner; a person donating a cat or dog that has been bred and raised by the person or who has owned the cat or dog for at least one year; or another research facility. The bill does not allow any research facility to obtain a cat or dog from a Class B dealer.

The PSP Act has been filed during every congressional session since 1996, covering six House bills and seven Senate bills. Each time, the bill failed to receive a committee hearing and failed to progress to a vote. But in the 110th Congress in mid-2008, Senator Akaka and Representative Doyle made a bold move to include the PSP Act language in the 2008 reauthorization of the Farm Bill that was passed by the Senate and the House of Representatives. With the passage of the Farm Bill, the language of the PSP Act had made its furthest progression to end the practice of pound seizure by Class B dealers nationally. Support for the PSP Act had also grown throughout the years. In the PSP Act from 1996, there were 26 House cosponsors but no Senate cosponsors. Now, fast forward to 2008 where the bill received 130 House cosponsors and 19 Senate cosponsors.

The joy felt throughout the animal welfare community was palpable with the passage of the 2008 Farm Bill. However, during the conference process to settle differences between the House and Senate language of the Farm Bill, the language of the PSP Act was summarily removed and replaced with a request to the National Institutes of Health to conduct a study on the use of random source cats and dogs in research. It was incomprehensible that the votes of the full House and Senate could be undone in one swift political move. The process was undemocratic in the minds of many people. A staffer from a House office informed me that the language of the PSP Act was removed due to last-minute maneuvering by a federal research facility and one congressional leader in the conference committee. A discussion of the congressional study starts in chapter 6.

At the state level, I have known for years that Michigan was ripe to stop the practice of pound seizure. But timing is always important when filing legislation. An effort was made in 2003 with a state bill to ban the practice.

Senator Valde Garcia introduced the bill. However, it died in committee, and I later learned that an animal welfare lobbyist requested that it not receive a hearing. The reasons behind this move are still unknown.

In 2007, the Humane Society of the United States filed an anti-pound seizure bill in Michigan, but the bill sponsor soon stopped his advocacy due to confusion as to its purpose. I was worried that another pound seizure bill on the heels of a failed bill would be detrimental. For most of 2008, I consulted with local animal advocates, animal shelters, and even some opponents on the prospect for success of a legislative bill in the 2009–2010 legislative session. I drafted the bill language that included some essential exemptions, such as allowing a veterinary training school to obtain shelter cats and dogs for spay-neuter training, and to perform other medical procedures such as setting broken bones or treating diseases, but then return the cats and dogs to the shelter for adoption; and to allow shelter cats and dogs to go to a state blood bank facility where the pets are provided blood donations and then, if healthy and adoptable, they are placed for adoption. The intent of the new bill would still allow some practices that are technically considered pound seizure, yet permit those cats and dogs to be returned to the shelter to find a new home, rather than be euthanized.

After drafting the language, I was able to secure the endorsement of a prior opponent, the Animal Blood Resources International in Stockbridge, Michigan. I felt it was important to secure the support of Animal Blood Resources since it was a worthy opponent on the 2007 bill. I was also personally knowledgeable of the facility. During my time as a shelter volunteer in Michigan, staff from Animal Blood Resources would come to the shelter looking for cats and dogs that were universal blood donors. At the time, the euthanasia and pound seizure rate was still quite high, and I advocated for certain cats and dogs to go into the program. I knew that the cats and dogs would be treated very well, including being allowed to live normally with sufficient space and would be adopted at the end of the service. A colleague from the Michigan State Bar Animal Law Section adopted her cats, Malcolm and Maureen, from Animal Blood Services. Therefore, I felt confident in placing an exemption for blood bank collection services into the bill knowing that the animals were well cared for and placed for adoption afterward.

On March 19, 2009, Representative John Espinoza filed HB 4663, a bill for Michigan to become the eighteenth state to ban pound seizure. (See appendix B for the bill language.) The following day I was in Lansing, Michigan, to present at the Michigan State Bar Annual Animal Law Symposium along with Representative Espinoza. I met with the congressman to discuss the anticipated opposition to the bill; he was determined to remain strong and stop the practice.

In the ensuing months, I have once again witnessed the Class B dealers run amok with the same tired, unproven, and undocumented arguments to maintain their business. Michigan research facilities also have spoken out against the bill with statements that their research is entirely dependent on random source animals from Class B dealers. I expected those opponents to voice objections to the bill and was abundantly prepared to defeat their claims with documented evidence. What was most shocking was that the Michigan Veterinary Medical Association launched an active lobbying campaign to defeat the bill. I had naively believed that veterinarians were interested in protecting animals from harm. That may be true, but what I failed to recognize was that the American Veterinary Medical Association (AVMA), along with many state veterinary medical associations, supports the practice of pound seizure.

In the meantime, Representative Espinoza is standing firm on the bill, my office is pushing forward on the Michigan bill in spite of the veterinarian opposition, and we are working to garner the support of individual veterinarians who do not support pound seizure.

ANIMAL WELFARE'S POSITION ON POUND SEIZURE

Every national animal protection organization, and numerous state and local organizations and shelters, have created policy statements condemning the practice of pound seizure. The following are just some national and state animal welfare organizations that have called for an end to pound seizure and have position statements against the practice:

American Anti-Vivisection Society
American Humane Association
American Society for the Prevention of Cruelty to Animals
Animal Law Coalition
Arizona Humane Society
End Pound Seizure Minnesota
Georgia Humane Society

Idaho Humane Society
In Defense of Animals
Last Chance for Animals
Michigan Humane Society
Michigan State Bar Animal Law Section
National Animal Control Association
National Anti-Vivisection Society
Nevada Humane Society
New England Anti-Vivisection Society
No Kill Advocacy Center
People for the Ethical Treatment of Animals
Physicians Committee for Responsible Medicine
The Humane Society of the United States

The Colorado State University College of Veterinary Medicine and Biological Sciences created a policy against pound seizure which states:

> College policy prohibits the acquisition of live animals from shelters, either directly or indirectly through third party vendors, for use in research or teaching. The College recognizes that many individuals in our society are opposed, on ethical and scientific grounds, to the release of animals from shelters (pound seizure) for use in research or teaching. This objection is founded in the understanding that pounds or animal shelters were not designed as facilities to supply animals for such activities. Rather, they were developed to be places where people may bring unwanted or stray animals in the hope of a new home being found. If not successfully adopted, the animals may be euthanized. The release of these animals for research or teaching may be interpreted as a breach of the public trust that could lead to loss of public support.[24]

There are twenty-eight university veterinary schools in the United States.[25] According to the Humane Society Veterinary Medical Association,[26] the following twelve university veterinary schools also do not purchase random source dogs and cats from Class B dealers:

Colorado State University
Iowa State University
Kansas State University
Louisiana State University

Mississippi State University
University of California, Davis
University of Missouri
University of Pennsylvania
University of Wisconsin, Madison
Virginia-Maryland Regional College of Veterinary Medicine
Washington State University
Western University of Health Sciences

Almost half of the veterinary training schools in the United States have opted to not accept random source cats and dogs from Class B dealers. Yet, the American Veterinary Medical Association still maintains a position statement in favor of the use of random source dogs and cats:

The carefully controlled use of random-source dogs and cats contributes greatly to improving the health and welfare of both animals and human beings. Therefore, the AVMA believes there is ample justification for prudent and humane use of random-source dogs and cats in research, testing, and education, provided that:

- The institution conducting such research, testing, or education has met all legal requirements and guidelines pertaining to the acquisition, care, and use of dogs and cats for these purposes;
- The investigators have thoroughly examined the need for such dogs and cats, appropriately justified the use of the species, and carefully determined the minimum number required to meet the needs of the protocol;
- Adequate safeguards are used to ensure that only appropriately screened dogs and cats are obtained legally; and
- Preventive measures are taken to optimize the health of dogs and cats used in research, testing, and education.[27]

In the summer of 2009 at the AVMA Annual Convention, the AVMA House Advisory Committee submitted Resolution 2-2009, titled "Revise Policy on Use of Random-Source Dogs and Cats for Research, Testing, and Education." The resolution struck the prior language and sought to replace it with this language:

While the use of animals contributes to improving the health and welfare of both animals and human beings, the AVMA believes that no live dogs or cats shall be procured from an animal shelter, or a dealer who provides live animals from an animal shelter, for the purpose of such research, testing, and education (with the exception of dogs/cats which may be used by students in veterinary programs for harmless procedures).[28]

The rationale supporting the resolution stated, "The AVMA should not support a policy whereby animals who are abandoned, neglected, or simply lost are relocated to a research or testing facility instead of a loving home or, where necessary, humanely euthanized. The present AVMA policy on random-source use runs counter to the public's concept of an animal shelter and may impede the surrender of pets to such a facility."[29]

Unfortunately, the resolution was pulled from consideration, and reasons for the action have not been provided. However, the AVMA readdressed the issue on January 9, 2010, and altered its position statement with these additions:

- Class B dealers are used to obtain random-source dogs and cats only when viable alternatives do not exist; and
- Alternative sources are explored and supported that will ultimately eliminate the need for Class B dealers as a source for random-source dogs and cats used in search, testing, and education.[30]

In spite of the enactment of federal and state laws to protect animals in research and thwart the activity of stealing pets and selling them to research, the issue of pound seizure is still fraught with suspicion, and random source Class B dealers are still highly regulated and often cited for violations of the AWA. Thus, all companion animals are in jeopardy of being victims of pound seizure until the system is abolished.

CHAPTER 4

Betrayal of Trust
Why Pound Seizure Is a Secret

Animal shelters, principally government-funded municipal animal control shelters, are mainly established to enforce state and local laws regarding animals. This includes enforcing stray dog laws, investigating cruelty and neglect complaints, puppy mills, hoarding situations, dog fighting, and a host of other crimes against animals. Open-admission shelters are required to take in stray dogs and, if enough evidence exists, to seize and house animals that have been abused or neglected. However, it is these same animals that can end up in the van of a Class B dealer for resale to a research facility.

Many states do not keep exact numbers of animals that become victims of pound seizure. However, USDA records for a one-year period covering November 2007 through November 2008 indicate that 947 dogs and 230 cats were obtained from shelters by Class B dealers.[1] The practice of pound seizure is America's dirty little secret because most citizens are unaware of the practice and that it may be happening at their local animal shelter. I frequently will mention the phrase "pound seizure" to people, and virtually 100 percent of people have never heard of the phrase or the practice. These same people are also shocked that such a situation exists in American animal shelters.

What surprises people the most is learning that if their pet becomes lost and arrives at their local shelter, their pet could be sold for experimentation in as few as five business days. If you are unable to locate your cat or dog in time, your pet that once snuggled in your bed may be sitting in a steel cage, waiting to be subjected to numerous scientific experiments or educational training that could result in its death at the hands of strangers. Because evidence now exists that animals are crossing state lines for research purposes, no pet in America is safe as long as pound seizures continue to exist.

People do not appreciate their local government keeping secrets or engaging in practices that betray public trust. Yet this is precisely what pound seizure presents for many communities. All states have stray dog (and some stray cat) laws that mandate people to bring stray and homeless dogs to the shelter for safekeeping until their owner is found. All states also have laws against animal cruelty, neglect, and various forms of animal fighting. We are taught that to be a good citizen we should report suspected cruelty and neglect, which often means that the pet is removed from the home and placed at the local animal shelter.

The betrayal of trust occurs when a shelter engages in pound seizure and keeps the practice secret. Rarely, if ever, will an animal shelter post a sign indicating that animals may be sold for research or experimentation. Therefore, if you act as a Good Samaritan and take a stray cat or dog to the shelter, the betrayal sets in when you learn that the pet has been sold for experimentation. If you call in a complaint of animal cruelty or neglect, or report an allegation of dog fighting, a hoarding situation, or a suspected puppy mill in the neighborhood, your act of kindness might result in yet another betrayal to those animals. Too many people do not realize that these pets could end up in a laboratory.

Even worse, imagine that you have to give up your beloved cat or dog to the shelter because you recently lost your job and/or your home, a scenario that is occurring at alarming rates due to the 2008–2010 financial downturn and home foreclosure crisis. You take your longtime companion to the shelter, filled with remorse, and believe that the shelter will find your pet a new home because your pet is friendly and loving. The shelter fails to tell you that it engages in pound seizure, and when you call a week or two later to check on your pet, you learn that it was sold for research. Or worse, the shelter attempts to cover up pound seizure and informs you that your pet has been "re-homed" or euthanized when it may actually be sitting at a Class B dealer facility waiting to be transported hundreds or thousands of miles to a research facility.

The betrayal of trust committed by taxpayer-funded animal shelters to their community defies comprehension and disregards the shelter's intended mission: to be a safe haven for homeless, abused, neglected, and surrendered animals. People who are aware of pound seizure in their community are more likely to refuse to take a homeless, abandoned, or abused animal to a shelter because they feel the current plight of the animal is better than what could await it at a research facility. Thus, the laws that were put in place to protect these animals are systematically undone solely because of pound seizure.

Having a microchip embedded in your pet or a tattoo identification can help to prevent your pet from ending up in a research laboratory. However, it is not guaranteed. Dr. Robert Willems with the USDA explains, "There have, however, been several occasions in which a dog sold by a random source B dealer (RSBD) to a research facility has subsequently been found to have such identification, and in those instances, either the research facility or APHIS has made attempts to trace the animal to an owner through its identification. Unfortunately, I do not believe that this has ever resulted in the dog being reunited with an owner. For the cases of which I am aware the dog either proved to be untraceable or, in one instance, it was traced to a municipal pound and no further."[2]

Currently seventeen states plus the District of Columbia have banned the practice of pound seizure. Yet thirty-one states still permit shelters to sell or give animals to Class B dealers, and two states mandate the practice of their shelters. When citizens learn of pound seizure in their community, that is when they take action.

A significant issue with pound seizure relates to the unlikelihood that families will be reunited with their pets. If a family pet is in the hands of a Class B dealer or a research facility and the family requests the return of their pet, the Animal Welfare Act requires the pet be returned. Complicating the situation is evidence now surfacing that Class B dealers trade random source cats and dogs among themselves. When the dealers trade animals, including transfers across state lines, it makes it virtually impossible for a family pet to be reunited with its family. Yet this is permitted under the Animal Welfare Act.

According to the American Anti-Vivisection Society, three Michigan random source Class B dealers have been found swapping animals. "Hodgins Kennels obtains dogs from Class B random source dealer R&R Research. Cheri-Hill Kennel & Supply obtains live dogs from local [Michigan] animal control pounds and subsequently sells or otherwise transfers the dogs to R&R Research. In some cases, dogs obtained from animal control facilities spend an extraordinary amount of time at Cheri-Hill. One rather extreme example is an adult male pit bull-hound mix that was released from Mecosta County Animal Control to Cheri-Hill on January 11, 2007. Almost one year later, on December 31, 2007, the dog was sold/transferred to R&R Research and sold to the University of Florida, where he arrived on January 10, 2008 after being driven over 1,000 miles in a truck. . . . In addition, LBL Kennels [Reelsville, Indiana] sells animals acquired from other random source animal dealers, including Mountain Top Kennels [Wallingford, Kentucky]."[3] When cats and dogs are transferred among random source dealers and cross state lines, the possibility of a family finding its lost pet becomes even slimmer. Yet, the USDA and the Animal Welfare Act does not address or condemn this practice.

In April 2009, my office at the American Humane Association conducted an online survey of more than 3,000 professional members and advocates to determine how widespread knowledge was about pound seizure and the impact of pound seizure on communities.[4] The results below are clear that communities do not want this practice in their local shelter:

Would you bring a lost animal you had found to a shelter that released unclaimed animals to research?

NO 97.1%   YES 1.7%   NO RESPONSE 1.2%

If there was a stray dog in your neighborhood, would you be less likely to report it to animal control if you knew it might end up in a research laboratory?

YES 91.1%   NO 7.3%   NO RESPONSE 1.6%

If you could not keep your own pet and brought it to a shelter that released animals to research, would you sign a form giving permission for your pet to be used for experimentation?

NO 98.4%   YES 1.4%   NO RESPONSE 0.3%

Would you donate money to an animal shelter that voluntarily sold or gave pets to laboratories?

NO 97.6%   YES 1.7%   NO RESPONSE 0.7%

If you could not keep your own pet and brought it to a shelter that released animals to research, would you feel betrayed if the shelter gave your animal to research without your prior knowledge?

YES 96.0%   NO 2.1%   NO RESPONSE 1.9%

If you knew of an animal that was being abused or neglected, would you be less likely to report it to animal control if you knew it might end up in a research laboratory?

YES 79.6%   NO 16.9%   NO RESPONSE 3.5%

Note: For the following "shelter staff only" questions, the percentages listed are based on the total number of responses to each question.
(For shelter staff only) Does your shelter provide animals to research?

NO 99.1%   YES 0.9%

(For shelter staff only) If you answered no to question 7, do you feel the public is more comfortable or more likely to bring animals to your shelter than to a shelter that does provide animals to research?

YES 93.7%   NO 6.3%

(For shelter staff only) Do you believe that citizens in your community approve of providing shelter animals to research?

NO 95.8%   YES 4.2%

(For shelter staff only) If there is another shelter in your area that provides animals to research, does the presence of that shelter affect your ability to gain the confidence of the community?

YES 51.5%   NO 48.5%

The above results are consistent with the same survey conducted in 1988 by the American Humane Association. The end outcome is that animal shelters that practice pound seizure will receive less donation dollars, less community support, and less compliance with stray dog laws and abuse/neglect laws. The practice could also result in a public health hazard with homeless animals running in the street, spreading diseases, and potentially biting humans. This public health hazard is one of many reasons why pound seizure must be discontinued.

Dr. Robert Willems shares these concerns about shelter cats and dogs used for research purposes:

> There is a very basic problem that I believe is inherent to the business of supplying random source dogs and cats for use in research. That problem is simply this: finding a steady, reliable, and constant supply of dogs and cats that is also legitimate. If the research community is going to use a dealer (vendor) as a supplier of these animals, that dealer must be able to meet the needs of his customers and be able to fill their orders. Finding sources of these animals is not always that easy. Finding legitimate sources is even more difficult.
>
> Historically, RSBDs [random source B dealers] have had problems complying with many of the other sections of the Animal Welfare Regulations— housing, veterinary care, feeding, etc. Proper and adequate recordkeeping

seems to be the biggest problem the RSBDs have as a group. What seems
to be unique to the RSBDs as a group, when compared to any other group
of licensees, is a high rate of acquisition of animals for resale coming from
non-legitimate sources.[5]

THE MYTHS AND FACTS ABOUT POUND SEIZURE

To fully comprehend the betrayal that pound seizure creates in communities, it is important to understand the arguments for and against pound
seizure. Although later chapters will describe the supporters and opponents of pound seizure, listed below are some common myths and facts
that were prepared by the American Humane Association for legislative
advocacy to stop pound seizure.

MYTH: Stopping pound seizure will prevent life saving biomedical research for both people and animals.
FACT: Even without access to shelter cats and dogs, researchers can
still obtain genetically diverse and purpose-bred animals from a variety
of legal sources, including: (1) Class A dealers that are already breeding
animals for research; (2) individuals who donate their pets for research;
and (3) research facilities with breeding programs and colonies. Banning
pound seizure simply cuts out the Class B dealer "middlemen," who have
been investigated for acquiring random source animals from questionable sources and then selling them, often for hundreds of dollars each, to
laboratories. It also stops former family pets, abused/neglected animals,
or stolen animals from being used for experimentation.

The issue with pound seizure is not to attack the value of medical research, but to question and end the practice of allowing Class B random
source animal dealers to obtain shelter cats and dogs for research. In
recent years, research and training facilities have moved away from live
animal research toward simulated, computerized, or in vitro research techniques. An even greater number are choosing not to use shelter animals
supplied by Class B dealers. According to the Physicians Committee for
Responsible Medicine, in 2008 the last U.S. medical school using dogs
for medical education ceased this practice. Currently, 151 of 159 U.S.
and Canada medical schools do not use any live animals for education,
and 198 of 208 surveyed programs do not use live animals for Advanced
Trauma Life Support (ATLS) courses. (See appendix C.) Many research

and training institutions, including all Department of Defense programs and the intramural research program at National Institutes of Health, have stopped using random source dogs and cats.

MYTH: Banning pound seizure will negatively impact the essential training that veterinary students must receive on cats and dogs.

FACT: Less than half of the veterinary schools conduct "terminal labs" on shelter cats and dogs.[6] A terminal lab is one in which often-healthy shelter cats and dogs are used to train the students on a variety of surgical techniques, but are then euthanized during the procedure. This is unnecessary and sends an inappropriate message to future veterinarians when they are required to kill their first clients. It is understandable that live cats and dogs are needed to help train our future veterinarians. It is possible to provide legal exemptions that would allow veterinary training schools to obtain shelter animals that are in need of medical or surgical attention, or to practice sterilization surgeries, then place the animal for adoption afterward rather than automatically euthanize the pet after the practice session is completed. For example, a legislative bill filed in Michigan by the American Humane Association included three important exemptions that are good for animals and good for veterinary training schools: (1) veterinary teaching opportunities to spay or neuter a shelter animal before it is placed for adoption; (2) veterinary teaching opportunities to correct a preexisting medical condition of a shelter animal (such as injuries or diseases) before it is placed for adoption; and (3) nonfatal blood-banking procedures of a shelter animal before it is placed for adoption. In these situations, the students receive the necessary training, and the animals receive the veterinary care that they need and then are placed in an adoptive home.

MYTH: If we do not conduct testing and education training on animals, then advances for the health and welfare of humans (and animals) will suffer.

FACT: Some scientists are beginning to question whether research and testing on animals is appropriate to determine what the human response will be to the same tests. Moreover, significant advances have been made in alternative research and training techniques that do not involve animals. As an example, in 2008, following recommendations from the National Research Council of the Academy of Sciences, three national governmental agencies (Environmental Protection Agency, the National Toxicology

Program, and the National Institutes of Health) signed a memorandum of understanding to replace the use of animals with in vitro methods for chemical safety testing.

MYTH: There is no need to stop pound seizure because pet theft is not really a problem and the USDA's enforcement of the Animal Welfare Act addresses these concerns.

FACT: The USDA has increased inspections of Class B dealers to include quarterly on-site inspections because they are deemed a "high risk" due to concerns about pet theft. These inspections include a "trace back" procedure that has verified that some random source animals were improperly obtained. As a result, the number of USDA-licensed dealers has decreased from one hundred in 1993 to only nine in 2010 through greater enforcement.

A congressional study conducted by the National Academies of Science in 2009 regarding the use of random source dogs and cats in research concluded that Class B dealers are not needed for supplying random source animals for research and training. The committee handling the study voiced concerns about the lack of USDA resources to properly oversee the dealers, animal welfare issues in the housing of animals at dealer facilities, and chronic violations of the Animal Welfare Act.

A USDA director has confirmed that, "We use a risk-based inspection system (RBIS) to target our inspections. RBIS encourages frequent inspections at types of facilities that, in our experience, have more problems and fewer inspections at types of facilities with consistent compliance. Random Source Class B Dealers are considered high risk in RBIS and are inspected at least quarterly. We had 10 licensed Random Source Class B Dealers in FY2008 and conducted 74 inspections. Five of the 10 licensed Random Source Class B Dealers have compliance issues that are under review."[7] In 2010, several of the nine dealers have inspection citations pending.

As an example of the nature of the Class B random source animal business, a 2006 HBO documentary called *Dealing Dogs* exposed the illegal actions of C. C. Baird, an Arkansas Class B dealer. An undercover investigation by Last Chance for Animals revealed that stolen animals were found being brokered by Baird, whose facility was shut down after subsequent criminal prosecution. Over the five month investigation, footage revealed that Baird paid "bunchers" (people who collect animals) to steal family pets or fraudulently acquire dogs and cats from "free to good home" ads. Baird faced felony charges relating to money laundering and mail fraud and was charged with hundreds of violations of the Animal Welfare Act. Responding to the need to eliminate such illegal activities of Class B dealers, the USDA authorized a standard operating procedure in 2008 to strengthen inspections.

There have been several examples where family pets, with identification tags, have been in the possession of two random source Class B dealers. These include:

- In fall 2008, a dog named Rusty was in the possession of a Michigan B dealer and had an identification tattoo. The dealer contacted the tattoo registry, but was uncooperative and gave a false name to the registry. The tattoo registry identified the caller as a Michigan B dealer through its caller identification and subsequently located Rusty's actual owner, who lived in Florida and reported that Rusty was stolen from his front yard in 2005. Through the quick actions of the tattoo registry, Rusty was retrieved from the B dealer and is now safe.[8]
- In 2005 the rabies identification tags were allegedly removed from a dog named Conan and thrown away by the dealer who seized the dog from Jackson County animal control. The family traced Conan to a New York laboratory where after an experiment he was killed. No one had contacted the family to retrieve Conan.[9]
- In 2005, a dog named Echo was allegedly stolen from his yard in Fayetteville, Arkansas, and traveled through five states before ending up at a research facility in Minnesota. Echo was in the facilities of two Class B dealers (Michigan and Missouri), and neither scanned him for an identification chip. The research facility scanned Echo, located a microchip, and returned Echo to his family.[10]
- In 1993, a dog named Sam from Ionia County was improperly obtained from the county shelter and concealed from the owner by a Michigan B dealer. Through a police investigation, Sam was eventually returned to his owner. A lawsuit filed by Sam's owners against a Michigan Class B dealer and others resulted in Judge Enslen of the U.S. District Court–Western District of Michigan stating, "According to the allegations, the [Class B dealer was] operating their business by paying the county animal shelter workers to illegally deprive pet owners of their pets by dispensing with the pets prior to the expiration of the legal holding period. Proof of these allegations' truthfulness is found in the report of the State Department of Agriculture, the testimony of the plaintiffs

that the shelter workers confirmed that their pets were immediately removed from the shelter, and the alleged admissions of [the dealer] to the effect that he was cooperating with [the shelter director] in covering up the goings-on at the shelter."[11]

MYTH: The USDA has sufficient resources to properly regulate Class B dealers.

FACT: The USDA admits it allocates too much of its limited resources in an attempt to regulate nine random source Class B dealers who re-sell dogs and cats for research. The USDA oversees about 10,000 total licensees and registrants that are in need of inspection and oversight. Those licensees received approximately one inspection per year, whereas random source Class B dealers now require at least four in-person inspections per year. In a meeting held in January 2009 at the National Academies of Science, a USDA representative stated that the USDA has prioritized its focus on Class B dealers because of allegations and investigations into "improperly obtaining animals," but a loophole in the Animal Welfare Act prevents them from doing the necessary job no matter how much money they have. He stated, "The oversight of random source dealers is the single most important thing USDA does based on public and Congressional expectations. Random source dealers have always been an issue over the years, even with declining numbers of dealers and animals involved."[12] The USDA admits "it is expensive" to regulate nine random source Class B dealers, who are each inspected in person more than four times yearly. A congressional study in 2009 into the use of random source cats and dogs in research demonstrated that the USDA is underresourced and unable to thoroughly and effectively monitor the actions of Class B dealers and assure the public that stolen animals are not entering laboratories.

MYTH: Stopping pound seizure will put Class B dealers and research facilities out of business.

FACT: Random source Class B dealers and research facilities will still be able to conduct business by legally obtaining dogs and cats from other sources such as other breeders who are already providing animals for research, people who donate their pets to research, and research laboratories with breeding facilities and colonies.

MYTH: Pound seizure has existed for decades and has support from scientists, communities, businesses, and citizens.

FACT: The National Animal Control Association and the Association of Shelter Veterinarians oppose the practice of pound seizure, as do all national animal welfare organizations. Moreover, seventeen states and the District of Columbia have passed laws banning the practice.

Given the economic difficulties facing American families, thousands of pets are being surrendered to shelters every day. Their owners do so hoping that the pets will be adopted by people who are able to afford pet care and provide a loving home. However, some of these pets are now being used in experiments unbeknownst to their former owners. This is a betrayal of trust even in the best of economic times.

Many state and local laws require that citizens report stray dogs to county or city officials in order to be reunited with their family. Citizens are also encouraged to call in complaints of animal abuse or neglect so that the pets can be brought to the shelter for safekeeping. Yet some people will not comply with those laws when they realize a shelter practices pound seizure.

In April 2009, the American Humane Association conducted a survey on how people feel about pound seizure. Responses were received from 3,044 individuals and included:[13]

- "Would you bring a lost animal you'd found to a shelter that released unclaimed animals to research?" More than 97 percent of the people survey responded by saying "No."
- "If there were a stray dog in your neighborhood, would you be LESS likely to report it to animal control if you knew it might end up in a research laboratory?" More than 91 percent of those surveyed answered "Yes."
- "If you knew of an animal that was being abused or neglected, would you be LESS likely to report it to animal control if you knew it might end up in a research laboratory?" Almost 80 percent of those surveyed said "Yes."
- "Would you donate money to an animal shelter that voluntarily sold or gave animals to laboratories?" Almost 98 percent of people surveyed said "No."

MYTH: Shelter cats and dogs that are given to Class B dealers are unwanted pets; thus, it is a better use of resources to use these animals in research rather than to kill them.

FACT: Shelters with high euthanasia rates do not need to rely on pound seizure. There is a growing movement in the United States to reduce shelter euthanasia rates by increasing foster care programs, spay-neuter programs, education, volunteer and rescue services, and general outreach. These efforts have proven to increase adoptions, pet ownership retention, and reduce euthanasia (all of which increases revenue and reduces costs to shelters). Most shelter cats and dogs are healthy and adoptable pets. There are a variety of reasons why animals end up at a shelter. For those families that give up their animals due to issues of hardship, many are not informed that their pet could be sent to research. Due to the recession, many people who love their pets are unable to care for them. People believe that an animal shelter is where you take your pet to find a new home. People may be informed that their pet could be euthanized, but they are *infrequently informed* that their pet could be used in experimental research. One Michigan dealer has stated, "[T]hey may have been a pet at one time, but at the point [a dealer] becomes involved, they are an unwanted, unclaimed animal about to be euthanized."[14] That statement is simply false. This attitude is particularly egregious in our current economic climate where people are being forced to make difficult decisions, one of which may be to reluctantly relinquish a beloved pet in the hopes of finding it a new home. Shelter animals taken for research are former family pets that are the friendliest and most trusting because they are the easiest to handle during experiments. Taking these former family pets in this way angers communities and violates the growing body of research involving the human-animal bond. It also violates the purpose of an animal shelter to be a safe haven for animals.

MYTH: It is financially sound for shelters to sell animals to dealers and research facilities and make a little money off of animals that otherwise would be killed.

FACT: Most states that allow pound seizure do not keep proper records of the number of animals sold to research. Michigan, however, does keep those records. Michigan law (MCL 287.389) allows shelters to charge a maximum of $10 per animal that is sold to research. Of the last two remaining shelters in Michigan that practice pound seizure, neither shelter is charging the $10 fee per animal. Rather, both of the shelters engage in a quid pro quo agreement with the dealer where the dealer provides other "free" services to the shelter (such as dead animal body removal or euthanasia by carbon dioxide barrel) in exchange for having the pick of the shelter dogs and cats for research. This practice breeds concern about greed and whether the shelter will give preference to the dealer over an adoption or rescue of the pet. Such scenarios have been documented in several former pound seizure shelters in Michigan.

Nonetheless, charging a fee would not bring a notable benefit to an economically challenged shelter in Michigan. According to records from the Michigan Department of Agriculture, there has been a significant decline in the past five years of shelter animals that have been given to Class B dealers. In 2004, animal shelters gave 2,344 cats and dogs to Class B dealers whereas in 2008 the number decreased to 721 shelter cats and dogs. Thus, at the $10 per pet limit, the maximum that could have been earned statewide in 2008 was $7,210. That amount is negligible and not worth the negative cost to society in maintaining pound seizure.

JACKSON'S STORY

Jackson, a pit bull mix six-month-old puppy, was found as a stray in the cold Michigan winter on January 2, 2002. The finder took the dog that she named Jackson to a mid-Michigan animal control shelter, as required by Michigan law, so that his owner would be able to find him. She also placed an adoption hold on Jackson in case the owner did not appear.

During an inspection of shelter records, it was learned that Jackson was sold to a Class B dealer in spite of the finder's written objection to selling Jackson for research purposes. The ability to object to an animal being sold for research was a new county policy that was put in place the previous fall by the county commissioners. Within months of the new policy, records showed that the policy was violated, and Jackson was sold to the dealer in spite of the finder's written objection.

The betrayal continued when the finder called the shelter one week later to inquire if the owners had been located and reclaimed Jackson. The shelter informed the finder that Jackson had been euthanized. According to shelter records, however, Jackson was not euthanized at the end of his seven-day hold period but, instead, spent an additional four weeks in the shelter isolation ward labeled "this animal is adoptable to the finder only." At the end of that four-week hold in the isolation ward, out of sight from potential adopters, Jackson was sold to a dealer on February 7, 2002.

Why must Jackson be adopted only by the finder? The shelter director was unable to answer that question. Jackson was also not given the opportunity to be adopted by the general public and was simply warehoused in an isolation ward until the dealer was ready to take him. Jackson's finder was betrayed twice: once in being told that she had the right to object to him being sold to research, and another time in being told that Jackson was euthanized.

After learning what happened to Jackson, I contacted the finder. I asked her about her conversations with the shelter staff, and she confirmed that she had placed an adoption hold on Jackson and called one week later to determine if she could adopt him. I broke the news to her about Jackson's fate. She was devastated and could not understand why the shelter had lied to her on two occasions. She felt guilty in taking little stray Jackson to the shelter and thought she had done the right thing. She believed that placing an adoption hold on Jackson would keep him safe if his family was not found. She was inconsolable, and rightfully so.

I then discussed the situation with the shelter director, including the violation of the county ordinance, as well as lying to the finder about Jackson's disposition. The director only said that he had made a mistake and that errors were bound to happen when handling 4,000 animals a year. I asked the director to have Jackson returned so that the finder could adopt him. The shelter director realized he had been caught in a crucial mistake and indicated that he would call the dealer to have the dog returned. Jackson was never returned, and the shelter staff never spoke of Jackson again.

Jackson's lesson indicates a system breakdown when the practice of pound seizure exists in a shelter. Jackson's finder took appropriate action by taking Jackson to the shelter so that his family could locate him. The finder also placed two protections on Jackson, one to prevent him from being sold to research and the other to allow her to adopt him. Those protections were violated, and Jackson paid the ultimate price.

CONAN'S STORY

Conan's story is another scenario of betrayal and should concern anyone who currently lives in one of the thirty-three states that allow pound seizure, or lives in a neighboring state. Conan was a young black and tan neutered male pit bull mix who was very loved by his family. In September 2002, Conan's family from lower Michigan went on vacation and arranged for a neighbor to care for him. Like any playful and curious dog, he escaped from his yard unbeknownst to the neighbor and ended up at the animal shelter in a neighboring county. The shelter engaged in pound seizure at the time. The neighbor did not realize that Conan was located in a neighboring county shelter.

Conan was held at the shelter for the minimum five days before being sold to a Class B dealer. When his family returned from vacation, they searched everywhere for Conan, but it was too late. As evident in his photograph, taken at the Class B dealer facility by an undercover investigator with Last Chance for Animals, Conan was sold to the dealer with his identifying rabies tags still on him. Yet no one had contacted the family to retrieve Conan. His family eventually tracked him to a research facility in New York where Conan was used as an experimental subject and subsequently killed. His family was devastated.[15]

The animal shelter and the Class B dealer had the information to contact Conan's family, yet the laws to protect pets like Conan failed once again. Information about Conan and his last days was obtained by Last Chance for Animals during an undercover investigation at the dealer's facility at the time that Conan was there.[16] The investigator confirmed that when the dealer's staff noticed that Conan still wore his identification tags, the staff removed them. Several months earlier, a German shepherd named Tootsie was at this same dealer's facility and had three identifying tags on her. According to Last Chance for Animals' investigative report, while Tootsie's family was embroiled in a legal battle for the return of Tootsie, the Jackson County (Michigan) Animal Control Shelter sold Tootsie to a dealer, who then resold Tootsie to a laboratory in Chicago, still with her identifying tags. The laboratory promptly returned Tootsie due to the tags. Fortunately for Tootsie, she was reunited with her family. According to the undercover investigator, the dealer began removing dog tags from that point forward, and the investigator was advised to do the same. Conan's tags were removed at the dealer's facility before he was sold to a laboratory in Utica, New York. This one act led to Conan's death and thwarted the law that was put in place to protect family pets from ending up in laboratories.

The protective measures of the Animal Welfare Act failed Conan and almost failed Tootsie. Conan lost his life because Michigan still allows Class B dealers to obtain stray and lost family pets from shelters for experimentation. Conan's story demonstrates that every household pet is in jeopardy of being the victim of pound seizure.

CHANCE'S STORY

Chance was a four- to five-month-old Labrador retriever mix puppy that was rescued from a neglectful and unsanitary home along with his four siblings by a Michigan animal control shelter in July 2005. A concerned neighbor had contacted the shelter in an effort to save the puppies from their bad situation.

Chance and his siblings were never given the chance to be adopted. According to Jackson County Volunteers against Pound Seizure,[17] the shelter had posted Chance and his siblings on Petfinder.com, a website for shelters to post animals available for adoption, but then quickly removed the posting, claiming they were listed by mistake. The shelter deemed the dogs "unadoptable" because they were frightened.

When the shelter briefly posted Chance and his siblings on the Petfinder website, two rescue organizations saw the postings and wanted to rescue Chance and his siblings. One woman who fell in love with Chance's photo wanted to adopt him. These requests came two days too late. Chance and his siblings were held for the minimum five days at the shelter and then sold to a Class B dealer. The rescue organizations placed many phone calls to the dealer and to the animal shelter, yet neither could agree on who had the authority to release the puppies for adoption. As the dealer and shelter gave contradictory information to the potential adopters on who had authority to release the puppies, days passed and eventually the puppies were sold to research.[18]

Chance and his siblings lost any hope of a loving home, and likely their lives, because a Good Samaritan called in a complaint of neglect. The shelter that was obligated to bring them to safety quickly labeled them unadoptable and chose to sell them for research rather than retrieve them and place them with a rescue organization. When people hear of Chance's story, they become less likely to call in complaints of neglect and abuse if the shelter engages in pound seizure.

SOUP'S STORY

On July 15, 2009, a beautiful one-and-a-half-year-old English setter female named Soup was taken from a mid-Michigan animal control shelter by a Class B dealer. Soup had arrived at the shelter on July 7, 2009, when her family surrendered ownership. Soup was the type of dog who loved to run. Her family had trouble corralling her, and Soup often would not return to the property even when called. A few weeks before arriving at the shelter, Soup had been hit by a car and sustained an injury to one leg. When Soup went on the run again and animal control received a complaint, the family surrendered ownership of the dog to the shelter in lieu of paying a fine that it could not afford.

The betrayal of Soup begins with animal control failing to inform the family that the shelter engaged in pound seizure. In an interview with the shelter director, she informed me that the family knew that research was an option for Soup. However, the surrender form that the family signed failed to state that Soup could be sold for research.

The form mentioned adoption and euthanasia as the possibilities for Soup's disposition, but research was not mentioned. The form also stated that "adoptions are strongly encouraged," yet the shelter gave Soup to the dealer knowing that a rescue was coming to the shelter to save Soup. A rescue organization had contacted the shelter and indicated that it would take Soup on the first day that the shelter would permit her to be rescued. The rescue organization had even scheduled a veterinary appointment for Soup to have her leg examined. When the rescuers arrived on the morning of July 15 to retrieve Soup, the dealer had already taken her.

Several Michigan advocates, including Richard Angelo, a Michigan attorney, and I, worked for several weeks in an effort to have Soup returned. A volunteer with Lake Haven Rescue in Newaygo, Michigan, telephoned the Class B dealer and offered him $200 for Soup's safe return. The dealer refused and hung up on the volunteer. Angelo then spoke by phone with the Class B dealer and offered him all out-of-pocket expenses, including anticipated profit. The dealer once again refused and stated that no amount of money would convince him to return Soup to the shelter.

Why was it so important for the dealer to have Soup? Efforts then turned to attempts to find Soup's previous owners to see if they would want to have her returned. Advertisements were placed in the local newspaper in hope of finding the family. One woman responded, believing that Soup was her dog. But when she visited the dealer's facility, she realized that she had the wrong dog. Eventually, in September 2009, Soup's owner was located by local advocate Sandy Carlton who had spent time with Soup in the shelter. Sandy learned that the owner's girlfriend had surrendered Soup to the shelter. When Sandy contacted the girlfriend, she hung up. Sandy then telephoned the owner; he was hesitant to speak with Sandy, too. Sandy learned through another family member that Soup's owner had been cautioned against talking with "animal activists" about Soup. We can only hope that Soup had a peaceful end to her life.

Part II

THE FACES OF POUND SEIZURE

CHAPTER 5

Exposing Dealers Who Violate the Law

In 2006, an HBO special titled *Dealing Dogs* exposed the criminal wrong-doing of one random source animal Class B dealer. Martin Creek Kennels, operated by C. C. Baird and his family, in Arkansas had been infiltrated by Pete, an undercover investigator from Last Chance for Animals, who wore a hidden microphone and camera while he was an employed staff person at the facility. This same undercover investigator infiltrated the Hallmark Westland livestock slaughter plant in Chino, California, in 2007–2008 and uncovered the atrocities associated with processing downed cows for food.

Pete was able to gain employment at the Arkansas Class B dealer facility for five months. During that time he gathered clear evidence that stolen dogs were being brokered to research facilities. The images of the dogs on the video are disturbing, particularly the area on the property called "the trench" where hundreds of dead and decaying dogs were found that had died from diseases or from overcrowded conditions.

He photographed staff slapping a dog that was being held up by a collar and dogs languishing in filth and near death with vacant looks in their eyes. During an off-the-record discussion with Pete, one of the bunchers bluntly stated that "he don't want to know anything" about whether Baird asked the bunchers for identification to verify the legitimacy of the animals.

In his field notes, Pete documented his job of spraying down the dog kennels with a hose, and scrubbing out buckets of water and food. He was in a prime position to view the welfare of the dogs that were awaiting sale to research or other laboratories. Many of his notes describe dogs that were in dire physical and mental condition. Some of the dogs suffered dog fighting wounds, a prevalent problem because of overcrowding in small cages. He noted the following during his time on Baird's property:

- Monday, December 3, 2001: Pete was hired by C. C. Baird to work at the kennel. Baird informed him that fighting was "common" at the kennel "and that I should expect to see three to eight dead dogs a week." Pete was shown how to hose down the cages. The technique resulted in feces being sprayed into the food bowls; the dogs were terrified of the hose stream. Pete noted that the stream was so extreme that it hurt his skin and could take out an eye if it hit one of the dogs. "Most pens house five to six dogs per pen, though some contain dogs all alone. 50% of the dogs appear to be hound, 30% beagles, and 20% mixed breeds, though mostly smaller and toy breeds."
- Tuesday, December 4, 2001: Pete witnessed numerous fights in the kennels; the dogs bled and received no medical care. An employee showed Pete how to feed the dogs. The food was mostly moldy and decomposing. Rats were so common in the kennel that Tim, another staffer, even put out rat poison. One dead rat was found inside a dog kennel.
- Wednesday, December 5, 2001: Pete found a dead beagle; another dog suffered from open wounds on its nose and tongue. Pete was ordered to feed the dogs moldy food.
- Thursday, December 6, 2001: "[A]bout a dozen fights broke out today between the dogs that I observed and acted to stop. In another fight, I saw Bill enter a kennel and whip at the dogs inside with a water hose three times. I [saw] way too many dogs with open sores on their faces and ears to count. . . . " Pete also noted, "I saw Tim on numerous occasions dragging dogs by their necks with a rope leash when they wouldn't walk. I also saw Bill pick up a small beagle mix from the indoor kennel by the scruff and throw her into a pen in a manner that could have injured the dog. At no point did I see any medical attention of any kind given to any of the animals."
- Saturday, December 8, 2001: Pete found a beagle/hound mix and four newborn puppies dead. He was instructed to place them near a gate with a wooden board over them. He saw numerous dogs in poor medical condition, including dogs with open scabs, mange, eyes and noses filled with mucus, and emaciation.
- Sunday, December 9, 2001: Pete was told to not feed the dogs that had been given food the day before.
- Monday, December 12, 2001: Pete noted, "I watched Tim on numerous occasions drag dogs [by] their chain collars, throw dogs into pens, kick dogs and slap dogs in their faces." He saw Tim load up a

white truck with a bunch of dogs, yet never saw the truck leave, suggesting that the dogs remained locked in the truck.

- Tuesday, December 11, 2001: Pete continued to document the poor medical health of the dogs, including numerous open wounds from apparent fighting. "I helped Tim draw blood and watched him repeatedly slap a hound in the face that was acting hyper while Tim tried to draw blood from it," he reported.

- Wednesday December 12, 2001: Pete found another dead beagle. Tim slapped a Dalmatian while drawing blood because the dog was hyperactive. "At one point," said Pete, "I saw Tim dragging a dog by its chain collar while using the collar to lift the dog's front legs completely off the ground."

- Tuesday January 1, 2002: Pete was informed that dogs in the outdoor kennels were being used for a whipworm study and could only receive water for five minutes once a day; Pete noted that the dogs were very thirsty.

- Wednesday, January 2, 2002: Pete noted that the winter weather was causing two to four inches of ice buildup in the outdoor cages. "I saw a beagle whose left eye was completely bulging out of his head and except for the pupil [was] totally red. I noticed a dog in pen #350 with [a] laceration on her neck, hinting her collar was too tight and had been removed, and that she had a 2-inch diameter bulbous fleshy growth coming out of her vagina. . . . I also saw a black hound lying in the gutter of its pen shivering and convulsing and unable to get out of the water." When filling the water bowls, Pete noted that the water was red from rust.

- Thursday, January 3, 2002: Pete pulled the body of the dead beagle out of her cage that had been convulsing the day before. He found three other dead dogs lying frozen in their pens. "I saw Tim yank dogs [necks] with a rope leash four times today, once picking [a] dog up by its chain collar and lifting its front paws off the ground. He then tossed it into a pen. In addition I saw Tim dragging a beagle by its neck with a rope collar when the beagle refused to walk. Most animals appear dehydrated when I lift up their scruff at the back of the neck and shoulders and watch it slowly fall back down. Dogs still have old and moldy food filling ¼ to ½ of their food buckets. Fresh food is simply thrown on top of this when the dogs are fed."

- Saturday, January 5, 2002: New dogs arrived from an auction house. "When we received dogs from the auction, we got 33 new dogs and 4 of ours returned. Of the 33 new dogs about 30 were emaciated and thin. Several were cagged 2 to a cage that is only 2 feet wide by 3 feet deep."[1]

This is a small summary of Pete's time spent at Martin Creek Kennels. Yet the notes are consistent that the staff was abusive, medical care was denied, food and water were inappropriate or withheld, the kennel conditions were filthy and dangerous, and the dogs were in poor medical and mental health. Remarkably, Martin Creek Kennels was providing these dogs to laboratories, and the USDA continued to license the facility. It makes me wonder what sort of research could be conducted on dogs in such a dreadful condition.

Tom Simon was one of the producers of *Dealing Dogs*. In an interview with *Newsweek*, Tom stated that the original intent of the documentary was to probe into animals used in research. What they found was that the procurement of dogs for research "was a complicated and somewhat shady business."[2] Tom further told *Newsweek*, "We found that the trade is not very well regulated, that there have been many, many allegations over the years that pets have been stolen from people's yards or strays picked up by people who were then selling them to these B dealers. In the film, there are [bunchers] speaking to an investigator who admit driving around rich neighborhoods in St. Louis [looking to] pick up dogs. We became very interested in this supply chain, and we began to reach out to animal-rights groups that were investigating this."[3]

After more than a year, C. C. Baird's facility was raided, and he was eventually held accountable for the atrocious acts of inhumane treatment and the brokering of stolen animals. In March 2004, a 108-page complaint was filed charging Baird with numerous civil violations of the Animal Welfare Act. The U.S. Attorney's Office for the Eastern District of Arkansas uncovered gross negligence on the part of the USDA-APHIS to properly enforce the Animal Welfare Act, including its inspection process and the oversight of how dealers acquire animals.

However, in the seventeen-month interim between the raid by federal law enforcement officials and pleading guilty, the USDA allowed Baird to continue his random source dealer operation. It was not until January 21, 2005, that Baird reached a settlement that included the permanent revocation of his Class B dealer license, his daughter Jeanette's Class B dealer license, and his wife Patsy's Class A dealer license, and a $262,700 fine. The fine was the largest in USDA history.

Baird was also criminally charged and in August 2005 he pled guilty to felony conspiracy to commit money laundering. Baird's wife, Patsy, pled guilty to misprision of felony mail fraud. Both entered into a sentencing agreement to forfeit $200,000 and more than 700 acres of property and to reimburse about $42,000 in investigative costs which were used to care for the animals seized from the property. Baird was sentenced to three years of probation, including six months of home detention, and his wife was sentenced to two years' probation, plus another combined criminal fine of $10,000. The Bairds were not convicted of animal cruelty, since that was only a misdemeanor in the state at that time, and instead were federally prosecuted for felony money laundering.

The USDA came under fire in the aftermath of the Baird case. The Committee on the Scientific and Humane Issues in the Use of Random Source Dogs and Cats for Research found that USDA/APHIS had not been able to properly enforce the AWA in regard to Class B dealers since the creation of the AWA more than forty years before.[4] The Committee made these comments specifically in regard to the C. C. Baird investigation:

> It is important to note that despite uncovering extensive evidence of gross mismanagement and animal suffering by an undercover investigator from the animal protectionist community rather than USDA/APHIS, it still required over a year of administrative procedure and due process for the government to investigate, prosecute and close this case, not to mention years of USDA inspections and approval of this dealer to remain in operation prior to the situation becoming public. Baird avoided imprisonment by agreeing to testify to USDA and others in regards to multiple other ongoing Class B dealer investigations. . . .
>
> When the Committee queried Dr. Jerry DePoyster, a Senior Veterinary Medical Officer with APHIS, he acknowledged the USDA/APHIS could not guarantee that a C. C. Baird–type incident would not be repeated, and reaffirmed the disproportionate effort and difficulties APHIS experiences in regulating Class B dealers. Likewise, Dr. Robert Willems, Assistant Director for the Eastern Region, testified that when he was involved in west coast operations, over 800 hours and 1-1/2 years was invested in the investigations of violations of a single dealer. He testified that Class B dealers are regulated more heavily than any other USDA licensee.[5]

In a rare view into the world of a Class B dealer, Baird was interviewed by his attorney.[6] Portions of the interview were contained in a documentary titled *The Case against "B" Dealers* which was provided to legislators of the 109th Congress where S 451 and HR 5229, the Pet Safety and Protection Act, was under consideration.

Baird stated he had been a dealer for fifteen years. His facility was raided by federal officials in 2003, and he admittedly was allowed to operate as a dealer for another seventeen months until his license was revoked. He acknowledged that one purpose of the AWA was to prevent stolen animals from being used in research. USDA-APHIS inspected Baird's facilities at least four times per year and on July 8, 2003, one month before the raid, he passed a USDA inspection. When asked if it was commonly known within APHIS that Baird was obtaining animals that were not bred and raised by the seller, Baird said, "Yes, sir, no question about that."[7] He admitted that he maintained fraudulent records of animals he obtained and that the animals did not come from people who had bred and raised the animals, a mandate of the AWA for Class B dealers.

Baird confirmed that when delivering animals to university research facilities, the staff would not question the source of the animals since USDA-APHIS was inspecting Baird, and he was passing inspections. The USDA-APHIS seal of approval on inspections validated that the animals were legally procured and, thus, the research facilities looked no further. Baird clarified, "USDA made no attempt to enforce the bred and raised . . . they gave a wink and a nod, would sometimes sit in my office and look at records and say 'this man sold you 10 dogs and obviously he did not breed and raise them.' With regard to the bred and raised rule, I think everyone in the industry, everyone at APHIS and all the dealers, both knew that the rule was not being applied and no intention to enforce it."[8]

When Baird was questioned whether the AWA was strictly enforced as to whether B dealers could stay in business, he responded, "If the Animal Welfare Act is applied to the nth degree, there is no way that a Class B dealer can stay in business and survive."[9]

Shortly after the Baird undercover investigation, a Michigan Class B dealer was targeted by Last Chance for Animals; an undercover investigator was placed at the facility. During this investigation, the dealer and his staff were found to be removing identification tags or collars from dogs before selling them to research. No attempts were made to reunite pet owners with their dogs. This happened to a dog named Conan who is featured in chapter 4.

In 1993, Chris DeRose of Last Chance for Animals interviewed Class B dealer David Stephens from Lebanon, Oregon, who was serving a ten-month sentence in federal prison. Stephens stated that he only brokered random source animals bought from bunchers. He confirmed that bunchers were "people that would go out and obtain the animals from wherever they could obtain them, be it from someone's back yard or free to good home ads."[10] Stephens had no doubt that other Class B dealers were brokering stolen animals and that the USDA knew of this practice. When the USDA inspected his records, Stephens believed that USDA had to know that he was brokering stolen animals. In regard to the system of Class B dealers, David Stephens poignantly stated, "I think it's pretty scummy to be honest with you. Because from what I've seen and experienced myself it's a pretty low shyster business."[11]

In an interview for this book, Dr. Robert Willems, assistant regional director, Eastern Region, USDA, APHIS, Animal Care, commented on his involvement in the Stephens case. "In the period prior to 2004, . . . I am personally aware of several such occurrences [of pet theft], two of which happened in the State of Oregon and in which I had some involvement. The first of these cases occurred in 1991–1992 and involved two RSBDs [random source B dealers], David Stephens and Brenda Linville. The thefts were by deception—answering free-to-good-home ads in local papers—and several of the dogs were returned to their owners. The second case occurred in 1995–1996, and the RSBD was Betty Davis (not to be confused with the actress). In both of these cases, stolen dogs were found either on the premises of the dealers, in research labs after having been sold, or where identified from records. Both of these cases were prosecuted criminally by the U.S Attorney's Office in Oregon, and both resulted in prison or jail sentences for the participants. In the first case both Stephens and Linville were sentenced to federal prison. In the second case, Davis's son was sentenced to federal prison, and nine of the bunchers that worked for him were sentenced to jail terms by the local authorities."[12]

On August 26, 2008, Class B dealer Henry Lee Cooper of Wewoka, Oklahoma, was placed on a five-year suspension by the USDA for numerous violations of the Animal Welfare Act. In a complaint dated August 27, 2007, some of the more egregious allegations from four separate inspections included creating false records on the acquisition of three dogs and failure to correct continuing violations regarding the minimal standard of housing, feeding, watering, and overall veterinary care of the animals in his possession. In reading the complaint, it becomes clear that the facility was a picture of filth and squalor. In the end, the USDA revoked Cooper's license for five years because of numerous and chronic violations of the AWA.

Dr. Willems stated that no Class B dealer has been prosecuted under the Animal Welfare Act statute (7 USC 2158) that relates to the procurement of animals. "All enforcement actions taken against RSBDs [random source B dealers] that I know of were taken by APHIS as administrative actions alleging violations of the AWA regulations contained in 9 CFR Subchapter A. These are handled by administrative law judges (ALJ) in administrative hearings. All criminal actions against RSBDs over the years have all been taken by either a U.S. Attorney's Office or a state court." As you will see below, the revocation process is either slowed through the administrative hearing process or is not pursued by the USDA.[13]

LICENSED RANDOM SOURCE CLASS B DEALERS AND USDA VIOLATIONS

The USDA admits the difficulty in tracing back random source animals to their origin. In USDA's 2007 Fiscal Year Animal Welfare Report, it states "there is concern that some of these dealers may be trafficking in stolen animals."[14] In spite of a ramped-up effort to conduct trace backs on animals in the possession of Class B dealers, it is fairly easy for the paperwork on the animals to be doctored to show that the animal came from an approved source. The USDA admits that this is a loophole in the current law and regulations.

As of mid-2009, there are 1,070 registered Class B dealers in the United States,[15] but only nine hold the title of "random source" Class B dealer and sell live animals to research facilities. At the same time, six of these nine random source dealers were under investigation for alleged violations of the Animal Welfare Act regulations. Based on the list of citations from the USDA,[16] many of them chronic and uncorrected, it is no wonder why pound seizure is so problematic for communities. Citizens should question why the Class B dealers are unable to correct citations and avoid future violations. Is it that they are incapable of understanding the law that is provided to them by the USDA, or is it that they flagrantly flaunt the law knowing the penalties are tame or nonexistent?

The USDA's 2007 Fiscal Year Animal Welfare Report provides the following information on what can occur after a violation is found during an inspection:

> If AC [Animal Care] inspectors discover conditions or records that are not in compliance with the regulations, AC typically establishes a deadline for cor-

recting these items and provides it in the inspection report. In conjunction with Investigative and Enforcement Services (IES), AC immediately investigates any situations that may have caused unnecessary animal suffering or death. Inspectors are required to reinspect any facilities where areas of noncompliance were found that have, or are likely to have, an impact on the well-being of the animals. If the conditions remain uncorrected, AC documents them for possible legal action. In cases of unrelieved suffering, AC may confiscate the animals or arrange for their placement elsewhere. With the assistance of IES, AC acted in 8 such situations in FY [fiscal year] 2007, resulting in the confiscation/surrender and placement of approximately 220 animals.[17]

In an interview for this book, Dr. Willems further clarifies the process as to what happens when a Class B dealer has been cited for violating the Animal Welfare Regulations. "The care of animals held by USDA licensees, including RSBDs [random source B dealers], is covered in the AWA regulations. (9 CFR Subchapter A.) If a RSBD is alleged to have violated those regulations covering the care of animals, the process for taking enforcement action against the RSBD is the same as it would be for any other USDA licensee. A noncompliance with the regulations found by an inspector during an inspection is recorded as a citation on an inspection report. If the noncompliance is severe, or if it is found to have been uncorrected on a subsequent inspection, or if a similar noncompliance is found on a subsequent inspection, the situation is referred to the Regional Office where it will be reviewed and a decision made as to what type of enforcement action will be taken. In some cases no action is taken if it is warranted. Enforcement can take several forms, usually (though not always) in the following sequence: 1) issuance of an Official Warning to the licensee; 2) issuance of a stipulation (generally a monetary fine); 3) issuance of a formal Complaint and a request for a hearing. In the last case, the complaint is given to an ALJ who will then schedule a hearing. The Complaint can be settled in a Consent Decision where the license might be revoked, or the ALJ can make a decision after a hearing and revoke the license. The agency does not have authority to summarily revoke a license."[18]

The system of Class B dealers is fraught with continued violations of the law, lack of resources for proper oversight, and the public's concern that a beloved family pet may end up in the possession of a Class B dealer or sold to a laboratory. The committee acknowledged that "acquisition and resale of animals by dealers, bunchers and individuals is profit-driven, which may foster corrupt practices and less attention to animal welfare issues."[19]

CLASS B DEALERS WHO BROKER DEAD SHELTER ANIMALS

Although this book is about dealers brokering live cats and dogs from shelters, it is important to understand that there are Class B dealers who go to animal shelters for the purpose of obtaining recently euthanized cats and dogs. Most people initially do not believe that selling already deceased shelter animals is a concern. However, as the next case explains, the practice of brokering dead shelter animals creates numerous issues, including the shelter being more willing to euthanize animals in order to fill an order from a B dealer.

Michael Sargeant is a licensed Class B dealer in California who brokers dead cats and dogs from animal shelters. In June 2007, Sargeant was arrested and charged with two counts of felony bribery, along with the Tulare County, California, animal shelter manager, and shelter employee. According to the Animal Legal Defense Fund, the charges stemmed from Sargeant buying carcasses from the Tulare shelter and selling them to research facilities. The charges included that Sargeant and the shelter had an "off-the-books" arrangement and that the shelter carried out unauthorized mass euthanasia of animals and falsified shelter records to cover up the deaths.

Sargeant admitted to the sheriff's office that his contract with Tulare County Animal Control ended in 2002, yet he continued to acquire cat and dog carcasses. Sargeant's business also purchased and gave the shelter manager gift certificates to restaurants. On May 13, 2009, Sargeant pled no contest to a lesser charge of engaging in anticompetitive practices and was placed on three years' probation.[20] While charges were pending, universities still engaged in business with him. According to Animalearn, the education division of the American Anti-Vivisection Society, those universities included the University of Pennsylvania and Michigan State University.[21]

The Sargeant case illustrates the unusual relationship that some shelters have with Class B dealers, which can result in shelter animals not receiving proper care, such as not being held a sufficient time until an adoptive home is found or not allowing a rescue organization to take the animals. Instead, some shelters appear to cater to the wishes of the B dealers. If a Class B dealer has an order to fill for a certain number or type of animal, shelters have been known to overlook their responsibility to the animal and choose to meet the supply demands of the Class B dealer's business instead.

The Animal Welfare Act was passed in 1966 for the primary purpose of protecting animals used in research and to prevent stolen animals from ending up in laboratories. We have to concede that little has changed since then to better protect animals used in research.

CHAPTER 6

Experiments Conducted on Shelter Cats and Dogs

During my medical education . . . I found vivisection horrible, barbarous and above all unnecessary.

—Carl Jung, M.D. (1875–1961)

I abhor vivisection. . . . I know of no achievement through vivisection, no scientific discovery that could not have been obtained without such barbarism and cruelty.

—Charles W. Mayo, M.D. (1961), son of the cofounder of the Mayo Clinic

Whether you believe in the benefits of animal research or are repulsed by the business, one thing that has been proven is that all animals (including rats, chimpanzees, cats, dogs, rabbits, mice, and other research animals) are sentient beings that feel pain, fear, jealousy, grief, and love, similar to humans.[1] Animals in laboratories suffer stress from being handled, undergoing blood collection, and other procedures. In a 2004 review of eighty published studies involving stress in laboratory animals, it was found that "animals responded with rapid, pronounced, and statistically significant elevations in stress-related responses for each of the procedures, although handling elicited variable alterations in immune system responses. . . . We interpret these findings to indicate that laboratory routines are associated with stress, and that animals do not readily habituate to them. The data suggest that significant fear, stress, and possibly distress are predictable consequences of routine laboratory procedures, and that these phenomena have substantial scientific and humane implications for the use of animals in laboratory research."[2]

The Animal Welfare Act and its related protocols address the issuance of anesthesia and pain medications for certain procedures due to the recognition that animals feel pain. However, when claims are made by the research community that animals in their facilities are cared for, treated humanely, and are not in pain or distress, what does this mean? In the pound seizure campaigns that I have worked on, no research facility has followed through on its claims of humane treatment with documentation, even when asked. So much of what lies beyond the laboratory doors remains a mystery.

Class B dealers and research facilities are generally reluctant to disclose their practices, to allow people to tour their facilities, or to provide information as to what the animals encounter during experimentation. Although university research facilities and USDA inspection reports are subject to the Freedom of Information Act (FOIA), requesting documents to learn the truth has proven to be a costly venture; most citizens can't afford it. The FOIA open-records process was created to make government and public facilities transparent to citizens. However, some FOIA requests to research facilities have resulted in fees of $800 or more to receive even minimal documentation of what happens to the research cats and dogs when the study is concluded, or how many shelter cats and dogs are received each year by the facility. Obtaining these records is financially restrictive for many people.

Research laboratories must comply with "the Three Rs," a voluntary set of principles incorporated into all laws, policies, and guidelines related to sentient research. The *Guidelines for the Care and Use of Mammals in Neuroscience and Behavioral Research* sets forth the Three Rs as Replacement (partially or fully replacing animals through the use of non-animal systems or less-sentient species); Reduction (only using the minimum number of animals required to obtain scientifically valid data); and Refinement (enhancing animal well-being through lessening or eliminating pain and/or distress).

The research community often states that it is appropriate to obtain unwanted shelter dogs and cats for research rather than to produce another dog or cat through a Class A dealer that breeds animals for research. In essence, why kill two animals when you only need to kill one? In relating the Three Rs to cats and dogs obtained from shelters, "some might argue that failure to utilize unwanted pound or shelter animals for research runs counter to the 'reduction' component of the 3-Rs principle. In contrast, others would argue that use of random source animals does not address the 'refinement' or 'replacement' components, or the 'reduction' of the overall number of animals being used. Thus, even this issue is not straight-forward."[3]

To aid in the oversight of animals in research, the Institutional Animal Care and Use Committees (IACUC) were created to evaluate the protocols of each research laboratory. In basic terms, the IACUCs determine whether using an animal is necessary for a particular study, whether a similar study has previously been conducted using animals, whether alternatives would be appropriate, and reviews pertinent documentation justifying why a particular animal species is needed. "Research involving random source animals may require more rigorous justification to satisfy IACUC and the institutional community that these animal models are not only appropriate, but that these models have scientific benefits that outweigh the use of purpose-bred animals. . . . [C]ost alone [of the random source animal] has not routinely been a sufficient justification for the choice of an experimental model."[4]

In May 2009, a report was issued by the Committee on Scientific and Humane Issues in the Use of Random Source Dogs and Cats in Research ("the Committee") pursuant to a congressional request[5] to study whether cats and dogs from Class B dealers are necessary for National Institutes of Health–funded research. The ninety-page report is fascinating to read and contains detailed information on Class B dealers and the animals they provide for NIH-funded research. The committee's findings are summarized as follows:

- Random source animals exhibit different characteristics not found in purpose-bred animals and may be more necessary for certain forms of research.[6]
- Random source animals cost less than purpose-bred animals. However, if a random source animal is conditioned (e.g., treated for parasites, dewormed, vaccinated), that adds to the cost. If the random source animal is not conditioned, then the laboratory could expend additional costs in bringing the animal to a particular level of health.[7]
- The demand for random source, and purpose-bred, cats and dogs has decreased in the past thirty years, and the number of Class B dealers has significantly fallen. The reasons include "research trends, alternate animal models, institutional policies, animal welfare, public opinion, animal rights pressure, regulatory and financial burden."[8]

- There are alternate sources for obtaining animals with qualities similar to random source cats and dogs (e.g., directly from animal shelters, Class A dealers, research colonies, and owner-donated animals).[9]
- In reviewing the forty-year history of the Animal Welfare Act, the Class B dealer system is not working as intended. The USDA has increased its enforcement of Class B dealers, though not completely effectively; the standards of care vary greatly among the current Class B dealers including some who flaunt the regulations and jeopardize the system; and the animals once in the care of Class B dealers do not meet the level of care required of research institutions.[10]
- Overall, "the Committee thus determined that Class B dealers are not necessary for supplying dogs and cats for NIH-funded research."[11]

There are countless ways that animals can be used at the hands of human researchers. Some of the different types of experimentation that shelter cats and dogs may be used for include medical testing of techniques (surgical techniques or medical tools), pharmaceutical testing (human and animal drugs), blood banking for other animals, cosmetics, industrial, and biochemical. Random source cats and dogs are also used by universities to train medical and veterinary students in surgical and other medical techniques.

According to the committee, "[r]andom source dogs and cats may possess a variety of desirable characteristics for research, including anatomic features, age, genetic diversity, and naturally occurring infectious disease, among others. However, they may also have undesirable features, such as unverifiable health status, zoonotic diseases and inconsistent research qualities (such as temperament)."[12] The committee acknowledged that the care of animals from pounds and shelters varies greatly across the country, with some animals receiving high-quality care and other animals receiving little if any care. These animals may have a variety of infectious viral diseases, parasites, and behavioral issues, and may be incubating some diseases that become known at a later time. Although some Class B dealers may "condition" animals through vaccinations, deworming, and other veterinary care, "random source animals may still have health problems, since not all infectious agents can be eliminated by antibiotics or deworming or prevented through vaccination. In contrast, purpose-bred animals have a higher degree of assurance of being microbiologically defined."[13]

Of further interest is that during the fact-finding and procurement of testimony from stakeholders, "[t]he Committee was unable to specifically identify research projects that used Class B animals, since [the National Institutes of Health] does not maintain records of the specific sources or numbers of research animals nor of grants that use Class B animals."[14]

According to USDA records for 2007, 7 percent of all research animals covered by the AWA were dogs and 2 percent were cats.[15] Of the total dogs and cats used in the research in 2007 to 2008, "approximately 4 percent of dogs and 1.2 percent of cats used in research were acquired from Class B dealers with a smaller percentage of those being random source animals from pounds or shelters."[16] Those numbers break down as follows:[17]

Dogs
• Source of dogs: 4,673 (2,297 from individuals such as a hobby breeder with hounds being the most common dog bought and sold),[18] 1,429 from other USDA licensees such as Class B dealers, and 947 from shelters (pound seizure)
• Purchasers of dogs: 4,058 (2,863 to research, 1,194 to other USDA licensees, and 1 to an individual)
• Sent to research facilities: 2,863 (2,568 to academic settings, 231 to laboratories, 64 to federal research facilities, and 0 to manufacturers)

Cats
• Source of cats: 378 (230 from shelters [pound seizure], 81 from other USDA licensees, and 67 from individuals)
• Purchasers of cats: 290 (276 to research and 14 to other USDA licensees)
• Sent to research facilities: 276 (247 to academic settings, 17 to laboratories, 12 to federal research facilities, and 0 to manufacturers)

The most common type of dog and cat used in research is a purpose-bred animal from a Class A dealer or a research colony. However, USDA provided the committee with information that showed approximately 20 percent of dogs and 61 percent of cats used in research come from animal shelters (i.e., pound seizure).[19]

The committee found that the extent of dogs and cats used in research, teaching, tests, and experiments over the past thirty years has dramatically declined. In 1973, there were 195,157 dogs and 66,195 cats used (this includes both purpose-bred and random source cats and dogs), whereas in 2007 there were 72,037 dogs and 22,687 cats.[20] "The use of animals to study relatively serious medical problems (e.g., cancer, heart disease, diabetes) tends to garner more support than their use for studying relatively minor problems (e.g., allergies), *while research involving the use of dogs and cats receives considerably less support than that involving the use of rodents* (Herzog et al., 2001)."[21]

In spite of the lack of documentation on what types of research use random source cats and dogs, "[a] common argument for the use of random source dogs is the need for larger, 27–37 kg (60–80 pounds), and older animals that are physically and physiologically similar to humans."[22] Tractability has also been argued to be an advantage through the use of random source cats and dogs. "[R]andom source animals were often behaviorally more predisposed than purpose-bred animals to training such as resting quietly for conscious animal studies or running on a treadmill. While tractability is certainly an important trait for studies requiring measurement of blood pressure, heart rate, and circulating hormones in conscious animal models, it is important to emphasize that this trait is largely a function of prior socialization with humans, and in no sense confined to random source animals. Poorly socialized dogs and cats, regardless of source, can be expected to be more fearful of, and resistant to, interactions with unfamiliar people including laboratory personnel. Conversely, when properly socialized, purpose-bred animals can be as tractable as former pets. Therefore, generalizations regarding tractability cannot be made, and depend upon individual animals, their socialization, and history."[23]

In its report, the committee noted the following areas where random source animals, though without supporting documentation, might be effective due to the anatomic and physiologic attributes of the dogs: cardiovascular (a dogs cardiovascular system is similar to humans in size and function); pulmonary (pulmonary artery and vein of the left lower lung lobe is more accessible in larger dogs); orthopedic (dogs are good models for prosthetic devices for hip and knee replacement, fixation devices and techniques, and tendon and ligament repair); age-related diseases (older random source dogs are more readily available than waiting for a purpose-bred dog to age, which adds costs to housing the dog until it's old enough for the study); genetic diversity from the random source population; naturally occurring infectious diseases (based on unknown medical history, including heartworm, Lyme disease, mange); and spontaneously occurring animal models of human disease (using random source animals to compare to purpose-bred animals for spontaneously occurring diseases such as sleep apnea, hemophilia, and muscular dystrophy).

For cats, the following research might be effective based on their anatomic and physiologic attributes: feline immunodeficiency virus (this is similar to HIV in humans; purpose-bred cats infected with FIV do not exhibit the disease like random source cats that are naturally infected); feline interstitial cystitis (random source cats develop cystitis which is similar to the human disorder); and feline infectious peritonitis (random source cats are a source of this often fatal virus which is helping scientists understand the mutation of other human viral diseases).

The committee examined the welfare of cats and dogs in laboratories and concluded that "random source dogs and cats used in research probably endure greater degrees of stress and distress compared to purpose-bred animals."[24] This conclusion was not based on studies as none were available on the topic, but rather was based on indirect evidence that former pets do not transition as well to laboratories as would purpose-bred animals. Many pets suffer physiological and behavioral changes when confined in a cage and can take two to five weeks before baseline physiological levels return to normal. The loss of social companions, stimulation, lack of control over stressors, and being exposed to unfamiliar people are all factors that cause chronic stress and can be immunosuppressive on these pets. "Given that some random source dogs and cats are likely to be former pets or strays and therefore not used to prolonged cage confinement, it is reasonable to infer that they may have more difficulty adjusting to laboratory conditions than purpose bred animals."[25]

ARE ANIMAL EXPERIMENTS EFFECTIVE?

In 2009, Dr. Ray Greek and Dr. Niall Shanks published *FAQs about the Use of Animals in Science*. They head Americans for Medical Advancement, an organization dedicated to promoting biomedical research and advancing methodologies that lead to effective cures and treatments for diseases in humans. Dr. Greek is a board-certified anesthesiologist, has taught at several medical schools, and has previously performed experiments on animals. Dr. Shanks is an expert in bioethics and the philosophy of science.

The book was written in layman's terms to explain when animal research is beneficial to humans and animals, and when it is not. The book focuses on all animal-related research and not just random source animals. But the opinions expressed certainly should cause everyone to pause and examine what is happening to animals in laboratories.

The authors first clarified the meaning of various types of "research."

- "When we use the phrase *animal research* we mean research involving animals when the research is meant to benefit the animal being used, or at least is not intended to harm the animal."[26]
- "*Animal experimentation* is used to indicate research that is not necessarily meant to benefit the individual subject involved. Animals used in the context of animal experimentation are typically euthanized when the study comes to an end."[27]
- "We use the phrase *animal model* to mean the use of an animal to model or represent humans."[28]
- "*Vivisection* literally means dissecting or cutting up the living."[29]
- "[T]he term *medical research* is reserved for attempting to find something new on the subject involved that will either be of benefit to the subject directly or at least not harm the subject."[30]
- "*Medical experimentation*, on the other hand, means attempting to find something new regardless of whether that new fact will be meaningful for the subject."[31]

To further clarify, "[U]sing animals as models for humans is an example of experimentation, not research, since the animals being used do not stand to gain any benefit from it, and are likely to be harmed in the process."[32] Drs. Greek and Shanks set forth that "[a]nimals are used in science in at least nine different ways:

1. Animals are used as predictive models of humans for research into such diseases as cancer and AIDS.
2. Animals are used as predictive models of humans for testing drugs or other chemicals.
3. Animals are used as "spare parts," such as when a person receives an aortic valve from a pig.
4. Animals are used as bioreactors or factories, such as for the production of insulin or monoclonal antibodies or to maintain the supply of a virus.

5. Animals and animal tissues are used to study basic physiological principles.
6. Animals are used in education to educate and train medical students and to teach basic principles of anatomy in high school biology classes.
7. Animals are used as a modality for ideas or as a heuristic device, which is a component of basic science research.
8. Animals are used in research designed to benefit other animals of the same species or breed.
9. Animals are used in research in order to gain knowledge for knowledge's sake."[33]

Drs. Greek and Shanks believe that the first two listed *are not* scientifically valid uses of animals in science; however, the remaining seven *are* scientifically viable.[34] They explain that the community of animal experimenters groups all nine of these areas into one general category and then extrapolates one successful area to the remaining eight areas. It is done in an effort to demonstrate that animal experimentation is viable. They argue, however, that scientific results have proven that using animals is not predictive of human response to drugs or learning how diseases progress.

"Living complex systems also manifest different responses to the same stimuli due to: (1) differences with respect to genes present; (2) differences with respect to mutations in the same gene (where one species has an ortholog of a gene found in another); (3) differences with respect to proteins and protein activity; (4) differences with respect to gene regulations; (5) differences in gene expression; (6) differences in protein-protein interactions; (7) differences in genetic networks; (8) differences with respect to organismal organization (human and rats may be intact systems, but may be differently intact); (9) differences in environmental exposures; and last but not least (10) differences with respect to evolutionary histories. These are some of the important reasons why members of one species often respond differently to drugs and toxins, and experience different diseases. These are the kinds of differences that are relevant to an assessment of animals as predictive models."[35]

For example, in response to the creation of Sulfanilamide, a drug in the late 1930s used to treat streptococcal infections that killed more than 100 people at that time, public outrage resulted in Congress passing the Food, Drug, and Cosmetic Act in 1938, which is administered by the U.S. Food and Drug Administration (FDA). "This law requires that all pharmaceutical drugs (as well as any chemical compound that alters the chemistry of the body) be tested on animals to prove their safety before they can be marketed to the public. We now know that safety testing on animals is not predictive for humans but animal testing seemed a solution at the time."[36]

The book provides many instances where animal testing to indicate human response proved to be ineffective, and sometimes harmful, in humans.

- "The National Institute of Allergy and Infectious Diseases (a division of NIH) acknowledged, at a summit they held in 2008 following the failure of a Merck AIDS vaccine in 2007, that the rhesus macaque system now used to test potential vaccines is not predictive and in fact has *not* been working out well for researchers. The Merck vaccine failed to protect against HIV infection in humans despite doing so in monkeys."[37]
- "Extracranial-intracranial (EC-IC) bypass procedures for inoperable carotid artery disease were tested or perfected on dogs and rabbits. Neurosurgeons performed thousands of EC-ICs before it was discovered the operation did more harm than good. More patients died or suffered strokes because of the operation than were saved as a result of it. This is the problem when using animals to predict human response."[38]
- "Thalidomide was a drug released in the late 1950s as a treatment for morning sickness in pregnant women. Unfortunately, the babies of the women who took the drug were born with phocomelia (the absence or deformation of limbs) as well as other anomalies. As least 10,000 children were affected. . . . Would extensive use of the animal model have predicted thalidomide's adverse affects? No. Not a single individual species or combination of species can be said to have predicted the effects of thalidomide."[39]
- "Think of the numerous drug recalls reported in the news because of previously unknown side effects. The animal models did not predict a vast majority of these side effects. Furthermore, animals are not even used in an attempt to predict subjective reactions to drugs such as nausea, headaches, dizziness, and so forth—which also happen to be some of the most common side effects."[40] And, "As of 1980, there were roughly 1,600 known chemicals that cause cancer in mice and other rodents. But only about 15 of these chemicals caused cancer in humans. What, prospectively, distinguished the 15 human carcinogens from all the others? Nothing."[41]

- More examples where humans were harmed from data using animal models include:
  - o "Asbestos and other environmental toxins were thought safe because of animal testing.
  - o "Animals did not suffer from artherosclerosis when fed a high cholesterol diet, so in the 1950s scientists said that cholesterol was unrelated to heart disease.
  - o "Artificial heart valves were delayed because dogs react to the valves differently than humans.
  - o "Penicillin was put back on the shelf for a decade because it was excreted too rapidly in a rabbit.
  - o "Medications such as Rezulin, Propulsid, Fen-Phen, and benzbromarone tested safe in animals but killed humans.
  - o "People who work in the animal labs have been killed by viruses such as Herpes B, which are benign in their nonhuman hosts but lethal to humans.
  - o "Hormone Replacement Therapy (HRT) was sold to millions based on animal tests. (While HRT is appropriate for some, it increases the risk for many diseases in most.)
  - o "The failed Alzheimer's vaccine caused some of the test patients to worsen.
  - o "The numerous failed AIDS vaccines, some of which increased risk.
  - o "HIV transmission through contaminated blood in France, which was caused in part because of reliance on animal models.
  - o "Lost cures for cancers because of adverse effects or lack of efficacy in animals.
  - o "Pharmaceutical companies have lost very large sums of money because animal tests led to development of drugs that were eventually stopped. That loss is passed on to the consumer.
  - o "The polio vaccine was delayed because of reliance on monkeys."[42]
- "One of the most stunning failures of the animal model approach in cancer research was its prediction that smoking was safe. Animal experiments largely failed to demonstrate a smoking-cancer connection."[43]
- "Former U.S. Secretary of Health and Human Services Mike Leavitt stated in 2007: 'Currently, nine out of ten experimental drugs fail in clinical studies because we cannot accurately predict how they will behave in people based on laboratory and animal studies.'"[44]

Drs. Greek and Shanks believe that "[a]nimals such as vertebrates can be viably used as a modality for ideas, education, a source of spare parts, incubators, factories and growth media, for the study of diseases affecting the same species, to study basic biological principles, and axiomatically to add knowledge to the world."[45] They also provided recommendations to increase the validity of results from research studies as follows:

> We propose: 1) that the EPA [Environmental Protection Agency] and FDA [Food and Drug Administration] ultimately eliminate animal testing requirements. Such tests are not predictive of either safety or efficacy; 2) that NIH [National Institutes of Health] and other funding agencies critically evaluate claims in grant applications concerning the predictive efficacy of animal models in the context of environmental toxicology, and disease and drug research. Such claims in grant proposals need serious justification, and should not be pro forma add-ons to keep those with oversight responsibility happy and content; 3) measures should be taken by funding agencies to develop methods to critically assess arguments supporting the predictive utility of animal models in specific contexts; 4) the practice of dressing up basic research proposals (antecedently known to be scientifically important) as proposals likely to be of direct and immediate predictive relevance to human medicine and well-being should be critically evaluated. A good place to start this critical process would be with the widespread use of weasel words such as *may, might,* and *could possibly* in research proposals.[46]

Drs. Greek and Shanks are not alone in the medical and research professions in regard to the ineffectiveness of animal research to benefit humans. Other physicians and researchers are questioning the validity of animal models being predictive of human response. The Physicians Committee for Responsible Medicine (PCRM), which was founded in 1985, is a nonprofit health organization that promotes preventive medicine, conducts clinical research, and encourages higher standards for ethics and effectiveness in research. PCRM researches, educates, and promotes the use of non-animal models to conduct research and training. For an informative discussion on the "Point-Counterpoint on Medical School Animal Laboratories," please visit the web link associated with this endnote. Below is an excerpt from that web link:

"Dogs will often be killed anyway in the pound."

If so, they will not be subjected to the trauma of continued confinement, shipping, preparation, and experimentation before death in the laboratory. Additionally, dog laboratories undermine animal control efforts, since many people will not bring animals to a shelter if they might be given up for experimentation. Therefore, many more animals are simply abandoned or left to the elements. Not uncommonly, dogs begin to wake up during the laboratory or are further traumatized by a faulty procedure. This often traumatizes the students as well.

"The more opportunities to practice a procedure before using it on a patient, the better."

Students are best prepared for procedures on humans by observing and taking a limited role in those procedures, under close supervision, and by manipulating lifelike human anatomical simulators and trainers. Most animal laboratories don't teach procedures anyway, they simply demonstrate the known effects of pharmacological or physiological agents. Computer programs, CD-ROMs, simulators, and videotapes also allow for repeated use and practice, according to the students' needs.[47]

Dr. John Pippin is a senior medical adviser to PCRM and consented to be interviewed for this book. In regard to the claims of Drs. Greek and Shanks, Dr. Pippin agrees that animal models are not predictive of human response. However, he and PCRM believe that animals should not be used in any form of experiment or training.

Dr. Robert J. Wall, a research physiologist with the USDA's Animal Biosciences and Biotechnology Laboratory, and Dr. Mordechai Shani, the director of the Gertner Institute in Israel, recently stated, "The vast majority of animals used as models are used in biomedical preclinical trials. The predictive value of those animal studies is carefully monitored, thus providing an ideal dataset for evaluating the efficacy of animal models. On average, the extrapolated results from studies using tens of millions of animals fail to accurately predict human responses. . . . We conclude that it is probably safer to use animal models to develop speculations, rather than using them to extrapolate.[48] And Dr. Stephen H. Curry, a professor of pharmacology and physiology with the University of Rochester in Rochester, New York, stated in a 2003 article, "The failure, in the clinic, of at least fourteen potential neuroprotective agents expected to aid in recovery from stroke, after studies in animal models had predicted that they would be successful, is examined in relation to principles of extrapolation of data from animals to humans."[49]

Although much progress has been made over the past decade, we still have a long way to go before researchers move away from using animals to test human response, especially on cats and dogs from animal shelters.

The old-guard research community clings to the use of animals because that is what has been done for hundreds and even thousands of years. Yet, have cures been found for the terrible diseases that plague humans today? Doctors Greek and Shanks sum up the arguments of the research community in a manner that I have personally experienced over the years, and continue to experience today in advocating to stop pound seizure. "If you have them on the facts, argue the facts; if you have them on the law, argue the law; if you have them on neither, attack their character. . . . By using the phrase *animal rights extremists* in the same diatribe about animal experiments, pro-animal experimentation interest groups seek to avoid engaging in true debate and instead imply that those who disagree with them are anti-science, inflexible, irrational, anti-human, and dangerous."[50] In the end, Drs. Greek and Shanks, and their organization, oppose "animal models as a modality for predicting or seeking cures and treatments for human disease based on overwhelming scientific evidence that animal models are not predictive for humans while acknowledging that animals can be successfully used in science in other ways."[51]

DYING TO LEARN

In 2009, Animalearn, the education division of the American Anti-Vivisection Society, released its findings on the supply and use of dogs and cats in higher education training institutions called *Dying to Learn: Exposing the Supply and Use of Dogs and Cats in Higher Education*. This section will describe some of the noteworthy findings regarding current-day practices that impact dogs and cats taken from animal shelters. Information on the use of dogs and cats at 175 public colleges and universities was compiled from Institutional Animal Care and Use Committee (IACUC) public records, USDA inspection reports and license renewal applications, and surveys of 150 university and college biology departments covering 175 institutions. Response rate to the survey was 20 percent.[52]

Dying to Learn identified three areas where dogs and cats are being used in higher education: dissection of dead animals, clinical skills training, and terminal surgery labs. Dissection became commonplace in high schools in the 1920s, involving a variety of animals, including cats. Fifteen states currently have laws or state education policies for primary and secondary education that allow students the choice of whether to dissect an animal: California, Florida, Illinois, Louisiana (education policy),

Maine (education policy), Maryland (education policy), Massachusetts (education policy), New Jersey, New Mexico (education policy), New York, Oregon, Pennsylvania, Rhode Island, Vermont, and Virginia.[53]

For clinical skills training, "a University of Georgia animal use protocol approved purchasing live dogs and cats from random source Class B dealers and acquiring animals directly from animal shelters. The dogs and cats are then euthanized for the clinic skills (emergency and non-emergency) laboratory in which students learn such procedures as fracture repair and chest tube placement."[54]

In terminal surgery labs, these once former pets are being killed at alarming rates in the name of education. "When animals are killed in surgery labs, students also miss out on the opportunity to learn post-operative care, including pain management, supportive care, assessing the healing process, etc. Such skills can be gained working with actual animal patients and are just as important as learning surgical procedures."[55]

For colleges and universities, twenty-eight schools have policies on student choice to select non-animal alternatives with more moving toward creating similar policies.[56] And veterinary schools are also seeing a growing trend in students objecting to harmful practices. In 1987, the first lawsuit of its kind was filed by two veterinary students against the University of Pennsylvania who won the right to obtain their degree without the required terminal surgery lab. The university ended the terminal surgery lab in the small animal clinic in 2002. Tufts University was the first veterinary school to end its small animal terminal lab in 2000–2001. Now "[m]ore than half of the 28 U.S. veterinary schools no longer require terminal surgeries in core courses, and many do not require them in elective courses."[57]

In reviewing records from ninety-two universities from 2005 to 2007, 52 percent are using both live or dead dogs and cats, while 26 percent are using solely live dogs and cats. In the survey of 150 universities (with only a 20 percent response rate), 63 percent are teaching anatomy and physiology by using dead cats.

Dying to Learn further looked at the sources of dogs and cats for educational purposes and found several universities practicing pound seizure. "Between January 2005 and July 2008, Texas A&M acquired 474 live dogs from local animal shelters, primarily Lehman Animal Shelter in Giddings, Texas."[58] Records indicate that the dogs were euthanized at the university on the same day they were acquired from the shelter. Between January 2006 and March 2008, Texas A&M acquired eighty-six dead cats from Lehman Animal Shelter. The shelter has since stopped the practice of providing live cats and dogs to Texas A&M and has confirmed that now only deceased animals are provided.[59]

Other schools obtaining cats and dogs directly from pounds and shelters include Colorado State University,[60] the University of Georgia,[61] Michigan State University,[62] Iowa State University,[63] and the University of Minnesota.[64] When dealing with pound seizure, universities are obtaining animals that are not accustomed to being confined in a cage, socially isolated, and dealing with strangers. Some cats and dogs may appear nonaggressive but end up being unpredictable, and they arrive with unknown medical conditions and a possible host of diseases.

Class B dealers were also investigated in *Dying to Learn* as a source of cats and dogs for educational purposes. In addition to discovering that random source cats and dogs are being transferred among the various random source Class B dealers, including being transported across state lines, Animalearn also discovered that animals are being transported in trucks for long distances (up to 1,000 miles) in order to fulfill an order received by the dealer. Regarding those dealers brokering in cadavers for education, "[o]ur findings show that greed can result in animals being euthanized and sold to these companies instead of being offered for adoption."[65]

INCIDENTS OF HARM CAUSED TO DOGS AND CATS IN LABORATORIES

In 2007, it was alleged that a researcher from the Cleveland Clinic subjected a dog, without anesthesia or pain medication, to repeated brain aneurysms in order to test a medical tool. The dog eventually died a painful, inhumane, and undignified death. The incident was portrayed in media reports because of the extreme nature of the situation. The USDA placed the doctor under investigation for violations of the Animal Welfare Act; the final resolution has not yet been made public. However, according to People for the Ethical Treatment of Animals (PETA), the USDA cited the Cleveland Clinic for two violations of the AWA, and the doctor who killed the dog was prohibited from working with animals for two years.[66]

In 2004, four veterinary students at the Center for Animals and Public Policy at the Tufts University School of Veterinary Medicine, a school that studies and promotes human-animal interactions, publicly complained concerning the treatment of laboratory dogs. "[R]esearchers at the school had surgically fractured the hind legs of six dogs, healed the legs, and then euthanized the dogs to study the results. The goal was to find better ways to mend broken bones in dogs, but the fact that an institution dedicated to healing small animals on one part of its campus could destroy those same animals on another part caused an uproar and reopened a long-simmering debate about how far is too far when it comes to using animals for research."[67]

Allen Rutberg, a researcher and assistant professor at the school, commented, "Most people like animals and support scientific research. They're able to balance their beliefs by not thinking about both at the same time or by justifying the research in a moral hierarchy—say, animal research to help heal children. But this particular experiment on this particular campus put those two values systems in direct conflict," says Rutberg. "We're sitting squarely on a fault line. It runs right through the campus, and we're trying to live with it."[68]

While the dogs were still alive, students were invited to meet with faculty to discuss options for the dogs in the study. The faculty invited the students to present an alternative solution that did not require the dogs to be euthanized in order to complete the study. The students suggested that "the researchers could have tested their methods on dogs that came into the hospital with legs already broken. They could have splinted some legs the standard way, others the new way, and compared the results. Barring that, at least they could have found a way to avoid killing them."[69] However, the researchers were growing nervous since the dogs' bones were healing. Time was running out to euthanize the dogs and microscopically examine the bones to see if the technique was successful.

While the students were on winter break, they received an e-mail communication that their alternative solution had been rejected and that the dogs would be euthanized weeks ahead of schedule. The students returned to campus early and worked with the New England Anti-Vivisection Society to issue a press release expressing their outrage. Nonetheless, the dogs were euthanized. The students felt angry and betrayed because this is not how Tufts has handled similar situations in the past. The dean ultimately held a meeting with students, amid tight security and worries of threats. The dean was angry because donors were threatening to pull support for the school. The situation had gone viral over the Internet. Tufts reputation was tarnished.

In the end, Tufts' policy remained the same. "It is both unfortunate and appropriate that the issue exploded at Tufts, a veterinary school that prides itself as a leader in the humane treatment of animals. It was the nation's first veterinary college to eliminate so-called terminal labs, where professors would repeatedly anesthetize a dog so their students could practice live surgery before finally euthanizing the animal. (Students now learn from cadavers and field experience.) It is the first school in the country to set up a 'client donor' program in which owners of deceased pets can will the bodies to science. The school even runs a bereavement hot line for pet owners."[70]

There are various levels of advocacy in the animal protection world, from conservative to extreme to outright illegal conduct. Other than the groups that engage in illegal conduct, I have learned that there is a place for all of the animal protection organizations. Although some people may get weary when they hear the word "PETA," organizations like PETA[71] and Last Chance for Animals[72] conduct undercover investigations in order to expose alleged abuses occurring in laboratories and with pound seizure. Whether or not you support the efforts and tactics of these organizations, it is worthwhile to review some of their recent investigations:

- PETA made a November 2009 investigation into the University of Utah's treatment of its laboratory animals. "For more than eight months in 2009, a PETA investigator worked undercover inside the laboratories of the University of Utah (UU) in Salt Lake City and documented miserable conditions for and terrible suffering of the dogs, cats, monkeys, rats, mice, rabbits, frogs, cows, pigs, and sheep confined there.

  "Our investigator learned that homeless dogs and cats—obtained for a few dollars from area animal shelters through an archaic Utah state 'pound-seizure' law, which requires government-funded shelters to turn animals over to laboratories that request them—were used in invasive, painful experiments and killed.

  "A pregnant cat pulled out of the Davis County animal shelter gave birth to eight kittens the very day she arrived at UU's laboratories. When the kittens were just 7 days old, a chemical was injected into their brains to cause fluid to build up. After the surgery, the distressed cat—who showed great affection for her kittens before they were taken for the experiment—stopped nursing her babies, and they all died.

  "In other experiments, a cat named Robert, who was also bought from the Davis County animal shelter, had a hole drilled into his skull and electrodes attached to his brain, and dogs bought from a local shelter had their necks cut open so that medical devices could be implanted inside."[73]

"The University of Utah (UU) paid the Davis County Animal Shelter $15 for this friendly, gentle orange-and-white tabby cat named Robert. Laboratory workers decided that Robert, now known as F09-017, would be used in invasive brain experiments.

"UU experimenter . . . cut into Robert's skull to implant electrodes in his brain. A large gash ran from Robert's forehead past his ears.

"Thus began a series of experiments in which electrical current was fired through the electrodes, stimulating nerves that caused Robert's legs to move involuntarily. After each experiment, Robert showed signs of trauma: He was tired and groggy, his pupils dilated and his eyes became glassy, and he vomited repeatedly. Over time, this affectionate cat became skittish and withdrawn.

"While PETA's undercover investigator eventually left the laboratory, Robert did not: He remained in his tiny cage, enduring experiment after experiment."[74]

- In the fall of 2009, PETA took action against Texas Tech University Health Sciences Center (TTUHSC) for its practice of purchasing live cats from Odessa, Texas, Animal Control for use in medical training courses. "PETA has filed a complaint with the university urging officials to replace the use of cats in this training with educationally superior medical simulation tools. In training exercises [at TTUHSC], cats are forced to undergo painful intubation procedures in which hard plastic tubes are repeatedly forced down their wind pipes by course participants. This can result in bleeding, swelling, scarring of the animals' throat tissue, collapsed lungs, and even death. In another procedure, the cats have air forced into their chest cavities so that course participants can repeatedly practice inserting a needle into the animals to remove the excess air. The American Academy of Pediatrics and the American Heart Association, which sponsor the most widely taught pediatric life-support courses in the country, exclusively endorse the use of modern, human-like manikins, not live animals, for this kind of training."[75] On November 29, 2009, PETA issued a statement praising TTUHSC for ending the use of homeless cats from the Odessa Animal Control and the overall use of any cats in its medical training courses.
- The Physicians Committee for Responsible Medicine reported in its online magazine about the March of Dimes experiment which

involved sewing the eyes of kittens shut in order to prove that the brain would be permanently affected by early visual deprivation. "A new Massachusetts Institute of Technology study shows that the March of Dimes' experiment was as pointless as it was cruel. The new study found that a young woman who was born blind and whose sight was restored at age 12 had almost normal vision 20 years later—showing that, in humans, early visual deprivation does not preclude the possibility of regaining sight. This finding also brings new hope to people with congenital blindness."[76]

Below are a few stories of shelter animals who were victims of pound seizure and died in laboratory experiments.

CRUELLA'S CRUEL ENDING

The story of Cruella was captured by the American Anti-Vivisection Society based on its investigation into the final days of her life.

There is little doubt that Cruella, a shepherd chow mix, was once someone's companion. Found wearing a purple collar, and already spayed, Cruella was roaming the streets of Carson City, Michigan, when she was picked up by Montcalm County Animal Control workers. She may have thought she was being rescued, but little did she know that the county had a contract with R&R Research, a random source Class B animal dealer that supplies animals to research facilities. In exchange for receiving free disposal of its euthanized animals, the shelter relinquished some of its dogs and cats to R&R Research. One of them was Cruella.

When Cruella was handed over to the R&R Research, she became known simply as E6993. There, she likely spent most of her time alone, confined in a cage with limited human companionship until she was sold to the University of Florida six months later.

She made the trip, traveling more than 1,000 miles, with 13 other dogs, a potentially frightening and high-stress experience. At the university, veterinary students named her Cruella, and she became the subject of their veterinary training exercises. Over a period of seven months, she was sedated or anesthetized seven times, often for hours at a time, and used in procedures to teach endoscopy, abdominal surgery, and ultrasounds exercises. She also underwent surgery with the intention to spay her, but once her abdominal cavity was opened, it was discovered that she had already been spayed.

During her last month at the University, Cruella twice experienced a lack of appetite, and passed up the food that was presented to her in her bowl. However, it was noted that she would eat handfuls of canned food, suggesting that the lack of human contact was taking its toll on her physical and psychological well-being.

On April 27, 2009, the Montcalm County Board of Commissioners voted to end the county's contract with R&R Research. But for Cruella, it was too late; she had been killed a year earlier at the University of Florida."[77]

KODA: THE FACE OF MICHIGAN HOUSE BILL 4663

Koda never realized that his ordeal would result in the 2009 Michigan House Bill 4663 being named after him. It certainly is not any consolation for what Koda endured, but it is a lasting legacy in hopes of changing Michigan's law on pound seizure.

On June 13, 2007, Koda's life changed forever. He was surrendered to a mid-Michigan animal control shelter. The reasons for Koda's surrender are unknown, and efforts to locate his family have been unsuccessful. Due to Michigan's hardship during the economic downturn, it is believed that Koda's family simply did not have the resources to care for him anymore. What Koda's family did not know is that the shelter engaged in pound seizure.

Koda was a three-year-old long-haired seventy-pound black and silver Malamute. When he was brought to the shelter, the family signed a document that stated in excruciating small print, "I request that the animal be disposed of as seems advisable in the discretion of the . . . Animal Shelter." Whether Koda's owner read that fine print is unknown; but what is known is that the shelter posted no signs and gave no indication that Koda could be sold to a research facility. On June 19, 2007, Koda left the animal shelter in the van of a Class B dealer. He was then transferred to the University of Michigan to be a subject in the Advanced Trauma Life Support (ATLS) program.

ATLS programs help to train medical students in emergency medical skills by allowing the student to practice on clearing obstructed airways, fluid removal from the sac surrounding the heart, and other procedures. These programs help to train our future doctors in life-and-death situations. Most ATLS courses use "manikins" which are based on the anatomy of a human; however, 12 out of 166 facilities offering ATLS that responded to a survey of the Physicians Committee for Responsible

Medicine are using and killing live animals in the process.[78] One of those programs was at the University of Michigan.

After Koda lost his life in the ATLS program, there was a public outcry from Michigan citizens and national animal welfare organizations. The Physicians Committee for Responsible Medicine filed a federal complaint against the University of Michigan's use of live animals, and led the charge for concerned citizens, doctors, paramedics, and alumni to contact the university to express their outrage. In the end, the University of Michigan issued a press release on February 26, 2009, indicating that it was ending the use of live animals during the ATLS program. The University of Michigan joined eight other Michigan ATLS programs, and a majority of other U.S. trauma training programs, in using human-based simulator programs.[79] The Physicians Committee for Responsible Medicine has filed other complaints with the USDA against the schools still using live animals in ATLS courses since the Animal Welfare Act requires the use of non-animal alternatives when available. Those alternatives are very much available and are, in fact, used by a majority of schools.

CHAPTER 7

Alternatives to Animals in Research and Education

I believe I am not interested to know whether vivisection produces results that are profitable to the human race or doesn't. To know that the results are profitable to the race would not remove my hostility to it. The pain which it inflicts upon unconsenting animals is the basis of my enmity toward it, and it is to me sufficient justification of the enmity without looking further.

—Mark Twain

I abhor vivisection with my whole soul. All the scientific discoveries stained with innocent blood I count as of no consequence.

—Mahatma Gandhi, statesman and philosopher

The issues associated with pound seizure often are intertwined with the legitimacy of medical research. An on-point debate about pound seizure should focus on the betrayal to the animals, former family pets, and the community's response to a shelter being the supply source of research animals. Contrary to the status quo research arguments, banning pound seizure will not stop the use of live animals in medical research. We have seen that in the wake of seventeen states and the District of Columbia banning pound seizure, yet medical research and educational training still continues, some even in those states. It is important to avoid getting off-track in debates on the legitimacy of animal-based medical research and keep the focus on the real issues of pound seizure. This chapter is dedicated to providing some information regarding non-animal testing choices.

Whenever the issue of pound seizure arises in a community or state, the medical researchers come out in full force to defend their use of animals.

The researchers and Class B dealers will parade cancer survivors in front of state and local officials in hopes that the tragedies of those illnesses will prevail over common sense and critical thinking. Some communities have banned pound seizure in spite of the power of the medical research community, whereas other communities collapse under the weight of medical research and university lobbyists. It is important to remember and convey the message that advocating to ban pound seizure is not a movement against medical research.

"The reason we use animal tests is because we have a comfort level with the process . . . not because it is the correct process, not because it gives us any real new information we need to make decisions," said Melvin E. Andersen, director of the division of computational systems biology at the Hamner Institutes for Health Sciences near Raleigh, North Carolina. "Animal tests are no longer the gold standard," he said. "It is a marvelously new world." "Some animal tests haven't changed in 60 years," said Thomas Hartung, head of the European group. "The tests are frozen in time. This is not science. Science is always moving ahead."[1]

RESEARCH FACILITIES MOVING TOWARD ALTERNATIVES IN ANIMAL RESEARCH

In 2008, three government agencies signed a Memorandum of Understanding that animal testing would be phased out over a ten-year period. This is the sign of the future. The Environmental Protection Agency, the National Toxicology Program, and the National Institutes of Health have agreed to collaborate to develop new methods of testing new chemicals and drugs without the use of animals.[2]

> Two NIH Institutes have formed a collaboration with the EPA to use the NIH Chemical Genomics Center's (NCGC) high-speed, automated screening robots to test suspected toxic compounds using cells and isolated molecular targets instead of laboratory animals. This new, trans-agency collaboration is anticipated to generate data more relevant to humans; expand the number of chemicals that are used; and reduce the time, money and number of animals involved in testing. Full implementation of the hoped-for paradigm shift in toxicity testing will require validation of the new approaches, a substantial effort that could consume many years. . . . The MOU and the plans articulated in the *Science* article provide a framework

to implement the long-range vision outlined in the 2007 National Research Council (NRC) report, "Toxicity Testing in the 21st Century: A Vision and a Strategy," which calls for a collaborative effort across the toxicology community to rely less on animal studies and more on in vitro tests using human cells and cellular components to identify chemicals with toxic effects. Importantly, the strategy calls for improvements in dose-response research, which will help predict toxicity at exposures that humans may encounter.[3]

Drs. Ray Greek and Neill Shanks have explained their theory of why animals are not appropriate test models to determine human response: "Animals and humans share many similarities in terms of the 'stuff' they are made from (all have cells, genes, lipids, proteins, and so on), but they also exhibit many differences. At the subcellular and genetic level, where the vast majority of research is now taking place, *organizational differences* between animals and humans outweigh the similarities in ways that are relevant to a discussion of prediction. (Recognition of organizational differences draws our attention to the way 'stuff' is put together, used and regulated.)"[4]

Drs Greek and Shanks believe that animals can be useful to train future doctors and veterinarians. But when it comes to laboratory research on animals, "[a]n experiment will always result in knowledge—even if we only learn what doesn't work. But if you mean 'Will the results from animals predict what a drug will do in humans or the natural progression of a disease—how the disease affects the body, what it does to the cell, what happens if left untreated?'—then the answer is *no*."[5]

Over the past two decades, advances have been made in research techniques such that live animals are no longer needed in many studies or training. There has also been a growing trend toward teaching techniques for high school students, college students, and medical and veterinary school students that do not include live animals. For those students pursuing medical or veterinary degrees, the first covenant that they learn is to do no harm. Yet, far too many universities ask students to kill their first animal clients for the sake of learning. Students have refused to complete educational labs involving live animals, and even dropped out of school because they could not resolve the moral dilemma of killing an animal in order to obtain a degree. It can be traumatic for some students to engage in training or research on a live animal because they may picture their own pet lying lifeless on a table. That interferes with the effectiveness of the training as demonstrated by the following story.

"Jaymie Shanker, M.D., a PCRM [Physicians Committee for Responsible Medicine] member in Shaker Heights, Ohio, will never forget her live animal lab experience either. She was studying at Case Western Reserve University School of Medicine in Cleveland. After refusing to participate in a cardiac physiology class that used animals, she was down the hall watching a computer simulation PCRM had provided as an alternative when some of her fellow medical students started trickling in.

"Some were dazed and others were crying from the trauma of seeing animals killed like that," Dr. Shanker remembers. "They couldn't learn what they were supposed to because it seemed like their pet was on the table. Instead, we all gathered around the computer and watched the video together. It was a better learning experience."[6]

There are moral and ethical issues involved for students who are required to conduct their training on live cats and dogs. Is the training on live animals beneficial, especially for students who have pets at home or love animals? Do the emotions of working on live animals interfere with the effectiveness of the education? For veterinarians in particular, who likely enter the business out of a love for animals, is it ethical to ask them to kill their first client? Many schools are now asking these same questions before they require a student to practice on an animal.

U.S. MEDICAL SCHOOLS THAT DO NOT USE LIVE ANIMALS IN TESTING OR EDUCATION

The Physicians Committee for Responsible Medicine (PCRM) and the American Anti-Vivisection Society (AAVS) have been leading the charge to educate universities on the use of alternatives to animal research. Each year, more schools are added to a distinguished list of universities that no longer use live animals in the curricula. Appendix C contains a listing of U.S. allopathic and osteopathic medical schools that use live animals and a listing of medical school Advanced Trauma Life Support classes using live animals, prepared by the PCRM. As of November 2009, only 8 medical schools are still using live animals in the curricula, whereas 151 have progressed to curricula that do not involve using live animals. The eight schools are Johns Hopkins University School of Medicine; the Medical College of Wisconsin; Oregon Health and Science University School of Medicine; Uniformed Services University of the Health Sciences F. Edward Hébert School of Medicine; the University of Mississippi School of Medicine; the University of Tennessee College of Medicine (Chattanooga campus only); the University of Virginia School of Medicine; and the University of Wisconsin School of Medicine and Public Health.[7]

As of January 2010, only 10 medical schools in the United States and Canada are using live animals in Advanced Trauma Life Support classes, whereas 198 schools use non-animal models. Those 10 schools are Baystate Medical Center in Springfield, Massachusetts; Elvis Presley Memorial Trauma Center/University of Tennessee Health Science Center in Memphis, Tennessee; Hartford Hospital in Hartford, Connecticut; Massachusetts General Hospital in Boston, Massachusetts; MeritCare Hospital/North Dakota State University in Fargo, North Dakota; Ottawa Hospital in Ottawa, Ontario; Tulane Life Support in New Orleans, Louisiana; the University of Massachusetts Medical School in Worcester, Massachusetts; the University of Texas Medical Branch in Galveston, Texas; and Vanderbilt University in Nashville, Tennessee.[8]

One example of a medical school still using live dogs in its training curricula is the Medical College of Wisconsin. In November 2007, PCRM along with the Wisconsin Humane Society and four Wisconsin physicians held a press conference in Milwaukee to call for the end of using live dogs at the college. PCRM reported that the following spring, the college was anticipated to use and then kill about sixty dogs in the first-year physiology course for medical students. At the press conference, Dr. John Pippin, senior medical adviser to PCRM, stated that a complaint had been filed with the federal government requesting an investigation into the use of dogs at the college. Dr. Pippin stated, "Department of Agriculture determined that alternatives to the use of animals exist and that a 'written narrative must justify why the alternatives were not used.'"[9] Dr. Pippin pointed out that various non-animal models are available to the school, and the school also owned four human patient simulators.

At the time, only two U.S. medical schools were still using live dogs in physiology courses: Medical College of Wisconsin and Washington University School of Medicine in St. Louis. Since then, the latter has stopped using live dogs in its course.

NON-ANIMAL TRAINING TECHNIQUES FOR HIGHER EDUCATIONAL INSTITUTIONS

According to the Physicians Committee for Responsible Medicine, many top-ranked medical schools have altered their surgery instruction to include "simulators such as Simulab's TraumaMan and laparoscopic surgery trainers, as well as didactic teaching, class and small-group case discussions, interactive computer-based methods such as virtual reality programs, and hands-on mentorship opportunities with faculty in anesthesiology, surgery, emergency medicine, and other clinical disciplines."[10]

In 2001, the American College of Surgeons approved the use of TraumaMan in Advanced Trauma Life Support (ATLS) courses. TraumaMan looks like a human body and has been used in training ATLS programs across the country. TraumaMan appears real and has lifelike skin, subcutaneous fat, muscle, and can bleed. It is based on human anatomy and allows students to practice over and over again until they perfect a technique. Doing this with animals would require the use of many animals, and euthanizing each animal afterward.

PCRM has helped to move medical schools toward acknowledging the effectiveness of non-animal training models through the use of the USDA inspection process and obtaining records under the Freedom of Information Act process. "The federal Animal Welfare Act requires schools to consider viable non-animal alternatives when those alternatives are available. The overwhelming use of non-animal teaching methods shows that these alternatives are not only available but are preferred by the vast majority of medical schools."[11] Pippin provided the chart below which compares where medical schools were in relation to using live animals, to where they stand now.

Dying to Learn outlined numerous non-animal educational models that are available at various phases of the schooling process. The Animal Welfare Information Center[13] with the USDA also has resources and in-

Table 7.1. Timeline of U.S. Medical School Animal Use (1982–present)[12]

Year	# Medical Schools LAL*/Total (%)	# Osteopathy Schools LAL/Total (%)	# All Schools LAL/Total (%)
1982	107/124 (86%)	Unknown	Unknown
1985	91/124 (73%)	Unknown	Unknown
1994	77/125 (62%)	Unknown	Unknown
2001	40/125 (32%)	Unknown	Unknown
2003	27/126 (21%)	Unknown	Unknown
2005	24/126 (19%)	Unknown	Unknown
January 2006	22/126 (17%)	2/25 (8%)	24/151 (16%)
January 2007	14/126 (11%)	2/25 (8%)	16/141 (11%)
January 2008	10/126 (8%)	0/28 (0)	10/154 (6%)
December 2009	8/131 (6%)	0/28 (0)	8/159 (5%)

*Live animal labs
Note: Percentages are rounded to the nearest one percent. All nine new medical schools opening 2007–2009 have animal-free curricula.

formation available on alternatives to animals, as does Animalearn's *The Science Bank*. As further discussed in chapter 6, the overall findings and recommendations in *Dying to Learn* were:

- That schools are engaging in harmful use of dogs and cats when teaching. "We discovered teaching exercises, such as terminal surgery labs at veterinary and medical schools in which dogs are killed following the procedure; clinical skills training labs for veterinary students, which involve euthanizing live dogs or cats in order to teach skills to students; and animal dissection, which involves using the cadavers of cats, dogs and other animals to teach anatomy and physiology."[14] The recommendations include allowing students to choose the use of non-animal models, changing curricula to have alternatives as the default procedures, and include shelter medicine programs for the therapeutic use of animals as well as accepting client-donated cadavers.
- Schools are obtaining dogs and cats from questionable sources, such as Class A and B dealers. Numerous violations of the AWA by the dealers, as well as the practice of pound seizure, contribute to the inhumane source of these animals. The recommendations include not using random source cats and dogs from shelters in education, encouraging USDA to consistently exercise its authority to revoke and not renew dealer licenses, and insisting that any animal obtained for education purposes should be from an ethical source and that it must be beneficial and therapeutic to the animal. Sources should not include dealers who breed animals since they promote the disregard of life and fail to foster compassion.

NON-ANIMAL MODELS FOR EDUCATIONAL TRAINING

The following is a description of some non-animal alternatives for educational training. For a complete description of each model, please consult *Dying to Learn*.[15]

Undergraduate Education

Dissection in undergraduate biology classes and learning human anatomy and physiology can be eliminated through the use of software, virtual dissection, and models, such as Neotek's Cat Dissection Laboratory CD-ROM, ITG Catlab, DryLab Fetal Pig, VH Dissector, Complete Human Anatomy Series on DVD, A.D.A.M. Interactive Anatomy, Anatomy Revealed, the Pregnant Cat Model, Anatomical Animal Models, and Bone Clones, as well as establishing a program for people to donate their bodies upon death or the bodies of their deceased pet.

Veterinary Education

Whether learning from cadavers or live animals, non-animal alternatives are available in the form of software, models, and skill-based and surgical simulators. Such programs include Canine Osteology CD, the Virtual Heart CD, Virtual Canine Anatomy, CLIVE (Computer-aided Learning in Veterinary Education), surgery videos, Veterinary Models by GPI, ethically sourced plastinated specimens, Canine Head Model, SimPooch, Hollow Organ Surgical Simulator and Skin-Suture Pattern Simulator, Skills-Based Simulators, Critical Care Jerry and Critical Care Fluffy, Virtual Reality Surgical Simulation, Live Surgery Simulator, Medical Education Technologies, Inc., and Human Patient Simulator. In addition, willed body donor programs, blood donor programs (where pet owners take in their pet a few times a year for blood donation), and shelter medicine programs (providing care to shelter animals, such as spay-neuter surgeries, that benefits the animal and aids with adoption of the animal) are also viable alternatives.

Medical Education

Medical schools have been consistently phasing out live animal labs because of other viable alternatives of software and human patient simulators, such as the Virtual Physiology Series, Live Surgery Simulator, Medical Education Technologies, Inc., Human Patient Simulator, Endoscopy AccuTouch, and Virtual Reality Simulators.

The work of PCRM and AAVS demonstrates that dogs and cats obtained through pound seizure are not necessary to train our future doctors and veterinarians, nor are they appropriate to test the human response to various drugs and procedures. Great steps have been taken in recent years toward eliminating the use of animals, particularly dogs and cats, in education and research, yet more work lies ahead.

CHAPTER 8

The Victims and Survivors of Pound Seizure and Pet Theft

In spite of protections put in place by the Animal Welfare Act, family pets, some lost and some stolen, are still ending up in laboratories. "Through an investigation by [the American Anti-Vivisection Society] and its education division, Animalearn, it was discovered that many animals who are transferred from shelters to dealers or universities are listed as spayed or neutered on sales transaction documents, and/or have animal control paperwork showing that they were taken in as strays."[1] In my research, I found that many legitimate research and training institutions are not interested in conducting studies on family pets. Therefore, until pound seizure is abolished, no family pet is safe, and legitimate researchers will be concerned that someone's beloved pet is now in a cage in their laboratory. Below are a few stories of former family pets that typify random source cats and dogs of pound seizure.

THE DARING RESCUE OF KARYN

Karyn's story holds a dear place in my heart because I was involved in saving her from an unknown future of pound seizure. Karyn's rescue also set in motion a volatile pound seizure battle in one Michigan county, and resulted in numerous personal and professional losses. But for Karyn, her life was saved. For me, although I experienced significant loss during this time, it thrust me to a place where I could be a better advocate for animals. If Karyn only knew how she forever changed my life for the better.

Karyn arrived at a mid-Michigan animal shelter in December 2002. She was a tiny black cat with gold eyes who cowered in her cage from the first day. Karyn had clearly been someone's pet. But the smells, sights, sounds, and uncaring cold steel cage likely added to her fright. Karyn was placed into the shelter's Cat Room. The Cat Room was supposed to be a safe room for cats. The volunteer organization assisting the shelter animals spent considerable time and effort on the cats in the Cat Room and had successfully adopted and rescued every cat from the Cat Room for almost two years. We took an interest in Karyn, including getting her spayed and fully vaccinated, services that the shelter was not equipped to provide. We also placed newspaper advertisements promoting her adoption on three occasions.

Karyn was at the shelter for fifty-two days, which is a lengthy amount of time for animals there. Many of us worried about Karyn's state of mind being in a cage so long, and worried that she would be euthanized or sold to the dealer without warning. The shelter director had refused our efforts to rescue Karyn and place her in a foster home. We were informed that it was the winter and that the shelter did not have sufficient cats for the public to view. I remember thinking to myself that the public was not rushing the doors of the shelter to view animals for adoption because the shelter was old, run-down, dirty, and some shelter staff were frequently unpleasant to visitors. Yet the more we advocated rescuing Karyn, the more I observed the director becoming obstinate.

It was during this time that I, another volunteer, and two county commissioners met and created a plan to finally rid the county of pound seizure. We began a marketing campaign to tell citizens of the practice. This included placing posters and flyers at local pet stores and veterinary clinics, and grew to include putting advertisements in the local newspapers. Prior efforts to have the shelter itself stop pound seizure had failed, as had prior advocacy to the county commissioners. An education campaign was needed.

The shelter director had publicly professed for years that he was simply following the mandate of the county commissioners in sending cats and dogs to the dealer and that he did not have a personal opinion about the practice. Yet, when our marketing campaign began in January 2003, I believed his true opinion on the topic emerged.

The dates and events surrounding Karyn are permanently etched in my memory. On January 17, 2003, the shelter director placed a rescue ban on the animals at the shelter. I was informed that there were not enough animals for the public to view, particularly younger animals like Karyn. The timing of the rescue ban seemed to coincide with the increased efforts to raise awareness. I felt that Karyn was trapped in the director's power play with volunteers like me. Efforts to reason with him failed. The volunteer group then placed rescue holds on the cats and dogs that we feared were in jeopardy of being sold to dealers, including Karyn. A rescue hold would prompt the shelter to contact the holder and allow twenty-four hours to rescue the animal.

The shelter director also informed us that the reduced-price rescue fee would not be honored during this "shortage" and that rescue organizations would have to pay the full adoption prices to rescue cats and dogs, which was a violation of a county ordinance that I helped to get passed in 2001. Nonetheless, we tried to rescue the animals but with little luck, and often used our own money to help pay the increased fees.

Then came strike three. We were told that if a foster home already had three pets, an adoption would be denied. The county had no pet limit ordinances, and the shelter even attempted to impose this new rule on rescue organizations outside of the county. I was frustrated and believed there was no reasoning with the shelter director or his dreamed-up mandates. The tactics seemed clear to me that our advocacy was touching a nerve.

As Karyn continued to languish in a cage, advertisements were placed in a local free newspaper that portrayed a photograph of a shelter animal recently sold to a dealer and an action request for people to contact the county commissioners to ask that pound seizure be stopped. Interestingly, the newspaper began disappearing from newspaper stands in the area surrounding the animal shelter. The day the newspaper was published, I received a phone call from the editor asking who might be behind the newspaper disappearances. I had a strong suspicion, and my belief was merited when the shelter director telephoned the newspaper and demanded to know who had placed the "offensive ad" and insisted it be removed.

The marketing plan was working. Many unaware citizens were now asking that pound seizure be prohibited in the county. But the shelter director went on the offensive against the animals, in my opinion to retaliate against our actions. I must admit that it was a smart tactic to get to the volunteers. As tensions increased, Karyn continued to shiver in fright in her cage.

On January 28, 2003, everything changed. Relations between our animal rescue group and the shelter director had been strained, at best, for years but quickly turned hostile on this day. I received a curt e-mail message from the director accusing my rescue organization of being a political action committee, rather than a nonprofit, and questioning whether the shelter would be willing to work with us in the future. What he failed to realize is that charitable organizations formed as 501(c)(3) nonprofits are able to engage in advocacy efforts. That is precisely what we were doing on behalf of the animals. Although the shelter rarely wanted our assistance with the animals, it soon became abundantly clear that we were unwelcome. Then the full-on assault began against the volunteers and the shelter animals.

On January 29, 2003, the shelter director sold Karyn, along with another cat and one dog, to a Class B dealer. Karyn was sold despite the rescue hold we had placed on her after our efforts to rescue her had been rejected and after our efforts to pay a full-price adoption fee were denied. The other cat had been sold on his first day available to be adopted, and we had not taken action soon enough to place a rescue hold on him.

I had grown accustomed to the so-called misunderstandings and miscommunications with the shelter staff. However, it seemed obvious that there was an active effort to prevent us from rescuing Karyn, which was contradictory to the director's prior declaration that animals were needed at the shelter for potential adopters.

When I received the frantic phone call from a volunteer that Karyn had been taken away in a dealer's van, my stress quickly turned to rage. Then I forced myself to calm down so that I could think about what to do next. We never believed we would get Karyn back from the dealer, but we did believe we could gather enough evidence to have a complaint filed against the shelter for violating the Animal Welfare Act in disallowing an adoption and preferring to sell Karyn to a dealer.

Knowing that the law only required that Karyn be held for five days at the dealer facility, we needed to act quickly. A friend of our rescue group, who I will call Sandy, offered to telephone the shelter to inquire about any recent disposition of black cats. Our purpose was to test whether the shelter would be honest about Karyn's disposition, which is required to help people be reunited with their lost pets. As expected, the shelter employee stated that Karyn had been adopted. What we did not expect was for the employee to offer to have Karyn returned from her "new owner." We had not even discussed that option with Sandy. But Sandy did not want to let an opportunity lapse to save Karyn, so she agreed to go to the shelter to see Karyn. I cautioned Sandy not to do anything that would cause her discomfort, even if that meant losing Karyn to the dealer.

The next day, February 5, 2003, Karyn was returned to the shelter. Life as I knew it forever changed on that day. Sandy viewed Karyn, told the shelter that it was her lost cat, and paid a $295 fee to cover her boarding at the shelter. It was a miracle that Karyn was safe, but then the real tragedy began. While I was in a courtroom prosecuting a stalking trial, the shelter director was lying in wait for both Sandy and Karyn.

Leaving the courthouse late that evening, I called a volunteer I will name Chris, who had Karyn safely at her house. Chris informed me that after Sandy dropped off Karyn, the director followed Sandy out of the county in an unmarked car, and things went very wrong. Chris was scared.

Everything became fuzzy in my mind when Chris was talking. I instinctively knew that things were going to get much worse. I instructed Chris to get out of her house and get Karyn to safety until everything could be figured out. I then called Sandy and arranged to meet her at a restaurant. Sandy was seated with her husband, wringing her shaking hands, as she described the situation. Sandy told me that when she arrived at the shelter, she had a sinking feeling because everyone in the office was staring at her. The staff were suspicious that Karyn wasn't Sandy's cat. Sandy was taken to the shelter isolation ward and saw Karyn curled up in the corner of the cage, shivering with fear. She told the staff that Karyn was her cat, even though, of course, she was not. Sandy stated that she was only concerned about keeping Karyn safe and did not focus on the suspicious conduct of the shelter's deputy director.

Sandy filled out some paperwork, which she did not read, and paid a $295 redemption fee to cover the fifty-two days Karyn was at the shelter. As Sandy described what happened, all I could think of was how smug the shelter director must have felt allowing Sandy to pay the fee knowing he was about to ambush her.

As Sandy left the shelter with Karyn, she said the shelter deputy director had an eerie smirk on his face. Sandy stated she was so nervous that she simply got in her car and drove quickly to Chris's apartment. After leaving Karyn with Chris, Sandy was still anxious as she began her drive home. About thirty minutes into the drive and after crossing the county line, she noticed that a car had been following her for the last ten miles. It was not a police car or an official car, but it was following so closely and the driver seemed to be staring at Sandy the entire time.

Sandy took an exit off the highway but the car continued to follow her even when she took a detour through a parking lot. The car then quickly pulled up next to her car, and the driver flashed a badge through his window. It was the shelter director, though not known to Sandy at the time. Yelling, he told her that she was under arrest. Sandy was not sure if he was legitimate: He would not allow her look at his "badge." He threatened her and told her that she had committed at least three felony crimes for stealing a cat. Sandy was shocked, as was I, because paying $295 to redeem a cat hardly qualifies as theft. Sandy added that the director acted aggressively. Terrified, she agreed to talk in order to avoid jail. She disclosed the entire plan to catch the shelter lying about Karyn's disposition and that when the shelter offered to return Karyn, she was not going to let the opportunity pass to save her. The shelter director told Sandy that if she turned over Karyn, he would let her go without any criminal charges. Although Sandy did not admit to disclosing Karyn's location, subsequent events led me to believe that she did tell the shelter director Karyn's whereabouts.

I was shocked to hear of how the shelter director had terrorized Sandy and abused his power. He had no authority to make an arrest, yet threatened Sandy in order to get a statement. I was sympathetic to what Sandy went through, yet I was angry that she quickly disclosed the plan. It was now late in the evening and I was exhausted from a long, and now emotional, day. As I made the long drive home, I telephoned my employer, the county prosecutor, to advise him of the situation and to seek his advice. I was met with an icy reception and a comment that he could not speak to me. As the snow started to fall on this dark night, it was then that I knew the shelter director had gotten to my boss. I had always enjoyed a wonderful relationship with my boss, which unfortunately ended on that night.

As I continued the drive home, Chris telephoned me and frantically screamed into the phone that someone had broken into her apartment. After calming her down, Chris told me that she had given Karyn to a friend who was supposed to keep her safe. Chris returned to her home, where she had cats of her own, and found the door kicked in and a search warrant taped to her refrigerator. The search warrant was for Karyn.

Still, to this day as I write this, I am astonished at the extremes that the shelter director engaged in to get Karyn back. The search warrant even listed that a microchip had been implanted under her skin before letting Sandy redeem her so that the authorities could track her down. Several attorneys that I spoke with after the fact agreed that the director abused his power. But the wheels had already been set in motion, and I was now the target. It was a clever plan to turn the focus against me and away from the misconduct of the shelter. If you shift the bright light onto others, then your own wrongdoing will not be uncovered. And that is exactly what the shelter director did.

In a surprising twist related to my position as an assistant prosecuting attorney, I was given an ultimatum by my boss that required me to apologize to the shelter director for the scheme, to back down on what I had discovered, and to return Karyn to the dealer. Sometimes the hardest position a person can take is to stay true to one's beliefs and not back down under pressure. All of my instincts told me to not turn away and certainly not return Karyn to the dealer. As much as I loved and thrived in my position as a prosecutor, I chose to lose my position and keep my integrity intact. It was one of the most difficult decisions I have ever had to make. Yet it was the right decision.

I believe that I came extremely close to uncovering something involving the shelter or the dealer, and maybe close to discovering why animals may have been hoarded for the dealer and not allowed to be rescued or adopted. But when one person attempts to stand up to government officials, some of whom I still believe had unclean hands in the process, it is impossible to keep the focus on the real story to discover the truth.

In an attempt to continue the pressure on me so that I would remain silent, the shelter director and my former employer attempted to obtain criminal charges on Sandy, Chris, and me. The Michigan attorney general reviewed the case and not only refused to issue criminal charges, but ordered my former boss to investigate the shelter. He refused to do that. Although I have no reason to believe that my former boss was involved in any wrongdoing involving the shelter or the dealer, his actions made me question his motives given that I was well-respected by him in my work. The shelter director also fired Chris's husband, who was an animal control officer. Chris's husband had received pressure from the shelter director to disclose any information from his wife regarding the rescue of Karyn, but he had no knowledge to disclose. Shortly thereafter, he was fired.

In the end, Karyn was safe and had an amazing adventure that evening. A friend of Chris's, who I will name Joe, took Karyn to his home that night. What Joe did not expect was that the shelter director and his posse of police would show up at his house in the middle of the night to retrieve Karyn. We never understood how they knew Karyn was at Joe's house. But Joe was able to sneak out of the house undetected, with Karyn tucked in a backpack, purring the entire time. Karyn was safe with Joe for several months and became the mascot to the now volatile pound seizure battle in the county.

But Karyn suffered an unnecessary tragedy. Joe was employed at a veterinary clinic. Many weeks later, and without notifying me or Chris, he euthanized Karyn because he said she had behavioral problems. Joe's actions were unforgivable and unnecessary because he had been informed on several occasions that many people would take Karyn into their home to keep her safe until she was adopted, including myself. His excuse for euthanizing her was reprehensible, and I still cannot rationalize it in my mind after all these years. Despite all we did to save Karyn, Joe took her life in one quick minute.

Although I am still sad over the loss of Karyn after all the tragedies and losses that occurred in saving her, her life and her story did help in the county banning pound seizure in June 2003, just four months after her harrowing rescue. Her short life also launched me into the world of pound seizure and working to stop the practice throughout the country. Karyn will never be forgotten.

KINGSTON

Kingston was a well-behaved yellow Labrador retriever who arrived at a Michigan shelter as a stray on March 20, 2003. He was wearing a collar, which showed that he had had a family at one time. He also knew basic commands, such as "come" and "sit." He was wonderful with children and desperately sought the attention of volunteers. Kingston was held as "unadoptable" for ten days by the shelter, for reasons unknown to volunteers. Then on his first day available for adoption, the shelter sold Kingston for $10 to a Class B dealer. What a shame for this very adoptable dog that was never given the chance to find another home.

TARRAGON

Tarragon was a handsome yellow Labrador retriever who was surrendered to a Michigan shelter by his owner, along with three other dogs in March 2003. Tarragon had a nice, stable temperament and walked well on a leash. He was very well-behaved. The volunteers quickly grew to love Tarragon. They arranged for him to be neutered, which would help him be adopted sooner. Six days later, while still recovering from the neuter surgery, Tarragon was sold to a Class B dealer. Records show that his family was not informed that Tarragon could be sold for medical research.

MITTENS' LUCKY DAY

In the fall of 2007, a dog was taken to a mid-Michigan animal control shelter and immediately recognized by a volunteer as "Mittens," a wonderful dog that had previously been adopted through a shelter in a neighboring county. Pictures were taken of the dog, and it was confirmed that the dog was the one-year-old spayed female black/white blue-eyed greyhound mix that the shelter had previously adopted and named Mittens.

A worker at the adopting shelter contacted the former adopters to inform them of the whereabouts of their dog so they could reclaim her. Unfortunately, the adopters never returned the calls. Instead, the adopting shelter told the shelter that was holding Mittens that if Mittens was not reclaimed by the owner, the original adopting shelter would be adopting/reclaiming the dog. The worker explained the circumstances that the adopting shelter's contract required a return of the dog to them, and even called the shelter daily to confirm that Mittens was still there.

Five days after Mittens was admitted to the shelter, and the first day she was available for adoption, the volunteer went to the shelter with proof of spay, rabies, and photographs that proved the adopting shelter's reclaim/ownership of the dog. By that time, though, the dog had already been sold to a Class B dealer. The volunteer's request to reclaim the dog had been ignored; Mittens was never given the opportunity to find a new home. When the volunteer complained, the shelter staff indicated they would contact the Class B dealer to see if Mittens could be returned. That day the volunteer and shelter staff were not able to get the Class B dealer on the telephone, and messages to the dealer were not returned. After several hours of attempts by the staff at both animal shelters, they were unable to reach the Class B dealer and messages were simply not returned. The USDA was then called upon to enforce a response and facilitate the return of the pet through their authority. Mittens was subsequently returned to the safety of the original adopting shelter and was quickly readopted to a permanent loving home thanks to great effort made by caring individuals and the USDA. It is still unknown why the shelter that had Mittens gave her to the dealer and bypassed the request to have Mittens returned to the original shelter.

ECHO'S ADVENTURE

In a newspaper report of October 20, 2005, titled *Why Is This Dog Smiling?* the *Fayetteville Free Weekly* published an exposé of stolen pets in research. In particular, a brindle lab-mix named Echo was featured in the story. Echo's family alleged that he was stolen from their backyard in June 2005. Two months later, a veterinarian at the University of Minnesota research laboratory, after conducting a scan, found a microchip in Echo. Echo had been sold to the laboratory by a Class B dealer from Michigan and had been in the possession of at least two Class B dealers, none of whom reported that Echo had a microchip or attempted to locate his family. Echo was returned to his family, and the USDA opened an investigation into a Missouri Class B dealer who originally obtained Echo. Last Chance for Animals estimates that approximately two million pets are stolen each year with only 10 percent being returned. Echo was one of the lucky victims of pet theft.

PRINCE: ONE VERY LUCKY DOG

Prince was a two-year-old black and white shepherd/Australian shepherd mix that arrived at a mid-Michigan animal control shelter on July 8, 2009. Prince had a wonderful temperament, was well-mannered, and quite congenial. At the time, the shelter was still engaging in pound seizure though the Class B dealer's pound seizure contract was due to expire on August 1, 2009. Animal rescuers were mobilized and working diligently to rescue as many animals from the shelter during this time period while the time dwindled on the contact.

Prince was a dog that should have been rescued directly from the shelter. A person who organizes rescue transports from Michigan contacted the shelter on July 14, 2009, to determine what date Prince and three other dogs were available for rescue. The rescuer was informed that Prince was not available for rescue until the next day, July 15. The rescuer informed the shelter that Prince would be rescued the next day unless he was adopted. The shelter's policy is to allow the public one business day to adopt any shelter animal when the animal's legal hold period is concluded. An animal rescue group is allowed to rescue an animal on the second day that the animal is available for adoption, and the Class B dealer was allowed to take animals on the third day the animal was available for adoption. However, the shelter allowed the Class B dealer to seize Prince on July 15, the second day he was available for adoption, even knowing that rescue was on the way to retrieve Prince. Why would a shelter give an animal to a Class B dealer knowing that a rescue organization was coming to retrieve the animal?

Advocates, including myself, quickly organized on Prince's behalf, analyzing the time span that Prince was at the shelter to determine if there was a violation of the AWA hold guidelines or the shelter's guidelines. In fact, it was discovered that the shelter violated its own guidelines by giving Prince to the dealer two days before allowed. Through the quick action of the rescuer and several other advocates, Prince was returned from the Class B dealer and placed with an animal rescue organization. Prince was then adopted to a loving home a few months later.

One interesting note about Prince's rescue from the world of pound seizure is that he tested positive for heartworm. It calls into question the use of random source animals in experimentation that have preexisting diseases, parasites, and ailments that could impact the legitimacy of the research.

CHAPTER 9

The Voices of the Research and Educational Communities on Random Source Cats and Dogs

A CONGRESSIONAL STUDY

In 2008, Congress ordered a study to be conducted on the scientific use of random source animals stemming from the Pet Safety and Protection Act of 2007. A committee of ten professionals (primarily researchers) was convened by the National Academies of Sciences, which included Stephen W. Barthold (chair) from University of California, Center for Comparative Medicine; Donald C. Bolser from the University of Florida, College of Veterinary Medicine; Kelly D. Garcia from the University of Illinois at Chicago; Joseph R. Haywood from Michigan State University; Stuart E. Leland from Wyeth Research; Lila Miller, veterinarian from the American Society for the Prevention of Cruelty to Animals; Randall J. Nelson from the University of Tennessee; James Serpell from the University of Pennsylvania School of Veterinary Medicine; Michael R. Talcott from Washington University School of Medicine; Robert A. Whitney, retired from the U.S. Public Health Service; and Christine Henderson (project director) from the National Research Council. The committee was tasked to evaluate the necessity of using random source cats and dogs from Class B dealers. Their report titled "Scientific and Humane Issues in the Use of Random Source Dogs and Cats" was released on May 29, 2009, during a congressional briefing.[1]

On January 12, 2009, I attended a committee meeting and observed as they received testimony from Dr. Robert Willems, the assistant Eastern Regional director for USDA's Animal Plant and Health Inspection Service/Animal Care. Dr. Willems addressed the committee about his experiences with random source Class B dealers (RSBDs). He was a USDA inspector in the early 1990s and was involved in the prosecution and license revocation of two RSBDs in Oregon. Both were convicted for having stolen dogs. Dr. Willems stated there are eleven RSBDs in the country that solely broker random source animals for live animal research, one of which is currently suspended for five years beginning August 2008. Nine of the RSBDs are in the Eastern Region. Dr. Willems stated that RSBDs may obtain dogs and cats from animal shelters, auctions (which are regulated by USDA), or from someone who breeds and raises animals. Although auction houses have not been a recent source for cats and dogs for research, they could be used as a means to legitimize illegally acquired cats and dogs.[2] He indicated that people can give their own pet to a RSBD, but this is very rare and is not covered in the regulations.

Dr. Willems testified that the oversight of RSBDs is the single most important thing the USDA does based on public and congressional expectations. He stated that RSBDs have always been an issue over the years, even with the declining numbers of dealers and animals involved. Those two statements impressed upon me that the USDA believes the time, resources, and money spent on oversight of RSBDs to be significant given that there are only nine remaining RSBDs.

Dr. Willems suspects that one RSBD is preparing to go out of business because that particular dealer has not had animals in many months. He also stated that a few dealers are acquiring more animals than they are selling. This is of concern to the USDA because the purpose of an RSBD is to have a high-volume business. The RSBDs bring in animals, then move them out quickly in order to make money. He did not have evidence as to why some dealers are keeping animals. I wondered if the RSBDs are breeding animals in order to maintain a sufficient source of animals given the dwindling supply of shelter cats and dogs across the country. If so, the RSBD would need to obtain a Class A license to breed animals for research.

Dr. Willems stated that the RSBD investigations are time consuming and costly and on average each investigation takes 800 hours. Random source Class B dealers now receive quarterly on-site inspections. The days of phone inspections are no longer allowed. The other nonrandom source Class B dealers only get yearly on-site inspections.

Trace backs are required for all RSBDs and must be done in person at each quarterly inspection. A trace back involves tracking an animal's ownership history back to the original source to ensure that the RSBDs are complying with the AWA in the procurement of animals. During a quarterly inspection, the inspector is required to look at all the records of the animals in the RSBD's care and select four to ten random trace backs.

When going through the documents, if a record appears suspicious, then that must be pulled for a trace back. If a trace back results in a dead end (without getting the original source of the animal), that automatically prompts a USDA investigation.

During each quarterly inspection, inspectors are required to look at every animal in the possession of the RSBD. That is not a new requirement and was required even before the C. C. Baird case (the Arkansas RSBD who was shut down and convicted). When asked how those dogs were allowed to languish and die at the Baird facility, Dr. Willems believed that Baird had a secret facility where he housed the dogs that were unknown to the inspector.

The USDA issued a new standard operating procedure in September 2008 that set better guidelines on trace backs, including that trace backs must be done on-site and not by telephone. With the new procedure, the USDA will conduct one 100 percent trace back session on each RSBD per year. This means that every animal in the RSBD's possession at the time of the trace back must be traced back to the original source. "[I]ncreased trace back oversight is working at discovering violations, but these ongoing events illustrate that the law continues to be violated."[3]

Dr. Willems explained that when he was an inspector in the 1990s in Oregon, he traced back the alleged surrender of pets in the possession of an RSBD and instead of going back to the owner's address, the trace back came back to the middle of a cornfield or a lake. Trace backs are very important in order to prevent stolen pets from entering the research system.

Animal auctions are licensed by the USDA, and RSBDs can purchase animals at auctions. There are three auctions in the East Region and two in the West Region. Unfortunately, USDA inspectors are unable to attend every auction. Anyone can take an animal to an auction for sale. Therefore, stolen animals can end up at an auction. When an RSBD purchases an animal from the auction, the trace back paperwork starts there. Thus, if an animal is stolen, it will not be discovered because all the RSBD needs is the auction paperwork to validate the trace back. Dr. Willems stated that RSBDs can get around the "original source" paperwork requirement for trace backs by purchasing animals at auctions. Auctions are primarily used to sell breeding animals. However, if someone takes his animal to an auction, he is not told that the animal could end up in research.

Dr. Willems stated that there were 1,429 animals purchased by RSBDs from other USDA licensees (auctions, Class B dealers) from November

1, 2007, to November 30, 2008. RSBDs also exchange animals with other RSBDs frequently.

The USDA has no legal oversight over flea markets. Dr. Willems stated that anything can happen at a flea market, which is where C. C. Baird received most of his animals. RSBDs cannot get a pet from a flea market unless it is from a breeder or a pet owner, and the paperwork validates that information.

Current USDA regulations do not require RSBDs or research facilities to scan for microchips in animals. If an animal shelter fails to scan, then family pets with microchips may enter the research system. This can be avoided if the USDA is allowed to institute a regulation to mandate scanning.

Dr. Willems had no evidence in the past eight years that RSBDs have been stealing animals although he did state that suppliers to RSBDs have been. Dr. Willems indicated that it is very difficult to find evidence of pet theft because the USDA has to find the original owner. This generally only happens if the original owner files a complaint with the USDA or the supplier to the RSBD is arrested and provides evidence to law enforcement on another supplier. Therefore, the USDA cannot assure the public that pet theft is not occurring and that stolen or illegally obtained animals are not entering the research system.[4]

Dr. Willems commented that inspections have been difficult with some RSBDs. Inspectors have been chased off their premises and sometimes inspectors go to an RSBD facility with armed law enforcement. When asked about penalties, Dr. Willems indicated that an initial violation will result in the inspector giving an on-site citation and allowing the RSBD to correct the situation if it is not severe. The standard is to give forty-five days to correct the issue. If the situation is not corrected, a repeat citation is given and the inspector files for enforcement action. If there are a high number of veterinary issues with the animals, the inspector can give time to correct or confiscate the animals immediately. The inspector can issue a fine on-site or start a full investigation. The maximum fine per violation is $10,000.

When asked what the USDA would like to see happen in regard to RSBDs, Dr. Willems was hesitant to answer. He did indicate that the USDA wants increased fines and more authority. It is restricted by the administrative code in processing complaints, and investigations can be frustrating. Moreover, the USDA investigators are outside staff that handle investigations of other government agencies. The USDA investigations take significantly more time than any other agency investigations, therefore having direct staff would help move the investigations along.

Dr. Willems was questioned about the C. C. Baird investigation, primarily the sanitation issues where the dogs were housed. He indicated that the housing from the Baird case is not typical with other RSBDs. However, it is somewhat typical for the larger RSBD facilities or the RSBDs that do not care to invest in good facilities.

Overall, Dr. Willems' testimony to the committee was damaging to the RSBDs. In the summer of 2009, the committee issued its conclusions: RSBDs are not needed in order to maintain the integrity of medical research or supply of dogs and cats to facilities.

The full report of the committee spans ninety pages. The committee cited its findings as to the advantages and disadvantages of using random source cats and dogs in research as follows. *Advantages* were that random source animals are genetically diverse, and some anatomic features and the presence of spontaneous disease (such as cancer or other infectious diseases) can enhance their value in the research. For example, random source dogs are often larger in size than purpose-bred dogs, thus making them appropriate for studying heart disease. The random source animals may be older which helps with research on aging. *Disadvantages* were that the health and history of the random source cats and dogs is unknown, and the quality of care of the animals at shelters varies greatly, thus impacting research. Since these animals may have parasites and other diseases, even the "conditioning" by the Class B dealers does not necessarily resolve the health issues or make them appropriate for some forms of research. Also, since many of these animals are former pets, they experience more stress and distress during research than would a purpose-bred animal that is accustomed to being confined in a cage. The distress and stress of the former pets can have implications on the research studies.

The committee evaluated the cost of random source animals versus purpose-bred animals and found that random source animals are less costly to laboratories, especially if they are not conditioned (no veterinary care). However, some random source animals are more costly in the end. "[T] he purchase price of a young, 20–25 kg dog runs $325–350 for random source and $600–900 for purpose bred. However, oftentimes dogs and cats from Class B dealers are not free from disease. In addition to being a potential threat to other animals and people in the research facility, they may need to undergo prolonged quarantine, socialization, treatment, or be removed from the study all together. These hidden costs may substantially increase the actual final cost by hundreds of dollars per animal. Additionally, the price of USDA/APHIS oversight of Class B dealers represents a substantial cost to the U.S. government and ultimately the American public that is not incurred by NIH, the research institution, or the research investigator."[5]

The committee made these additional findings:

- The need for random source animals in research has steadily declined over the past thirty years. Research techniques have evolved and changed, alternatives to animal research are available, animal welfare considerations and institutional policies have changed, as has the regulatory and financial burden of using random source animals.
- Less than 1 percent of laboratory animals are cats and dogs, and most cats and dogs are specifically bred in research colonies or by Class A dealers. "[T]he majority of dogs, but not cats, sold by Class B dealers are not random source animals, and are therefore similar to animals provided by purpose-bred [Class A] animal dealers."[6]
- For dogs, 48.8 percent came from individuals, 30.8 percent from other Class B licensees, and 20.4 percent from shelters.
- For cats, 60.9 percent came from shelters, 21.4 percent came from other Class B licensees, and 17.7 percent came from individuals.

In evaluating the Class B dealer system, the committee found that the original system for overseeing RSBDs and the animals in their care may not be operating as intended. The committee also voiced concerns regarding the care of animals at RSBD facilities. "Dogs and cats acquired by Class B dealers are destined for research, but the standards of care at some dealers are discordant with key guidelines for the care of laboratory animals, including U.S. Government Principles, PHS Policy, and the Guide. Instead of adhering to standards of care specific to laboratory animals, Class B dealers and their facilities are governed only by the Animal Welfare Act. Although in principle these various standards are similar, in practice they are not. This dichotomy of standards colors public perceptions of [National Institutes of Health] and USDA, and brings into question the welfare of animals under the care of Class B dealers."[7]

The committee found that other options are available for obtaining random source cats and dogs for research, including working with pet owners who have pets with diseases that could be studied and providing experimental treatments to the animal; partnering with breeders, veterinarians, and working dog organizations to identify animals with recurring genetic diseases that need to be studied; working with breed and hobby clubs to receive donations of animals; continue working with Class A dealers; directly acquiring animals from shelters (pound seizure), although the committee noted that states are disallowing this practice; and using animals from research colonies. Such colonies exist at the University of California (Davis), the University of Florida, and the University of North Carolina.[8]

In the end, "the Committee could not reconcile the serious unresolved Class B compliance issues, and felt that these issues, as well as humane concerns, were major factors in the Committee's final recommendations."[9] The committee concluded that Class B dealers are not required to maintain the use of random source cats and dogs in research.

Dr. Robert Whitney, a member of the committee and a veterinarian who spent twenty-two years with the National Institutes of Health and served as the director of the National Center for Research Resources, has also been vocal on Capitol Hill against the use of random source animals in research from Class B dealers. In a letter dated July 27, 2007, to the U.S. House of Representatives in support of the Pet Safety and Protection Act, he stated, "The continued supply of dogs and cats by random source dealers is a blight on the biomedical community that can be eliminated."[10]

Dr. James Serpell, also a member of the committee, graciously agreed to be interviewed for this book.[11] Dr. Serpell is a professor of animal welfare with the University of Pennsylvania in Philadelphia. His work involves research on the behavior and welfare of dogs, including working dogs (e.g., guide, service, and search and rescue dogs), pets, and shelter dogs. All of this work is conducted in the "field" and does not require the use of laboratory-housed animals. This research has been conducted "only with a view to improving their welfare."[12]

When asked about his position on pound seizure and the use of random source cats and dogs for medical research, veterinary training, or other experimentation, Dr. Serpell stated, "I am not categorically opposed to using shelter dogs and cats for these purposes, if the specific scientific or educational need for these types of animals has been fully and properly justified, if the welfare of these animals during transfer to user institutions meets a high standard (e.g., PHS guide or better), if all reasonable efforts have been made to rehome the animals or reunite them with their former owners, and if the animals have already been scheduled for euthanasia. However, since I doubt that such a system would ever be able to comply with these conditions, I do not currently support a policy of pound seizure." He is opposed to obtaining random source animals from Class B dealers, and he has never obtained a cat or dog from a Class B dealer for his work. "History has demonstrated that the USDA does not have sufficient manpower and resources to police the activities of Class B dealers adequately. Consequently, the animals are always at some risk of neglect or abuse, and it is not possible to close all of the potential loopholes through which Class B dealers may continue to obtain animals from illegal sources. Given the small number of B dealers still operating, and the cost of regulatory oversight, it makes no sense to continue to support an inherently flawed system for obtaining random source animals for research."[13]

When asked about the discussions of the committee in arriving at its conclusions for the report back to Congress, Dr. Serpell was not at liberty to divulge details. However, in regard to the arguments for or against using Class B dealers to obtain random source animals, he stated, "in general terms those in favor were concerned that shutting off this source of animals would impede progress in important areas of medical research, while those against felt that the Class B system was inherently flawed and could never properly ensure that animals were obtained legally or cared for appropriately."[14]

In regard to whether dogs and cats suffer or are in pain during experiments, Dr. Serpell elaborated that "[t]he use of animals for research is more heavily regulated and policed than any other area of animal use. While this cannot entirely prevent occasional abuses, the system does tend to ensure that the vast majority of research animals are treated humanely. Occasionally, studies are approved that inflict a limited amount of pain and distress on animals. Such studies require special justification as to why pain/distress cannot be controlled by analgesia/sedatives, and in terms of their perceived importance to medical knowledge, etc."[15] However, Dr. Serpell agreed that there are currently non-animal alternatives available for medical and veterinary students, and those alternatives have been successfully implemented in schools.

RESEARCH AND EDUCATIONAL FACILITIES THAT RELY ON RANDOM SOURCE ANIMALS

Animalearn, the education division of the American Anti-Vivisection Society, conducted an investigation into university records from 2005 to 2008 to determine, among many queries, whether training universities accepted random source cats and dogs. The investigation found that the following universities had purchased random source cats and dogs from Class B dealers: Michigan State University, Ohio State University, Oklahoma State University (updated information shows that the veterinary school no longer uses random source animals), Purdue University, the University of Florida at Gainesville, the University of Georgia at Athens, the University of Illinois at Chicago, the University of St. Paul, and the University of Oklahoma.[16]

The research community believes that random source cats and dogs are less expensive, which then saves on the overall cost of studies. "However, according to the University of Michigan Medical School, 'non-conditioned dogs [such as those obtained from random sources and not vaccinated or tested for parasites] often have an unknown health status; thus, no guarantees are provided for such animals.'[17] These animals are usually used in a teaching lab shortly after their delivery to the school and are subsequently killed, or they are killed upon arrival at the school for use in dissection labs."[18]

When a random source cat or dog is "conditioned," that means "vaccinating an animal against a single disease and holding it for observation to ensure it is healthy enough for a short-term experiment. If the animal is needed for a longer term project, conditioning may be more extensive. It may include quarantine of the animal for up to six weeks, and treatment and prevention of disease including a range of vaccinations (against rabies, distemper, etc.), antibiotic therapy and frequent monitoring tests, as well as a special nutritional regimen."[19]

The Michigan Society for Medical Research (MSMR) provides the following explanation as to why facilities require the use of random source cats and dogs from animal shelters, including Michigan shelters: "Although pound dogs and cats comprise only a tiny percentage of all animals used in biomedical research and education programs in Michigan and throughout the United States, they are critically important to those programs for both scientific and economic reasons. Less than 2 percent of the more than 10 million unwanted animals in the United States and 500,000 in Michigan that are otherwise put to death in pounds and shelters each year, are released for research. These unwanted animals play a vital role in studies on health problems such as heart and kidney disease, brain injury, stroke, blindness and deafness, and for the education of future veterinarians and physicians."[20]

The Michigan Society for Medical Research states that random source shelter dogs and cats make excellent research models due to their diverse genetic pool. "Randomly outbred dogs, the type most commonly found in pounds, have widely divergent genetic backgrounds. Their diverse genetic makeup is analogous to the variations in genetic backgrounds among humans, especially in the U.S., where immigration and intermarriage among ethnic and racial groups has produced what may be termed a randomly outbred population." Moreover, the cost of acquiring a pound seizure cat or dog is 80 to 90 percent less expensive than obtaining a cat or dog bred for research. For example, an unconditioned random source animal costs $60–100, a conditioned random source animal costs $200, and a purpose-bred research animal costs $422–580. "If researchers could no longer use pound-source animals, they would have to purchase similar animals from breeders. The resulting increase in the cost of research could retard or halt the progress of research in some vital health areas such as heart disease, simply by pricing it beyond the reach of many research institutions."[21]

The Michigan Society for Medical Research estimates that less than 2 percent of research animals are pound seizure cats and dogs, amounting to approximately 138,000 dogs and 50,000 cats annually. The society is firm in stating that "[o]nly animals that have not been reclaimed by their owners or have not been adopted are used in research and education."[22] However, the USDA continues to cite certain Class B dealers for the improper procurement of animals for research, thus contradicting the broad-sweeping claims of the MSMR. Moreover, my experience with several shelters has shown that pound seizure was preferred rather than allowing for the adoption or rescue of the dog or cat, again contradicting MSMR's statement.

The society points out that pound seizure animals are used in education and research. For instance, Michigan veterinary schools use pound seizure animals to hone surgical skills, and MSMR estimates up to 75 percent are pound seizure animals. In medical schools, MSMR points out that physiology and pharmacology courses *require* animal experimentation and demonstration, as well as surgical residency programs. However, as of November 2009, only eight medical schools, none in Michigan, utilized live animals in their training.[23] Thus, animal experimentation and demonstration is no longer a *requirement*.

The Michigan Society for Medical Research further states, "[M]ost current medical and surgical methods for treating heart and kidney disease have been, and continue to be, developed through research with dogs. Because the cat's nervous system is the closest animal system to the human's, cats are frequently the best animal models for research on the brain and on visual and auditory function and disease. Cats are also essential to promising research into improved treatment for stroke victims. As a part of recent research leading to a vaccine for feline leukemia, cats played a critical role in the identification of the virus believed to cause Acquired Immune Deficiency Syndrome (AIDS) in humans."[24]

In regard to stolen pets ending up in laboratories, MSMR has posted this statement on its website to refute those claims: "Because universities and research institutions acquire animals directly from pounds or licensed dealers, there is virtually no market for trade in stolen animals for research purposes. A survey of police departments and animal control agencies in the 10 largest U.S. cities, conducted by the Foundation for Biomedical Research, revealed no reports of thefts of animals for resale to research for education. When a pet animal is stolen, it is usually for resale as a pet, guard or hunting dog, or for illegal gaming activities. Stolen dogs tend to be pure-bred animals, such as German Shepherds, Doberman Pinschers or Pit Bull Terriers, which can be sold illegally to private individuals at prices far higher than those for random-source animals used in research or education."[25]

The Michigan Society for Medical Research has likely obtained no evidence or reason to suspect that stolen animals are ending up in laboratories or teaching institutions; however, the USDA and other undercover investigations have proven that stolen animals are still brokered into the research system in spite of the protections of the Animal Welfare Act. Individuals who steal animals for resale into biomedical research or training institutions generally do not operate out of large U.S. cities, but instead work in rural areas where it is easier to remain undetected. Moreover, when someone reports that his pet has been stolen, the report is generally not made that the pet was stolen for research. Families of missing or stolen pets do not know what happened to their pet and, therefore, do not have the knowledge or information to make such a claim.

The American Physiological Society (APS) also supports the use of random source animals in medical research. However, on October 26, 2009, the APS voiced its support for the congressional study findings that Class B dealers are no longer necessary for NIH-funded research facilities. "The American Physiological Society endorses the recommendation of the [National Academies of Science] report that alternate vendors replace Class B dealer sales of random source dogs and cats. Immediate actions are required to ensure that random source dogs and cats remain available so that all medical and veterinary research, teaching, and testing endeavors that require these animals may continue without disruption."[26]

The Foundation for Biomedical Research (FBR) is the nation's oldest and largest organization dedicated toward advancing human and animal health through animal research. FBR states on its website that it also monitors the activities of animal activists, including maintaining a report of illegal incidents. The organization has also compiled a document for its website titled "The truth about cats and dogs." The document describes twenty-five areas where animal research has benefited both humans and animals, including feline diabetes and heartworm in dogs.[27] In reading through this list, I could not help but wonder if a person had a dog or cat with one of the afflictions listed in the report, why couldn't that owner have his pet undergo treatment as part of a study? Potentially the pet could benefit from the experimental treatment, the pet would go home after each treatment and remain in the comfort of his or her home and with his or her family, the laboratory would not have to incur the resources to obtain, condition, and house research animals, and no shelter cat or dog would be required for these studies. Maybe that is a simplistic way of looking at a complex situation, but sometimes a simple commonsense solution is the most sound. Let me give an example.

In September 1998, Chyna, my ten-year-old pure white cat whom I adored above all else, was suddenly stricken with paralysis in three of her limbs. I rushed her to my veterinarian who suggested that I take her to Michigan State University's Veterinary School for possible treatment. The veterinary training hospital examined Chyna and indicated it could test an experimental drug to see if function could be restored in her limbs. Chyna suffered from an undetected heart disease and was passing blood clots that were causing the paralysis. The treatment was approximately $1,800 to start, and there were few guarantees for success. The cost was not an issue. Chyna was alert and seemed very confused regarding her paralysis. I was told that we would know in twenty-four to thirty-six hours whether the treatment was working. So I left Chyna at the clinic and prayed that the experimental treatment would work. The next morning, filled with hope, I sat in the examination room with Chyna who was still paralyzed, yet alert and wanting affection from me. The veterinarian explained that the treatment was not working. It was not reversing the paralysis. There was no solution.

I was then left alone with Chyna in the examination room to make a life-changing decision. As I type this, my eyes well up with tears even though eleven years have passed. I did not want my once-active and vital Chyna living with paralysis. She deserved better. So I said my good-byes. As I now reflect back on that situation, I realize that Chyna was part of a university veterinary experimental process to not only train veterinary students in the care of critically ill pets, but also to test experimental drugs. Although the experimental treatment did not work for Chyna, maybe her participation has led to refinement of the process and a successful drug to reverse paralysis.

This brings me back to my prior statement about the option of having family pets with illnesses (cancer, diabetes, seizures, etc.), injuries (broken bones), or genetic conditions (hip dysplasia) receive treatment at university veterinary clinics. There are countless family pets that currently suffer from a number of ailments that could contribute to the education of students, and the creation of better treatments. If a training school also offered a reduced price to have a pet enter a clinical trial, that might result in more pet owners trying experimental treatments to save their pet and advance veterinary medicine at the same time. All of this can be done without the taking of shelter cats and dogs for the procedures. Humans volunteer themselves for clinical trials everyday and for every possible illness. Why not offer the same alternative to pets and avoid the terrible stain on a community of pound seizure?

CHAPTER 10

Shelters and Pound Seizure

Why do shelters engage in pound seizure? Is it the money they can receive selling animals for experimentation? Is it a benevolent belief that the animals are truly saving other animal and human lives by being research tools? Are there other benefits for the shelter in exchange for providing these cats and dogs to research? Over the past ten years, I have found few shelters that are willing to discuss their practice of pound seizure. In writing this book, I attempted to interview seven shelters that engage in, or recently ended, pound seizure without success. Efforts to know which shelters across the country are practicing pound seizure have resulted in shelter workers sounding hesitant on the phone to confirm the practice, and silent regarding details of where the animals are sent. Thus, learning which shelters engage in the practice has been difficult to determine. Pound seizure continues to be America's little secret.

To tackle this issue for advocacy on the federal Pet Safety and Protection Act of 2009, the Public Policy Office that I oversaw at the American Humane Association conducted a national pound seizure survey in late 2009 in an effort to estimate how many shelters engage in the practice.[1] Of the thirty-three states that allow pound seizure, we contacted five to ten animal random shelters and animal rescue organizations throughout each state to survey whether pound seizure was occurring. Only a few states, like Michigan, are required to file annual reports with the state that report disposition numbers of animals. In Michigan, shelters must specifically report pound seizure numbers. However, we did not locate any other state that had a similar reporting requirement. A majority of states do not require shelters to report to the states. Many shelters either report to their county government or maintain their records in the event of an inspection. Thus, it is difficult to determine precisely which shelters and states are actively practicing pound seizure. We hoped that our survey would uncover word-of-mouth information about the practice.

As of December 2009, the survey has resulted in the following information on pound seizure activity. The results astounded me for two reasons. First, I expected to hear of more shelters engaging in pound seizure, although I was pleasantly surprised to see the number is dwindling. Second, I was surprised at how many shelter and rescue workers had never heard of pound seizure. That led me to conclude that those shelters and rescue groups are not working in an area where pound seizure occurs, but also that they are not tuned in enough to know if it is occurring in other parts of the state. We also sensed that shelters were unwilling to disclose the practice when it did occur. Although the survey produced interesting results, we still do not have an accurate grasp on the extent of pound seizure in this country. This is what we have learned:

- Alabama: Three state veterinary schools obtain shelter cats and dogs. However, a representative of the Alabama Humane Federation is unaware of any state shelters engaging in pound seizure.
- Alaska: An individual with the state veterinary office indicated that he does not know of any state shelters practicing pound seizure. Nor are there any research facilities in the state. A representative of the Alaska Animal Care and Control Association stated that she has not heard of pound seizure (of live or dead animals) being practiced. Anchorage's city code specifically prohibits pound seizure for its local shelters. An employee at the Valdez Animal Shelter is unaware of any state veterinary school training on shelter animals.
- Arizona: Four separate animal shelters indicated they have not heard of pound seizure being practiced in the state.
- Arkansas: Three individual animal shelters stated that they are unaware of pound seizure being practiced in the state; however, representatives at each shelter indicated they would not be surprised if pound seizure was active in some shelters.
- Colorado: The Colorado Federation of Animal Welfare Agencies and the state veterinary office were unaware of any shelters practicing pound seizure.

- Florida: Representatives of five animal shelters indicated that they are unaware of pound seizure being practiced in the state. Miami specifically has an ordinance prohibiting pound seizure.
- Georgia: A representative from the Humane Associations of Georgia, Inc. and the state veterinary office indicated that they have not heard of pound seizure being active within the state. Athens has an ordinance specifically banning pound seizure. However, the Georgia Humane Society is concerned that pound seizure is practiced secretly since there are three veterinary schools nearby that use shelter cats and dogs for training exercises.
- Idaho: The Post Falls Animal Control had a past practice of paying a local veterinary school to take shelter cats and dogs. However, a representative of the Post Falls Animal Control shelter confirmed that the practice stopped in 2009 since it was too difficult and time consuming to coordinate the transfer of shelter dogs to the veterinary school. According to the shelter, dogs were transferred to the veterinary school for spay-neuter training, and many dogs were scheduled to be adopted afterward. Now the shelter has a growing rate of rescue for the dogs and does not need to transfer dogs to the veterinary school. The Pocatello Animal Shelter also ended a recent practice of sending shelter cats and dogs to a local university as a result of advocacy pressure from the Physicians Committee for Responsible Medicine and People for the Ethical Treatment of Animals. Moreover, a representative of the shelter indicated that the mayor has requested that the shelter stop pound seizure. For 2009, no pound seizure occurred at the shelter. A representative from the Idaho Humane Society and two other municipal shelters indicate that they are unaware of any other shelters practicing pound seizure in Idaho.
- Indiana: According to the state veterinary office, there is one random source Class B dealer in Indiana. The dealer is only required to document animals that come in from other states and does not have to document when animals come from local shelters. There are also no records that list from which Indiana shelters the dealer may obtain cats and dogs. Two shelters and one rescue organization indicated no knowledge of pound seizure being practiced in the state.
- Iowa: According to the state veterinary office, there has been no noticeable pound seizure activity since 1993. However, state reporting requirements for shelters do not require that shelters indicate if

cats and dogs are being provided to dealers or research facilities. A representative of the Iowa Federations of Humane Societies has not heard recently of any shelters engaging in pound seizure, yet suspects that it is occurring. Pound seizure officially ended in 2009 at the Des Moines animal shelter.

- Kansas: According to the state veterinarian, pound seizure is not actively practiced in the state. However, shelters are not required to file annual reports with the state. Several shelters and rescue organizations contacted had not heard of pound seizure and were unaware if it was being practiced elsewhere in the state.

- Kentucky: Kentucky was home to one random source Class B dealer. Representatives at the state Veterinary Office and state Animal Control Advisory Board have not heard of any shelters engaging in pound seizure in recent years. Several shelter representatives indicated they were unaware of pound seizure within the state, but were concerned that some smaller county shelters may engage in the practice.

- Louisiana: According to the East Baton Rouge Parish Animal Control, shelter animals that are scheduled for euthanasia are sold to a local veterinary school for teaching purposes. Those animals are euthanized after the training according to a shelter representative. The training program has been significantly scaled back, but has not ended: As a result, the school now uses non-live animal models. According to the Louisiana Animal Welfare Commission, which was legislatively established to inspect and investigate shelters, pound seizure was quite frequent in the state in past years but has declined as a result of decreased demand.

- Michigan: Michigan has three random source Class B dealers. As a result of strategic advocacy, only two shelters now engage in pound seizure. Mecosta County Animal Control is a privately run shelter under contract with the county and engages in pound seizure. For 2007 and 2008, the shelter gave, at no cost, 319 dogs to Class B dealers. The shelter received 934 dogs during those years, with more than 34 percent being subjected to pound seizure.[2] The Gratiot County Animal Control shelter also practices pound seizure. From 2007 through 2008, the shelter received 3,076 cats and dogs and gave, at no cost, 633 cats and dogs, or 20 percent, to Class B dealers.[3] At both shelters, there were more pound seizure pets than adoptions. As of 2003, there were fourteen shelters engaging in pound seizure. Successful advocacy has reduced that number to two shelters as of late 2009.

- Minnesota: According to state records, no shelter has engaged in pound seizure since 2001 in spite of the mandatory pound seizure law. Minnesota is home to one random source Class B dealer, however.

- Mississippi: The state veterinary office and several shelters indicated that pound seizure is not publicly practiced or known of in the state. Several animal shelters indicated that they are unaware whether pound seizure is occurring within the state, but that they have not received any information that it is ongoing.

- Missouri: Missouri is home to one of the random source Class B dealers. The state veterinary office does not know of any shelters practicing pound seizure. A representative indicated that shelters are required to submit annual disposition records that include adoptions, euthanasia, and transfers, but that there is no specific reporting requirement for pound seizure. The Animal Care Facilities Act coordinator stated that two animal control shelters contacted him recently to ask about the legality of pound seizure.

- Montana: Several shelters, including the state veterinary office, are unaware of any shelters practicing pound seizure. However, shelter annual reports are not required to be filed with the state, so it is unknown whether pound seizure is active.

- Nebraska: Several shelters and the state veterinary office have stated that pound seizure is not active in the state. Again, the state does not require animal shelters to file annual disposition reports, so it is difficult to know whether any shelter is engaging in pound seizure.

- Nevada: The state veterinary office and several shelters have not heard of pound seizure being practiced in spite of a large national and international research facility in Reno.

- New Mexico: Advocates from New Mexico have vocalized a concern that New Mexico shelter pets are being transferred to Colorado for research purposes. This information is difficult to obtain and has not been confirmed. An investigation is underway to determine the accuracy of this complaint. The Animal Protection New Mexico (APNM) organization is responsible for keeping state records for shelters and it is unaware of any shelter engaging in pound seizure. According to APNM, Albuquerque was the last shelter engaging in pound seizure and it ceased that practice in 1989. One shelter worker stated that if pound seizure were being practiced in a shelter, it is kept secret to avoid bad publicity.

- North Carolina: North Carolina is home to several corporations that broker animal carcasses for research. Currently there are some shelters suspected of practicing pound seizure with live animals, but obtaining specific information has been difficult due to the lack of state reporting requirements.
- North Dakota: A representative of the state veterinary office had not heard of pound seizure and was not knowledgeable of any shelter engaging in the practice. Several animal shelters also indicated that they are unaware of any shelters practicing pound seizure.
- Ohio: One random source Class B dealer resides in Ohio. Several shelter representatives were unaware of live animals being brokered for research from any shelter, but that some shelters sell carcasses for research. The state veterinary office indicated that there is no state requirement for shelters to file disposition records, so the state does not have information on pound seizure.
- Oklahoma: In surveying several shelters, none were aware of any that are providing live cats and dogs for research.
- Oregon: The Humane Society of Eastern Oregon transports cats and dogs to a Washington veterinary school for free spay-neuter services from the students, but the animals are returned and placed for adoption. The state veterinary office does not require state annual shelter reports and does not inspect shelters, so knowledge of pound seizure is unknown. Several animal shelters believe that pound seizure is not occurring within the state.
- South Dakota: Several shelters indicated they have not heard of pound seizure being active in the state. The state veterinary office does not require annual shelter reports that would indicate pound seizure, but does not believe it is being practiced.
- Tennessee: The state veterinary office had no information that shelters were practicing pound seizure, although annual reports are not required to be filed with the state.
- Texas: According to the City of Giddings Lehman Animal Shelter, the shelter only provides already-deceased cats and dogs to Texas A&M University and no longer provides live cats and dogs, as indicated in *Dying to Learn*.
- Utah: A recent investigation by PETA discovered that three shelters engage in pound seizure: Davis County Animal Shelter in Fruit Heights, North Utah Valley Animal Shelter in Lindon, and Tooele

City Animal Shelter. When requests were made to each shelter for specific information, phone calls were not returned and requests for documents were not responded to by the Davis or Tooele shelters.

- Washington: Many cities such as Seattle, Everett, and Walla Walla have specifically prohibited pound seizure. According to the state veterinary office, a state veterinary school receives live cats and dogs from Oregon for spay-neuter training, but the animals are returned for adoption. Several shelters indicated that they are unaware of shelters engaging in pound seizure within the state.
- Wisconsin: According to the Wisconsin Federated Humane Societies, pound seizure is not practiced within the state and has been closely monitored since the late 1980s.
- Wyoming: According to Black Dog Animal Rescue, a community college obtains shelter animals for veterinary technician training, but then the pets are adopted afterward. The state veterinary office has not heard of any pound seizure activity and indicated that shelters are not required to file annual reports with the state.

Although this state-by-state information appears to indicate that pound seizure is not widely practiced throughout the country, except in Michigan, I also know that shelters are hesitant to disclose pound seizure information for fear of negative public perception and pressure from outside advocates to stop the practice. Therefore, many shelters keep the information secret and do not keep paperwork on pound seizure unless required by law. As detailed in the congressional study on random source animals, 947 dogs and 230 cats were victims of pound seizure in just a one-year period covering November 2007 to November 2008.[4] Where are they coming from? If you are in one of the states listed above, do not presume that all shelters in your state have banned pound seizure. Some shelters may also change policies on pound seizure depending on financial constraints or new management. Instead, make an inquiry to your local shelter to find out the facts.

From 2000 to 2003 when I was actively advocating to prohibit pound seizure at my local shelter in Michigan, the most common defense that I heard from the shelter director was that only animals that were truly unwanted were sold to the dealer. Only the animals that had been given every opportunity at adoption or rescue and were then slated for euthanasia would be sold to the dealer. I hear similar statements from other pound seizure shelters today. Based on my own observations, I never believed those statements to be true. When the pound seizure campaign came to a boiling point in early 2003, I decided to gather the evidence to determine what was true and what was false.

In a Freedom of Information request to the shelter, I requested inventory cards of all shelter cats and dogs that were sold to the Class B dealer for 2001 through 2002. I was not surprised that the documents proved that the shelter director was incorrect.

In 2001, the shelter reported that eighty-three dogs and eighty-two cats were sold to the dealer. The shelter was only able to provide the inventory cards for 142 of those animals. Inventory cards for twenty-three animals were "missing" and nine other cards failed to indicate that the dealer obtained the animal. Of those 142 cards, 35 percent of the animals were sold to the dealer on the first day available for adoption and 18 percent were sold on the second day available for adoption. Two dogs were sold to the dealer one day before they were available for adoption, thus not allowing any adoption opportunity for those dogs. Another 32 percent of the animals were sold to the dealer within their first week available for adoption. A shepherd that was sold to a dealer on March 21, 2001, had a collar grown into his neck and was part of a neglect complaint. Two nursing cats were sold to the dealer in 2001, and their newborn babies were euthanized. There were nine additional animals where the shelter had the owner's name, claimed that the owner had not been located, and presumed that the owner wanted his or her pet sold for research. Three finders of lost dogs turned the dogs over to the shelter with a request to adopt if the owner was not found. Records indicate that those three finders were not contacted about adopting the dog that was found, and instead the dogs were sold to the dealer.

In 2002, the shelter recorded selling twenty-six dogs and twenty-one cats to a dealer. At this point, the efforts of the volunteers and outside animal rescue organizations were being noted in fewer animals going to the dealer. The shelter provided forty-five of the forty-seven inventory cards, and indicated that two were "missing." Of those forty-five cards, 29 percent of the animals were sold to the dealer on the first day available for adoption and 16 percent were sold on the second day available for adoption. Another 42 percent of the animals were sold to a dealer within their first week available for adoption. One dog was sold to a dealer on June 4, 2002, after being removed from the owner due to neglect. The inventory card prevented the dog from being adopted due to a notation that only the owner was allowed to have the dog. So that dog was never afforded the opportunity to be adopted. There were eight additional animals where the shelter had the owner's name, claimed that the owner had not been located, and presumed that the owner wanted his or her pet sold for research. The owners of two animals were not asked or informed about research when surrendering their pets, and those pets were sold to the dealer. And Jackson, who was featured in chapter 4, was sold to the dealer in spite of the finder's request to adopt Jackson, and objecting in writing to Jackson being sold for research.

During a county commissioner meeting on June 9, 2003, I presented these findings to the full commission in an effort to refute the claims of the shelter director. It is a very powerful argument for a shelter director to claim that animals are given every possible opportunity to be adopted and that only in the event of imminent euthanasia will they be sold to the dealer. Any reasonable person would understand that argument. Showing the shelter documents to the commissioners was a powerful tool to refute the claims of the shelter director. I could see that opinions were starting to change based on what the shelter's documents stated. In the end, later that evening, the county commissioners voted twelve to three to end pound seizure.

According to Dr. Robert Willems of USDA/APHIS, it is believed that very few animal shelters are selling animals directly to research facilities, and those practicing pound seizure are using the services of Class B dealers. In the past, providing animals directly to facilities was common; however, that is not the case now. Currently, Dr. Willems knows of no private animal shelter that engages in pound seizure. He also confirmed that "regulations promulgated under the authority of the Pet Theft Act of 1990 require that pounds or shelters that sell random source dogs and cats to RSBDs hold those animals for a period of not less than five full days, not including the day of acquisition or any time spent in transit. That five-day holding period must also include a Saturday. The purpose of this requirement is to allow the public time to claim any pet dogs or cats that the pound or shelter may have picked up or that may have been sent to it."

Although it is clear that pound seizure is on the decline, it is unknown precisely how many shelters continue to engage in this practice. While some pound seizure is considered beneficial (such as transporting shelter animals for spay-neuter clinics or to receive care for injuries and diseases, and then returned for adoption), too many shelter cats and dogs throughout the country are still victims each year.

CHAPTER 11

Voices of the Advocates to Stop Pound Seizure

When advocating to ban pound seizure, whether at the local, state, or national level, there are two main requirements to establish a solid foundation for success: First, having accurate facts on the practice of pound seizure for the area covering your advocacy; and, second, selecting decision makers (county commissioners, state legislators, or federal congressmen) who are educated on the issue, both proponent and opponent arguments, and steadfast enough to withstand the opposition and move the issue through to a vote. Below are the stories of advocates at the national, state, and local levels and what they found to be successful.

NATIONWIDE AND BEYOND

Dr. John Pippin,[1] senior medical and research adviser with the Physicians Committee for Responsible Medicine (PCRM), has been advocating to end pound seizure and the use of animals in laboratories and teaching institutions for many years. When addressing proponents of pound seizure in the medical and research community, Dr. Pippin is someone you want on your side. He will scrutinize the medical and scientific arguments and address them with straightforward facts and win-win proposals. This is why Dr. Pippin and PCRM have been successful in their efforts to transition medical schools away from the use of live animals as teaching tools.

In the area of pound seizure, Dr. Pippin agrees that progress has been made and that the pound seizure advocacy of ten or twenty years ago is different from today's. This is primarily because pound seizure is different on both sides of the issue. Pound seizure requires a willing source and a willing user, and both sides have undergone changes in the last few decades. On the supply side, largely due to public education, there is a growing and now very strong sense among the public about what pound seizure is, and there also is strong opposition among this same public regarding pound seizure as a practice. Today there are fewer shelters that provide animals. The supply is shrinking. On the other side, the way that cats and dogs are being used is disappearing, such as using animals to test cosmetics, in dissection classes, and in medical schools (where the last dog lab ended in 2008). The iconic "dog lab" endured by students for decades is now in the historical dustbin, as none of the 159 accredited U.S. medical schools has a student dog lab.

Dr. Pippin explains that in medical research, rather than using random source dogs through pound seizure, many researchers are using smaller species, genetically modified species, or non-animal methods to do their research. Good examples are the trauma courses in medical schools and hospitals, where it is now very uncommon to use dogs to teach students and physicians. As of the end of 2009, 95 percent of Advanced Trauma Life Support programs in the United States and Canada do not use animals at all, and the animals used in the remainder are typically pigs or goats. Those programs that would use pound seizure animals have dried up.

To put progress in perspective, Dr. Pippin states, "What we forget sometimes is that when we look at the moment, we still see two states that mandate pound seizure, thirty more that allow it, there is still some research institutions and schools and trade groups that promote the use of random source animals, and some shelters willingly send animals for research. But if you look at where we are compared to where we used to be, we are steadily getting there." So what are the barriers to banning pound seizure nationally? Dr. Pippin believes that the Class B dealer system will be eliminated before pound seizure. "Dealers have a deservedly bad reputation. They use bunchers, they acquire animals in a variety of ways, some legal some not legal. There have been exposés, including the HBO *Dealing Dogs* documentary. The U.S. National Research Council has declared that Class B animal dealers are unnecessary for the conduct of research. Formerly numbering in the hundreds, as of 2009 there remain only [9] Class B random source animals dealers in the U.S., and [six] of those are under investigation for animal welfare violations." With the 2009 reintroduction of the federal Pet Safety and Protection Act in the U.S. Senate by Hawaii senator Daniel Akaka and in the U.S. House of Representatives by Pennsylvania representative Michael Doyle, the opportunity to eliminate Class B dealer status has never been greater. As for the overall practice of pound seizure, Dr. Pippin foresees an environment in which the perceived reasons for pound seizure are no longer present. "Those four areas of progressive change—decreased demand for animals, decreased supply of animals, burgeoning public advocacy against pound seizure, and effective federal legislation—together will eventually get us to the time when animals in shelters are no longer at risk to end up in laboratories."

The advocacy work of PCRM and other organizations is also changing the way medical scientific research is performed, which simultaneously eases the pressure on the animals and helps put pound seizure out of business. Dr. Pippin explains, "For so many aspects of our history—such as slavery, civil rights, and women's suffrage—we look back with the wisdom of hindsight and we are ashamed. That's how we are going to feel about using animals in this way. I hope I live to see it. As scientists and researchers, we are going to look back on our history of using animals as a shameful part of our past that persisted far beyond the knowledge to end it. What were we thinking? Before we get to that point, we have to get beyond this blind period, and then we will see that we should have seen it sooner. People by and large don't think with a future perspective; they only live in the present. I am confident this is going to happen, but I am frustrated by how long it takes."

In educating the medical profession to transition away from using animals, Dr. Pippin attributes PCRM's success to three areas. "First, we look to what is left to do rather than to what we have done. Second, while we are of course driven in important ways by the ethics of animal use, I feel strongly that the perception that animal welfare concerns contribute importantly to progress is incorrect. It's not a part of the decision for the other side. I have not seen that researchers and educators care about animals at all. They are scientists, educators, and teachers, indoctrinated willingly to see animals as tools. We have not won any of our animal-related campaigns during my tenure based on others' concerns for animal welfare. PCRM seeks abolition rather than just welfare—not just ways of treating animals better, but abolition of animal use. Sadly, concern for animals has not been part of the equation in our dealings with researchers, schools, and institutions."

The third and final reason is that sometimes schools and programs will move away from animal use for practical reasons, such as pressure from the public or negative attention from the media. In some instances, economics comes into the equation. Dr. Pippin elaborates, "Simulation is not only a better way to learn, it is also a potential revenue source. Many facilities and programs will use their simulation centers to provide train-ing to nonaffiliated professionals and students, and also to do refresher courses for doctors in practice. It can be a revenue center. What we have learned at PCRM is to always frame this as a win-win proposition because that's what it is if you do it properly."

If animal welfare is not a concern in stopping the use of shelter cats and dogs in research, Dr. Pippin states that raising public awareness of non-animal alternatives is crucial. In other situations it requires finding a decision maker who sees the big picture and understands it's a win-win situation. "Better education, better research, and better ethics run together. Often we have to go beyond the course director, to a department chair, IA-CUC chair, or university administrator to get that done. That is part of our approach." Dr. Pippin clarifies, "We try to never make it an adversarial process. We try to make it win-win. But there is never the need to give up. There is more we can do even when we get rebuffed."

On a hopeful note, Dr. Pippin has noticed an interesting and encouraging phenomenon in the past few years. He states, "Some schools have undertaken curriculum reform to change the way medical students are taught. Much of this reform focuses on making medical education more directed to patient care than to older ideas about basic science, which typically means moving away from the use of animals and getting students into clinics and hospitals sooner. Reform is moving us away from the less relevant basic science approach of using animals for biology or pharmacology."

Overall, appealing to ethics of the medical profession has been unsuccessful in Dr. Pippin and PCRM's advocacy. "How do people get in a position where they are using animals for these purposes? These are people who came to their positions because of who they are. They have less concern for animals than they have for what they believe they are doing with them. I don't fret over this lack of ethics, because it's a given among vivisectors. By the time you're dealing with them, ethics is not part of the discussion. We have success because we are doctors and scientists at PCRM. I have been an animal researcher, a physician, and an educator. While we are driven by ethics, we come at this with expertise in science and medicine, and we approach it from the practical medical, scientific, and educational points of view. That's the only thing, plus external pressure when necessary, that works. I cannot think of a single instance where ethical concerns were the driving force for replacing animals in medical school education or trauma training. If you put up a billboard or do a TV interview informing the public of what's happening to dogs and cats that does get public support. There is a difference between the public and the people who use animals. If you can bring the public to bear on the schools and researchers, it puts what they are doing in a public light and usually they cannot stand the public light. We don't like for it to get to that point, but we will not give up on the animals without trying external pressure. Sometimes getting to that one person in the chain of command who can make changes also helps. But it's not always easy to find that one person."

In the end there still is much work to be done to abolish pound seizure and ensure that all cats and dogs are safe. Dr. Pippin sums up the issue beautifully: "Pound seizure erodes public confidence, and many people won't take animals to shelters that practice pound seizure. From my perspective, from the ethical point of view, it seems that this goes to the very core of our relationship with animals. If an animal shelter cannot be a refuge from misuse, abuse, suffering, and death, or at least provide a painless death, then the whole human-animal relationship comes apart. I think you must have a level of core ethics, baseline ethics that you won't violate. And I think when you convert a refuge—that's what an animal shelter is supposed to be, and a place of humane treatment—into an underground railroad to send animals into situations where they will suffer pain and a bad death, then you have gutted the core of the whole human-animal relationship."

Other national animal welfare organizations that are consistently working to end pound seizure include the American Humane Association, the American Anti-Vivisection Society, People for the Ethical Treatment of Animals, and The Humane Society of the United States (HSUS). In November 2009, HSUS issued a statement urging fifty research institutions to stop purchasing random source cats and dogs.[2] HSUS surveyed institutions and discovered that seven no longer purchase random source cats or dogs from Class B dealers, whereas five institutions confirmed purchases and another forty-five institutions failed to respond to repeated requests for information. According to HSUS, they suspect that the forty-five institutions are still purchasing animals from Class B dealers and do not want to publicly confirm the information. Gathering information on which institutions are purchasing cats and dogs from Class B dealers is an essential component to a successful advocacy campaign, and HSUS, along with other national organizations, continues to gather information.

STATE OF MINNESOTA

Amy Draeger[3] and a group of advocates are prepared to tackle Minnesota's mandatory pound seizure law in 2010. A website titled *End Pound Seizure Minnesota* was created to be a clearinghouse of information on pound seizure in Minnesota, and to draw in the support of citizens throughout the state. For sixty years, Minnesota has had a law that mandates shelters to turn over cats and dogs to research institutions or educational facilities upon demand. Minnesota is one of two states that mandates pound seizure.

Some of the techniques Amy and her group are using to spread the word about pound seizure in Minnesota include an online petition that will add you to the list of supporters for a ban and notify you when the state bill is filed; online tools on how to contact your state representative to voice your opinion about pound seizure; a brochure that can be downloaded that explains pound seizure and why a ban is needed in Minnesota; and, if a donation is made, you can receive a pet ID tag that states that your animal cannot be used for research, or bandannas, and T-shirts for pets that say "Ban Pound Seizure: I Am Not a Research Tool."

As previously discussed in chapter 3, Minnesota is ripe to change its pound seizure law in 2010 or in the coming years primarily because pound seizure has been a dormant practice in Minnesota shelters since 2001. Specific strategies for the 2010 (or beyond) legislative session include being meticulous in the history of pound seizure in Minnesota through credible sources. Amy states, "Minnesota's pound seizure law was passed in 1949, but my research took me back to 1939. I spent many hours in the archives of the Minnesota Historical Society. In addition to reviewing legislative history and materials preserved by archivists (like letters to elected representatives from stakeholders), do not ignore newspaper archives, especially 'letters to the editor' sections of newspaper archives." Another strategy is to ensure that the public face of the campaign remains mainstream and is not labeled as an extremist animal rights movement. For example, no board members of the coalition are members of PETA. Although PETA has its place in the animal rights movements, the name alone can cause lawmakers to turn away from hearing the factual arguments to ban pound seizure. Also, no graphic images are placed on the website. People do not need to be persuaded with shock techniques of images of animals in various stages of the experiment process. Amy clarifies, "Focus on pound seizure as a violation of pubic trust in animal shelters, not pound seizure as part of an anti-vivisection campaign."

Additional strategies include obtaining national and local endorsements for the bill. Contact local animal rescue groups to help spread the word. The more support that is available at the time of the bill filing (or making a presentation to local lawmakers), the stronger your arguments will be received. Be sure to check your state bar association to see if there is an animal law section. Amy is a member of the Minnesota State Bar Animal Law Section, and I have been a longtime member of the Michigan State Bar Animal Law Section. It can be very effective to mobilize the section lawyers, especially when drafting Freedom of Information requests.

STATE OF UTAH

Anne Davis[4] has been advocating on behalf of animals for more than twenty years. Until March 2010, Utah was one of three states that mandated pound seizure. With Anne's assistance, 2010 became the year to finally overturn Utah's mandatory pound seizure law and leave pound seizure to the discretion of the shelters.

Anne became involved in animal advocacy, including pound seizure, because of Utah's weak laws to protect animals. She joined an organization called Citizens Against Mandatory Pound Seizure (CAMP), which became defunct after a 1989 loss to change the pound seizure law in Utah. Anne then started the Utah Animal Rights Alliance and has been working steadily to change Utah's laws. She enjoyed success in 2008 when Utah passed its first-ever felony animal cruelty law, after thirteen years of planning and strategizing for success. The law is called Henry's law, after a little mixed-breed dog who was chased with a leaf blower by his owner, causing a rock to hit him in the eye and blind him instantly. Two weeks later, Henry was put in a 200-degree oven for five minutes. His pads were fused together when they touched the oven coils and his chest was burned over 75 percent of the surface. Henry survived, is now in a loving home, and became the mascot for Utah, which passed its first-ever felony animal cruelty law. Through that campaign, Anne learned that Utah politics moves very slowly and that patience is the key to success.

Why did Anne believe that 2010 was the year to rid Utah of mandatory pound seizure? In late 2009, media reports detailed an investigation by PETA into research conducted by the University of Utah on shelter cats and dogs.[5] Anne states, "We all feel that since [PETA's] naming of Utah shelters which participate in pound seizure, and shining the light on these 'little known secrets' that really angered the public gets us on the road for success this year even if it means only removing the word 'mandatory' from the current code." But much public education needs to be done in Utah to ensure success. Anne and other advocates prepared a plan to conduct outreach to community organizations to educate citizens about pound seizure and why overturning the mandatory law is in the state's best interests.

Anne and other advocates laid the groundwork for a successful legislative campaign, such as securing a legislator who sponsored and filed the pound seizure bill; writing the legislative bill, including providing exemptions that still allow veterinary students to provide treatment to shelter animals and place them for adoption; surveying the state to determine the extent of pound seizure; and garnering support before the bill is filed. Anne expected to receive opposition to the legislative effort from research facilities and universities. Advocates were also prepared to receive opposition from the state veterinary association and possibly the state animal control association. The key was to be well-prepared with information, statistics on the frequency of pound seizure in the state, and evidence-based answers to arguments in favor of pound seizure. The American Humane Association assisted Anne with these efforts and provided support and advocacy through to a win in March 2010.

Anne's advice to advocates is to "recognize that you will never be able to stop animal research. Although we have made strides in limiting live dissection from the public schools and that more and more people learn anatomy in computer models, there are still die-hards out there that will not give you the time of day. They are simply fearing change and perhaps fearing that they may become dispensable as a result of the ever-changing technology. We can make it difficult for Class B dealers to obtain animal by changing the pound seizure laws. Every impediment that we put in their path will either cost them money, time and perhaps reputation. It's like putting a chink in the armor or like an itch that HAS to be scratched or you will go nuts. Our answer to them would be 'we can make this easy on you or difficult: You choose.'"

INGHAM COUNTY, MICHIGAN

Holly Sauvé and I were volunteers with Friends of Ingham County Animal Shelter (FICAS), a nonprofit organization helping our local animal control shelter. Like me, Holly was deeply involved in the campaign to end pound seizure at the shelter. Holly[6] recounts how she first learned about pound seizure: "I heard on the Internet that animals were being put down at our local animal control due to lack of inmates (the inmates cared for the animals). I thought I could help by cleaning some cages and helping to feed. After my second visit, I was befriended by a volunteer who told me about the B dealer. Up until that point, I was absolutely clueless our local shelter sold animals to research. I was also clueless as to what a B dealer was. If I hadn't gone in there, I would have never known . . . much like the rest of the population of Ingham County didn't know either."

After starting her volunteer work at the shelter and learning about pound seizure, Holly became an advocate to stop pound seizure. "It was bad enough to see faces in the shelter that I knew would be put to sleep and I would never see again. But when I found out some of those disappearing faces were going off to research, it made me unable to sleep."

When Holly's advocacy started, she noticed a change in how the shelter staff interacted with her and other volunteers. "I remember the 'secrecy' involved. The shelter didn't openly give us information about the animals being sold. We were forced to spend money to file FOIAs [Freedom of Information Act] to find out where the animals went. I remember the shelter staff fighting us to keep doing what they were doing. It was like they were so opposed to change that they'd prefer the animals go to the dealer."

Holly describes one key method in advocating against pound seizure: public education. "Making sure that the public is aware what is going on around them is most important. Getting the citizens involved in letting the lawmakers know that they oppose pound seizure and they do not want it in their county/state." Holly knew that citizens were unaware of pound seizure at the shelter, just as she initially was. After launching ads with the local media and newspapers, posting printed literature at stores, and hosting rallies before county commissioner meetings, Holly and others were able to reach the average citizen and let them know what was happening at the shelter.

The education campaign was successful, especially for Mike Severino[7] who was a county commissioner during the pound seizure campaign from 2001 through 2003. Mike had not heard of pound seizure in his many years in that position, but when his constituents began contacting him as a result of the public education campaign he learned of the practice and became a vocal opponent. Mike works in the medical professional and understands that there are alternative training tools available to teach students rather than use pets.

FICAS received many donations to help in the education campaign. A generous citizen donated $2,000 to help place four quarter-page ads on the front page of the classified section of the *Lansing State Journal* that depicted photos of shelter cats and dogs recently sold to the Class B dealer and a call to action for citizens to attend county commission meetings. These ads ran a few days before several important commission meetings where the issue of pound seizure was an agenda item. The ads were successful; citizens began appearing at meetings and voicing their objections. Many of the citizens were not typical animal advocates, but simply were concerned citizens who did not want pound seizure in their county shelter. Severino agreed that the issue caused many citizens to appear at meetings to advocate for the end to pound seizure. He had not seen any other county issue generate more passionate pleas for reform than the issue of pound seizure.

Mike recalled one particular commission meeting that was preceded by an organized rally. "It was a rainy afternoon/evening before a board meeting and yet about a hundred people showed up with their pets (primarily dogs). It was a wonderful sight to see all these local dogs enjoying the fertile grounds of their county courthouse and seat of county government. At that time we had no idea how long, or if we would ever succeed in getting pound seizure banned, but it did send a message to the commissioners cowering upstairs in their meeting room that our voices and the voices of our pets would not be silenced."

FICAS also received the assistance of an out-of-county rescue organization that created a flyer and a postcard for citizens to sign for mailing to the county commissioners. This leafleting campaign occurred every weekend. Dozens of volunteers worked the entire county by going house to house to hand out flyers and postcards. At one point, the clerk for the county commissioners had received several thousand postcards. Mike recounts, "Various groups put out e-mail alerts so we on the board of commissioner were inundated with e-mails from all over the world. I did receive many calls at home about this issue, and the only one that was in favor of keeping pound seizure was a Class B dealer."

Holly mentioned another effective effort that involved mobilizing the rescue of the animals before the dealer arrived at the shelter each week. While I was marshaling the cat rescue organizations throughout Michigan to assist us in rescuing cats from the shelter, Holly was organizing the dog rescue organizations. We also coordinated to advertise pets for adoption in the local newspaper, which helped to increase the adoption rate at the shelter.

To put the impact of the volunteers in perspective, the shelter's own annual reports showed success in reducing the number of animals subjected to pound seizure. In 1998, before volunteers assisted the shelter, there were

4,026 animals that came to the shelter, with only 477 being adopted and 567 sold to research. In 2000, the first year of volunteers and the formation of FICAS in September 2000, the shelter received 4,393 animals, of which 1,041 were adopted and only 149 were sold to research. In 2002, the shelter received 3,980 animals, of which 1,797 were adopted and only 47 were sold to research. Our primary effort of getting the shelter pets adopted or rescued from the shelter was working to reduce the supply of cats and dogs available to the dealer. That tactic helped to maintain the sanity and perseverance of all the volunteers throughout the three-year campaign.

Holly attended and spoke at many county commission meetings on pound seizure. "I remember the first time I saw [a dealer] at the court-house. He looked like anyone's grandfather. It shocked me that he could be a B dealer." Holly also witnessed some interesting debates among the county commissioners, several of whom continued to cling to the practice of pound seizure.

Holly, like others, was subjected to name-calling by the opposition. "I remember getting called a PETA activist in the local newspaper by a county commissioner because I wrote a letter to the editor about a situ-ation at the county shelter that involved the B dealer. The commissioner also said that my 'story' was just that . . . a story, when, indeed, it was not a story and my letter was factual. Yet the commissioner got the last word and was able to lie about my status and the facts." PETA was not involved in the campaign in Ingham County and was specifically asked to let local advocates handle the situation. We needed to keep the focus on the issue and avoid labeling or name-calling.

Mike Severino confirmed that two commissioners in particular were steadfast in supporting pound seizure. He also believed that the shelter di-rector at the time was interested in maintaining the practice. Mike stated, "Over the course of the debate, my perception was that [the shelter direc-tor] had a very poor relationship with the shelter volunteers and a very good relationship with the Class B dealers with whom he dealt. Both of these relationships made me uncomfortable."

As for commissioners who supported pound seizure, Mike felt that their tactics were not in line with the democratic process. Mike explains, "One commissioner was rather public and vocal in his disdain for the shelter volunteers who showed up at our meetings advocating change in the shelter policy. His issue was simply control, and in my opinion, he didn't want to cede any of his inherent power on the board to 'outsiders' or the democratic process. The other commissioner was, in my opinion, rather sinister, devious, and self-serving in his approach to the pound seizure debate. While trying to appease those that wanted to end pound seizure, I discovered during the process that he was doing the bidding of [a university] in their attempt to support the Class B dealers with whom they provided plenty of business. His actions delaying, obfuscating the issues, and playing games with the lives of these pets were perhaps the epitome of the self-serving, two-faced politician. In my opinion, he was the biggest obstacle in not only changing the pound seizure policy, but the reason why Ingham County failed to pass a pure ban on pound seizure."

In a commission meeting that lasted more than six hours and ran past midnight into June 10, 2003, the final vote was twelve to three in support of banning the Class B dealer from the shelter. The vote unfortunately would still allow state universities to obtain shelter animals. However, it is believed that no university has gone directly to the shelter to obtain cats and dogs, other than for practicing spay-neuter techniques and returning the pets to the shelter for adoption. Holly, Mike, and I, along with more than a hundred other advocates in attendance, were overjoyed with the final vote. But it was not an easy road for the advocates or the animals.

What was the one key to success? Holly says it was intense public pressure. "We wore down the commissioners. I think they truly got sick of sitting through very, very long meetings. It seemed like the vast majority of them fought it, but when it came down to taking time away from their families (and they knew we weren't going away) they caved. We also did have some very good, supportive commissioners and do not want to discount the time and effort they put in. Without their starting support, we would have been nowhere." Holly and I both agree that the internal support of commissioner Mike Severino, along with a few other commissioners, played a large part in our success.

Along the way, it can become frustrating and tiring to maintain an advocacy campaign against pound seizure. In Ingham County, our campaign took three years. Holly's words of advice are echoed by me and many others who have followed down this path: "You will get very frustrated, but don't give up. They are hoping to frustrate you enough to make you give up. Don't. Be prepared to fight for what you know is right. It won't happen overnight so be prepared for the long haul."

Holly is now working on pound seizure advocacy at the state level and in the two remaining Michigan counties that engage in pound seizure. In 2009, she formed Voiceless-MI, a 501(c)(3) nonprofit aimed to help companion animals in Michigan and to lend a voice to advocacy campaigns.

She and her organization have been a tremendous help to me and my staff at the American Humane Association in mobilizing the grassroots campaign on the 2009 Michigan pound seizure bill.

JACKSON COUNTY, MICHIGAN

Judy Dynnik[8] is a force to be reckoned with when it comes to advocacy on behalf of animals. For decades, the Jackson County Animal Control in Michigan practiced pound seizure, and citizens battled to stop the practice. Judy had known about it for years. As an avid animal lover and rescuer of a variety of pets, Judy knew she needed to get working to stop pound seizure once and for all.

Judy formed a volunteer group in 2004 called Jackson County Volunteers against Pound Seizure. Although I had already moved out of Michigan by then, Judy found me, and I gladly and humbly agreed to be the pro bono attorney for their campaign. Judy surrounded herself with a small but dedicated group of residents, and she was the heart and soul behind the group. I am honored that she agreed to be interviewed for this book.

Judy and I had many discussions about pound seizure campaigns and how to avoid any legal liability. With my assistance, Judy created a volunteer agreement for everyone to sign. "I required all volunteers in my group to sign a document stating that if they were ever disrespectful or broke the law their membership was immediately canceled. We were always polite and professional in spite of inappropriate behavior by some of the opposition." This tactic protected Judy and her organization from any rogue tactics of a volunteer gone astray.

Judy states, "I became involved in my community after a dog named Conan (featured in chapter 4) from a county south of Jackson got loose while his owners were on vacation. He crossed into our county, was picked up, and ended up in our county shelter. He had rabies tags on him yet was sold to research and killed in New York before his people could find him. His owners were devastated. That incident made me very fearful for our dogs since no system of identification is fail-safe. What if I was incapacitated after a car accident on the way to the vet's with our dogs in the car? They would be taken to our county shelter. This could happen to anyone."

"Secondly, our large terrier mix was the first dog we ever had who would not come when called in spite of every training method we tried. It terrified me that she could get loose, get into our shelter, and end up lost in the huge research system, because as long as pound seizure was allowed in our community I felt there was extreme risk to her safety as well as to our other dogs, especially after the Conan incident."

Judy was involved in the 2003 Ingham County pound seizure campaign and had worked on a Jackson County campaign prior to the 2004 failed vote. "Then I formed my own group in 2004 because I wanted to try a different approach. The Jackson County Animal Shelter is currently being further reformed under new leadership which is wonderful. People have told me that our work helped to shed the spotlight on our shelter and helped to make shelter reform here possible. Our humane society publicly thanked us for our work on a local TV show. Recently, I was even invited to sit on a county spay/neuter committee for our shelter."

She also advocates on state and federal bills addressing pound seizure and has been helpful to me and my office at the American Humane Association on the 2009 Michigan pound seizure bill. "Sometimes I write letters or make calls for state and national campaigns to stop pound seizure because no pet is safe as long as pound seizure is allowed. The majority of county facilities, regardless of their location in the U.S., are mostly understaffed and overworked and so the statistical chances of someone's beloved pet accidentally ending up being sold to research I believe is very great. It has happened before sadly. The only way to be certain that NO lost pet will end up in research is for a county shelter to not sell to research or places where they may end up in research."

Judy realized that people in the community were unaware of pound seizure, so she and her group set out on an education campaign. Unfortunately, the local newspaper was not very interested in publicizing the issue, so that made widespread media efforts more difficult. Judy also created a website to post information and raise awareness. She even sold some of her special dog and horse statues in order to raise money to create T-shirts and print bumper stickers. Judy also learned about county politics. "My group attended and spoke at county commission meetings for about two years, wrote letters to the editor, and worked on convincing all the news media that this was an important community/pet safety issue. I was interviewed by a local news station at my home about our cause. I held library meetings to educate people and even put signs on my car and would see people reading them at my vet's office, at the grocery store, etc."

At the county commissioner meetings, Judy came up with an innovative and visible plan for the commissioners to know who in the audience was supporting a pound seizure ban: wearing red ribbons. "Before each county meeting, I would put the basket of red ribbons at the door of the commission chambers, close to the agendas, with a note saying to please wear a ribbon if you supported stopping pound seizure. People wore them from our community who I didn't even know, who just sat in the audience to show support for our side." Judy was vocal in stating that failure was not an option in our campaign. The campaign would not cease until pound seizure was banished from the county shelter. Judy and her group were fiercely determined to win.

Judy was creative in spreading the word. "We got flyers and signs out to businesses, and I carried them in my car to hand out if I got into a discussion with someone. I remember once going through a drive-through, and a woman saw my signs on my car and yelled for me to pull over. She had just moved here and was very upset to learn our county was selling pets to research. We spoke for about twenty minutes, and she left with a bunch of information and a promise to me to contact her commissioner. We tried to get flyers out at any public place that dogs were being walked. My group had fund-raiser garage sales and handed out info there too. Most people, especially pet owners, were horrified to know that this was allowed in our community.

"We were one of only eight counties at the time in Michigan still allowing pound seizure out of eighty-three counties total in our state. People began writing letters to the editor to stop pound seizure and many began contacting the county commission and/or attending county meetings. One of the commissioners running for reelection told me that he was surprised at the number of people in his district who made it a point to introduce their dog to him as he went door-to-door. He thanked me for educating him and said he didn't realize how many people really cared for their pets. Some people didn't understand the issue in my opinion (that this was about pet safety, not stopping animal research)." Judy also hosted booths at local community events and with her own funds bought life-sized, realistic stuffed dogs wearing signs to educate the public about pound seizure.

Keeping on top of an advocacy campaign can take many hours and an emotional toll. Judy recounts one of the saddest moments she encountered during her 2004–2006 campaign. "Probably one of the saddest incidents was a litter of cute lab mix puppies who ended up being sold to research even though there was a rescue lined up to take them as well as one woman who called me from out of state wanting to adopt one. She had fallen in love with his photo on Petfinder and wanted my help to adopt him. Due to our county's policies at the time, we could not save them sadly, but the story was in our newspaper and picked up by the Associated Press so it was circulated all over the U.S. I believe this helped our cause tremendously."

During the campaign, Judy's group also made an effort to help the shelter. The group donated a $500 gift certificate to the animal shelter so that digital cameras could be purchased to assist with criminal abuse and neglect investigations. They also purchased a TV/DVD player; that way educational programs could be played in the shelter lobby while customers waited. Her volunteers, as well as other groups, also rescued animals from the shelter to help reduce the number being sold to research, as well as to re-duce the workload of the staff and cost to the shelter in housing the animals. The goal was to make a positive impact on the shelter and to not merely be seen as doing something against a shelter practice. Their work continues to improve the shelter—recently by just getting the word out they raised more than $8,000 to improve the shelter walls in the large dog room, which will reduce the spread of diseases and improve safety for staff.

In the heat of the battle, the opposition began to surface at the county commission meetings. The Class B dealer would appear at meetings, and other supporters began to attend. "Several people identifying themselves as farm bureau members spoke in support of pound seizure at a few county meetings. There were a few in the community who felt shelter pets were needed to further research, but others voiced the opposite opinion as well as concern for their pets. One commissioner in particular was very adamant that pound seizure should continue, and he was the only one who voted against us in the end. A local psychologist on our side debated a dog dealer and a [university] representative on a local radio station."

In July 2006, the Jackson County commissioners voted to end the prac-tice of pound seizure at the shelter. The joy for the advocates, especially Judy, could be seen in the front-page newspaper article of the *Jackson Citizen Patriot* titled "Board Outlaws Selling of Strays." The photo showed Judy with an apparent look of shock and her hands held up to her face. Another advocate seated next to her raised both arms in the air as a sign of victory. Judy said, "We had heard rumors before we were getting the vote and nothing would happen so I almost couldn't believe it when if finally did happen. There were many hugs and tears of happiness. I was so proud of my wonderful volunteers and the citizens who had the courage to speak out against an injustice and stand up for their rights as citizens of our great community."

Judy's word of advice for current and future pound seizure advocates is simple: "I would say to believe in yourself first of all and be willing to work to win a campaign. Many people told me we would never win this issue because it had been tried before. I had never worked on anything like this before in my entire life. I only wanted our community to be one where pet safety was important along with other things we care about like the safety of our children, care of the elderly, community safety, etc. Pets are family members and need our protection. People need to educate others that stopping pound seizure does not stop animal research. Whether we believe that animal research is needed or a waste of valuable time and money, research has other places to obtain lab animals if they must. By using other sources they don't compromise the safety of our pets. I didn't want Conan's death to be meaningless—change had to come from it."

Judy continues, "It is also important to become knowledgeable about local politics and get to know the 'movers and shakers' in your community. Keep the issue very public—use any media you can think of from small local papers to the Internet to TV stations to signs on your car. Also, learn to 'direct' the media. A famous politician was quoted in an interview years ago (paraphrasing) saying to always give the media the answer to the question you wish they would have asked you, instead of the actual question they did ask you. So if they ask you a question, use that moment to give them the 'sound bite' that you would want to see on the evening news."

To encourage others, Judy has these final words. "I am no one special. I am a former law enforcement secretary, and I believe in a higher power—I'm just a regular person. Who was I to go against the wisdom of others who have fought this before? But, with this knowledge, how could we then argue this was about pet safety and only ask for a partial ban? We used truth as the basis for our argument, and the truth not only got us a vote of 10–1 but a complete ban, which I am told is rare. I think we need to realize the worst enemy of any cause is the word 'can't.'"

EATON COUNTY, MICHIGAN

The advocacy approach in Eaton County was strategically different than the campaigns in the neighboring counties of Ingham and Jackson. Judy Oisten and two other concerned citizens headed the campaign from 2007 to 2009. Judy's approach to ending pound seizure in Eaton County offers a different perspective, and I am grateful that she agreed to be interviewed.[9]

Judy's story of getting involved in a pound seizure campaign could have ended badly, but fortunately did not. "The summer of 2005 (my husband and I) were in our front yard watching our two yellow Labradors play. We heard a man in the passenger seat of a white panel van that started driving by our house yell out, 'There's a Lab.' We quickly called our dogs up to us and watched as they proceeded to drive slowly down our dead-end road and slowly back by. We waved and then thought it was odd they didn't give us a telephone number if they lost their Lab. Then after they were out of sight and it was too late to get a license plate number, we realized they were looking to steal our two Labs, as they are both friendly and would have jumped right in to go for a ride. This made me angry enough to get on the Internet and start finding out as much information as I could about 'pet theft.' I learned that 'bunchers' travel through neighborhoods and steal animals to sell to a random source Class B dealer. This is when I discovered Eaton County Animal Control, that was a mile from my home, sold unclaimed lost pets to a random source Class B dealer. Information I read also mentioned that pet theft increases in areas where animal control practices pound seizure. This is also when we got both of our dogs microchipped, just to give us one slight chance to get them back, if they were ever stolen."

Before forming the campaign strategy, Judy found me, and we discussed various techniques that might be successful in Eaton County. The initial stages were similar: Judy and her group needed to educate the community about pound seizure. As expected, residents in the county were unaware of the practice. "It was amazing most of the public was not aware lost unclaimed pets were being sold to research, and some had lived in Eaton County all their lives. It had been kept so quiet that nobody knew that out of eighty-three counties, Eaton County was one of five counties at that time still selling to a random source Class B dealer."

In 2007, she hosted a booth at a pet show and displayed materials about pound seizure and pet safety. Letters were written to the editor of the local newspaper encouraging citizens to attend the commission meetings. "It was really hard to get other people involved that would publicly stand up against pound seizure in Eaton County. I kept hearing the phrase 'Good luck, you will not get anywhere and will just waste your time.' Back in 1996 several Eaton County citizens protested and tried to get the shelter to stop selling to research and were no longer allowed to volunteer at the shelter after that."

In February 2008, the shelter underwent tremendous public scrutiny from an incident involving two dogs and five cats abandoned outside a home in the cold Michigan winter. Photos of one dog, with an obvious head injury, were displayed over the local newspaper showing that the dog was also tethered and unable to seek safe shelter. The shelter declined to help the animals because neighbors were feeding them and, therefore, the animals were not abandoned. The outcry was tremendous. The dogs were eventually rescued by another shelter and nursed back to health. The cats did not fare well and were euthanized. But this incident shined a spotlight on the shelter.

Following that incident, in March 2008 Judy and her group attended a county commission meeting and offered to help the shelter. Although the offer met with defensiveness, the shelter staff still listened. Judy showed them information about pound seizure and why it was wrong. Judy and her group asked the commissioners if they would establish a task force to assist the shelter with essential changes. In April 2008, the task force was established, and Judy and Helen Schneider, who had been advocating together with Judy, were appointed as citizens. One commissioner, who led the task force, was also an advocate for the animals and against pound seizure. Judy credits this commissioner with the progress that they made. In the end, the task force came up with eighteen recommendations, some of which have been instituted and some of which are still pending. However, Judy and the other volunteers still struggle with the shelter staff in that they are forbidden to take photos of the animals and they have to be escorted by the staff to see the animals. "It feels like you are entering a prison."

The strategy that made a difference in Eaton County was that the commissioners were agreeable to the formation of a task force that would make recommendations to the shelter. Also, the county sheriff was officially in charge of the shelter, although the commissioners had some oversight. Thus, it was the sheriff who allowed pound seizure to continue. In 2008, the position for sheriff was up for election. A candidate running against the current sheriff publicly stated that he would stop pound seizure. Soon thereafter, in May 2008, the current sheriff issued an order to stop the practice at the shelter. This was an interim order that still required eventual approval from the commissioners. So although the shelter animals were safe, the work was not complete.

With a win in their pocket, yet significant work still to accomplish at the shelter, Judy knew what tactic would work best for the long haul.

"Our motto was to take baby steps. We were very careful to win over the support of the commissioners and everyone we could. Give them as much documentation as you can, as they don't have time to do any research on the subject. We gave them a booklet we made with as much information as possible to educate them on changes where universities and medical fields were not using live animals in research any longer. That it would be more profitable for the shelter to do adoption events and bring in money from that rather then sell them to a Class B dealer. This would bring in public support and donations. We also toured other animal control shelters, took pictures, and provided a power point to each commissioner to review. In the meantime there were others speaking against us at commission and public safety committee meetings on how it was important for Michigan State University to continue receiving animals, but they didn't have any documentation and were speaking from past practices that they thought needed to continue. Basically they were stuck in the 1960s."

As expected, some supporters of pound seizure appeared at the commission meetings. Surprisingly, a local veterinarian and the leader of a local animal rescue group spoke in support of pound seizure. "They felt that it was necessary to use live animals in research as they felt it would help with future medical treatment. The heart valve was one example they used, but we had previously give them documentation that the National Heart Institute and others were using simulators and more advanced research that didn't require the use of live animals."

On November 5, 2009, the county commissioners officially voted and passed a resolution to ban pound seizure in the county. Judy and her team deserve endless accolades for their patience and effort. Judy's final words of advice to other advocates are well-reasoned: "Lots of patience, being firm, exposing to the public that pound seizure is going on in our county, and educating the public as a lot of them have no idea what happens to their lost pets. Being honest and taking baby steps were really helpful. Proving ourselves with documentation to educate the commissioners on the issue was also a way to show we were honest in what we were saying, and we earned their trust. Most of the commissioners didn't have any idea this was going on in Eaton County, and they didn't even know what it was all about. Some of the commissioners even took a tour of animal control with us to see the inside. Going in with a respectful attitude gained us respect back. We do have a good group of commissioners here in our county to work with, which we have been grateful for."

MONTCALM COUNTY, MICHIGAN

Montcalm County Animal Control engaged in pound seizure for more than thirty years. During the 2008–2009 campaign to end the practice, it did not appear that it could be stopped. Sandy Carlton[10] has been an advocate against pound seizure for more than thirty years, whereas Frances Schuleit[11] learned about it in the spring of 2008 while running for county commissioner and quickly became involved. I have engaged in numerous conversations with both Sandy and Fran on strategies for one of the most hostile pound seizure campaigns I have encountered. I thank both Sandy and Fran for offering their wisdom and experiences on this issue.

Sandy Carlton has lived in Montcalm County, a rural community in the center of the state, since 1972. She first heard about pound seizure in 1976 when a local Class B dealer approached the county commissioners about taking unclaimed animals from the shelter for use in research. The dealer's first attempt resulted in no agreement, but the next year an agreement was given to the dealer over protests from Sandy and others in the community. It was then that Sandy became involved at the shelter, not only to stop pound seizure, but to correct what she believed to be subpar conditions at the shelter, which is still an ongoing issue.

Sandy has been a longtime advocate against pound seizure. "My campaign against pound seizure in Montcalm County started in 1976. I also actively participated in Ionia County's successful bid to end this practice in 1994. I wrote letters, attended meetings, and shared information with Newaygo activists when they conducted a successful campaign against pound seizure in 1995. I traveled to Ingham County to show support for their efforts and to speak on behalf of ending pound seizure in 2003. During this time I continued to learn about pound seizure by gathering information, attending seminars, and meeting with anti-pound seizure activists throughout the United States as well as Michigan."

Sandy reveals how tactics with the county commissioners changed over the years. "Over the years, beginning in 1977, we tried many tactics. We started by being very reasonable and trying to work with the commissioners. That got us nowhere. They saw us as absolutely no threat, and while everyone was cordial, nothing changed for the animals. In going through some old notes, I came across one of my early statements to the Board of Commissioners. In that statement I said, 'It has always been my tactic to avoid argument and arrive at solutions through cooperation and mutual

understanding—above all, I have always sought to be reasonable. . . .'
My, my how things changed! As we watched other counties around us
launch aggressive campaigns against pound seizure and win, we noticed
that the common denominator for success involved significant numbers of
people who were willing to attend every commissioner meeting and point
out problems with the shelter while continually hammering the message
to end pound seizure. It appeared that it wasn't as much about the content
of the message as it was about the amount of pressure being exerted on
the commissioners and the number of people exerting that pressure. In
Montcalm County it was nearly impossible in the early days to get people
interested enough to attend commissioner meetings (which were and continue to be held at 1:00 p.m. on weekdays) on a regular basis or to speak
out in opposition over an extended period of time. Until we could get the
numbers we needed, we felt anything we did would be unsuccessful. The
arrival of the Internet and new blood in the community would bring us the
people with the determination and fortitude we needed."

There have been numerous pound seizure campaigns in Montcalm
County over the past three decades. However, the most intense effort occurred in 2008–2009. Sandy credits public education and an intense dis-
like of bad publicity by the county leaders as the tipping point for change
in Montcalm County. Even though previous attempts at ending pound
seizure had failed, many residents thought the practice had ended years
ago. The new campaign ramped up efforts through ads and news stories
in the local newspaper, leafleting campaigns door-to-door, and posters
throughout the community.

A defining moment during Sandy's introduction to pound seizure was
an invitation to visit the dealer's facility. During that visit, the dealer was
very pleasant and seemed to be a very caring and kind person. She was
shown one of the buildings where dogs were housed, which at that time
wasn't any better than our current county shelter. After visiting the building he invited her into his kitchen where he continued to extoll the virtues
of pound seizure and the lives that are saved or made better because of it.
She thanked him for the invitation and left. A few days later, it dawned on
Sandy that it might be nice to know if he had a contract with the county
to take these animals. Because he was so eager to give her information
she didn't think anything of calling him. When she asked him if he had a
contract, he went ballistic. He screamed that she was stupid and was being
led "down the primrose path" by animal rights zealots and threatened her
with an order of protection if she ever set foot on his property again. It

was then she knew that this man and his business were not what they were portrayed to be and set out to learn the truth about pound seizure.

Sandy recounted several successful tactics in the 2008–2009 campaign, one of which was the large number of people that appeared at county commission meetings, as well as the overwhelming number of letters, faxes, and e-mail communications being sent to the commissioners. Residents from outside of Montcalm County attended the meetings, including Holly Sauvé, Judy Dynnik, and Judy Oisten mentioned earlier. National animal welfare organizations such as the American Humane Association, the American Anti-Vivisection Society, People for the Ethical Treatment of Animals, Physicians Committee for Responsible Medicine, and the Humane Society of the United States all mobilized their organizations' membership to write letters to the commissioners. This was no longer Montcalm County's little secret; the entire nation knew what was happening to shelter animals, and everyone wanted it to end—everyone except the dealer and a few commissioners.

Other successful tactics included:

- Creating a website for Concerned Citizens Coalition, one of the two groups that spearheaded the movement. This website promoted its position against pound seizure, provided calls to action, linked to other activist websites, and provided an opportunity to sign an online petition;
- Circulating petitions and flyers throughout the county calling for an end to pound seizure in the county;
- Going door-to-door with information and distributing handouts at local events;
- Hosting booths at area festivals to distribute information;
- Sending Freedom of Information requests to the county and local research institutions to gather information on the extent of pound seizure and the use of Montcalm's cats and dogs in research;
- Working with numerous state and national animal welfare groups and activists to get their thoughts regarding strategy and share information;
- Working around the clock with animal rescue organizations and transporters to keep as many shelter animals from the dealer as possible;
- Keeping a watch on the activities at the shelter and being vocal about problems that were identified;
- Creating ads for the local papers, including writing editorials regarding the problems with pound seizure;

- Making pound seizure an issue in the 2008 elections by having people attend political forums and asking candidates their position on the issue. Most of the candidates challenging an incumbent said they would not support pound seizure if elected;
- Sending e-mails and postcards to supporters reminding them of important meetings and asking them to attend to show support;
- Sandy and two members of her core group attended every Board of Commissioners meeting for nearly two years. At every meeting they would provide the commissioners with comments and/or pertinent information on pound seizure or problems at the shelter.

Pound seizure campaigns invariably run into situations that seem insurmountable. In Montcalm County, the issue started in November–December 2008 before a key vote when the two local newspapers refused to run any advertisements or letters about pound seizure. It was discovered that the dealer's attorney had sent a stern letter to both newspapers threatening them with legal action if they advertised anything associated with pound seizure or his client. These small-town newspapers were frightened and opted for the easy way out. Through their website the advocates located a First Amendment attorney in New York who offered to assist the local newspapers, but the offer was declined. This was a devastating blow, but the advocate group contacted a weekly shopper publication that agreed to run their ads. "Our first ad came out in the *River Valley Shopper*, and it was a winner! People in that area were all talking about the ad, and they were angry about pound seizure. While it would have been nice to have had the ads placed in the daily as well as the weekly newspapers, we got a good response so our efforts were not completely foiled. We will always be grateful to the *River Valley Shopper* for standing with us on this issue!"

Sandy credits much of the success to a small core group of longtime advocates against pound seizure. On January 26, 2009, the commissioners met to vote on the contract with the Class B dealer. The meeting room was filled to capacity with people who opposed pound seizure. Rather than take a vote, the commissioners agreed to form an ad hoc committee to review the dealer's contract. Sandy remembers the chairman of the commission making it clear that the committee was not to work toward abolishing pound seizure, but to find a way to work with it and that all members appointed to the committee must be willing to accept a modified contract with the dealer. The chairman also appointed the Class B dealer and the dealer's veterinarian to the committee. The appointment of these two people to the committee would prove to be a move that helped the cause more than if any advocates had been appointed to the committee.

"The forming of this committee provided the commissioners with an opportunity to put off making a decision on the (Class B dealer's) contract while support for ending it was strong. We believe that the commissioners hoped that by the time the committee came back with a modified contract our supporters would be gone. It also allowed them to extend the contract with the dealer for an additional six months with no public outcry. But the creation of this committee helped us as well. It gave those commissioners who supported us additional time to try and bring other commissioners to our side, and it gave us time to compile some information that would help turn the vote in our favor." During this time, the chairman of the commission began attending township meetings to promote the practice of pound seizure. However, those opposing pound seizure were quickly on his heels to present the other side of the story to the township leaders.

The ad hoc committee went back to the county commissioners, complete with a shelter survey conducted at no cost by Dr. Wendy Swift, the veterinary medical director for the Humane Society of Kent County in Grand Rapids, Michigan. In her 100+ page report, numerous recommendations for improvement were outlined, including banning pound seizure. The ad hoc committee now had solid and unbiased positions supporting everything that pound seizure opponents had advocated presenting to the commissioners. The county commission had nine members. So it became essential to know the breakdown of the votes before the vote occurred. Sandy recounts that there were four commissioners supporting the ban on pound seizure, of which two were actively lobbying their colleagues to gain one more vote. Sandy further noted that one commissioner, who initially supported a pound seizure ban, changed his opinion after attending an open house at the Class B dealer's facility. However, after the commissioners were provided a list of USDA inspection citations over the past several years, that commissioner switched his vote back to support banning pound seizure. Additionally, the Class B dealer's practice of taking "the Fifth Amendment" at commission meetings and refusing to answer questions regarding the disposition of the animals in his care served to sway one more commissioner to vote in favor of a ban. At that point, there were six votes to ban pound seizure, enough to win.

On April 27, 2009, the county commissioners voted six to three to end the contract with the Class B dealer. It was almost too good to be true. And in a way it was. The dealer was given an additional three months on his contract before the official end date of August 1, 2009. Those final three months were some of the more taxing times for the pound seizure opponents who were relentless in getting as many animals out of the shelter and out of the grasp of the dealer. One particular tragedy involved an English setter named Soup (who is featured in chapter 4). Sandy was the one volunteer who knew Soup and advocated the most to guarantee her safe return. Even months after that fated date in July 2009 when Soup was given to the dealer, Sandy never gave up. Sandy placed ads in the local newspaper attempting to locate Soup's original owner. But when the owner was finally located, the owner refused to talk about the dog. Reportedly someone had forewarned the owners that "animal activists" might ask them to change their mind on surrendering Soup to the shelter and warned them not to speak with any of them.

Sandy's words of advice for future pound seizure advocates are simple: "Get large numbers of vocal people who are not intimidated by authority. You need a strong core group of workers dedicated to the cause and willing to put in hours of legwork, computer work, homework, and some of their own money. Your core group must be prepared to be lied to and ridiculed, and they must be willing to forge ahead in spite of significant drawbacks while constantly retaining their dignity and credibility. Know your message, stay on message, and repeat your message over and over again. Make sure all your facts are correct and you can support them. Hang together because the opposition will try and split you. Be fair but be tough. Your core group does not have to be large (we had four), but your support group must be huge though not necessarily local. The harder we got pushed, the harder each of us pushed back. We would not have won this battle without them!"

It was the county's practices of pound seizure and inhumane euthanasia that propelled Frances Schuleit to run for county commissioner in 2008. When Fran lost by 0.5 percent of the votes, she contacted the person who won the election and urged him to learn about the practice of pound seizure. He quickly became an ally for the shelter animals. Fran worked collaboratively with this new commissioner to end pound seizure in the county.

Although Fran knew that the community did not understand what pound seizure entailed, she was surprised at the number of supporters for the practice. "I am quite certain that the community did not understand the concept of pound seizure, since so many people supported the notion that using the 'leftover' animals for research was acceptable. This required a lot of research and a great deal of education of the public in open settings, by many people."

Fran started the community education process by working with her local veterinarian who supported the campaign to end pound seizure. She also worked with the local media to raise awareness. One local newspaper was particularly helpful in reporting on county commission meetings that involved discussions about the animal shelter and the Class B dealer who had a contract with the county. The dealer's contract with the county allowed him to take cats and dogs from the shelter for free. In exchange, he would remove the carcasses of euthanized animals at no cost.

Fran also met with the chairman of the county commissioners and provided information and resource materials explaining why pound seizure was both an outdated and inappropriate practice for the shelter. She offered suggestions for enhancing operations and shelter improvement ideas, including the appointment of an animal control advisory committee. Throughout the entire process, the chairman was the staunchest advocate supporting the contract with the Class B dealer.

In February 2009, the commissioners appointed a nine-member animal control ad hoc committee to review shelter practices and make recommendations to the commissioners. Fran was placed on this committee, along with a local veterinarian who was opposed to pound seizure. The chairman also appointed the dealer to serve on the committee. The mission of the committee, according to the chairman, was to work collaboratively with the dealer and to "find a way to work with the dealer." Fran and several committee members argued that in order to make a recommendation about pound seizure, the entire shelter operation would need to be assessed. The committee then proceeded to push ahead with massive shelter reform, including a pound seizure ban.

The committee sought the assistance of Dr. Wendy Swift, who, as previously mentioned, had conducted a pro bono survey of the shelter and issued a 100+ page report to the commissioners. One of the recommendations was to end pound seizure. This survey reinforced the committee's recommendations.

Still, three county commissioners continued to block any efforts to ban pound seizure. The committee persevered in pushing its recommendations forward anyway. On April 27, 2009, Fran led the ad hoc committee's presentation of its findings and recommendations to the Board of Commissioners, amid a room filled with local advocates, including Sandy Carlton.

When a vote was taken, the commissioners voted not to renew a contract with the Class B dealer.

For those remaining months, advocates worked endlessly to rescue the cats and dogs from the shelter, with little support or help. Six months later, the shelter was well on its way to making improvements. Fran continues to implement positive change at the shelter. The carbon dioxide barrel, which was once used to euthanize ill, aggressive, or unadoptable animals, was removed. Euthanasia by injection was adopted. There is still much work to be done at the shelter, and Fran is still involved in helping to implement positive change for the animals.

Fran's advice to advocates: "Follow your heart, do what is right, and be sure that you have done your homework. Know the facts, do the research, and know the personalities you are dealing with. Above all, don't give up. The key to success for this entire process, which has been highly emotionally charged, is to treat everyone respectfully."

Part III

TAKING ACTION

CHAPTER 12

Lawsuits, Threats, and Intimidation

One of the most unnerving aspects of advocacy to stop pound seizure is the possibility of being threatened, intimidated into silence, or worse yet, sued. This information is being provided solely to protect you, the reader and advocate, and not to frighten you away from becoming an advocate. Threats and intimidation are not common, but they can occur. And lawsuits are even rarer.

The number one rule in any advocacy to ban pound seizure is that only documented and factual evidence can be publicized. Publicizing information involves speaking to a citizen or public body, an e-mail, a letter written to lawmakers or the local newspaper editor, or information contained in flyers, brochures, or a website. Engaging in speculation, unproven accusations, or spreading rumors that are unproven could result in a lawsuit for defamation. Even if a lawsuit does not result, such conduct can impact your credibility and tarnish the campaign's effectiveness. If you are misquoted by the media, immediately send a written response to the reporter and the editor of the newspaper correcting the misinformation and requesting a written retraction. Sending a letter will help protect you and will demonstrate that you took immediate action to rectify the issue.

In writing this book, at the forefront of my mind as I typed each word, was to make sure there were facts and evidence supporting each statement. To some extent, being so cautious may have impacted the book's power and emotion. At the same time, my legal training and pound seizure advocacy have helped. I have come to form beliefs about why pound seizure exists in some shelters and not others; however, I do not have evidence to support these beliefs. Although my theories would make for interesting reading, it is important to state only the facts. The same is true for any individual involved in animal advocacy, particularly regarding pound seizure.

I have been honored to provide pro bono legal advice to several volunteer groups that were working to ban pound seizure in their county. My initial advice to the volunteers was always the same: "Only speak of, write about, and publicize information that is factual and documented. Never engage in conjecture, speculation, rumor, or innuendo. Pound seizure is a serious issue that requires serious consideration before speaking."

Too many times I have heard advocates speak of the perceived fate of shelter animals taken in pound seizure that I knew was not proven. I also have received countless e-mail messages over the years containing unproven information about those individuals and institutions directly involved with pound seizure cats and dogs. In 2009, I was alarmed when an advocate friend forwarded to me an e-mail from a former animal welfare lobbyist who made a bold statement about improper conduct between supporters of pound seizure in a particular campaign to end the practice. When asked for documentation, this advocate stated, "I wish it were documented. But in some of the counties I helped, it was obvious to us that he had made payments to local officials (probably legally via campaign donations)." I cannot stress enough that tactics like that are forbidden in any advocacy. If you cannot speak the truth, then do not speak. Had this e-mail gotten into the wrong hands, this former advocate could have legitimately faced a lawsuit for defamation, and the pound seizure campaign could have been irreparably harmed.

In my advocacy role as a private attorney assisting citizens, and in my previous employment as the vice president of public policy for the American Humane Association where we advocate eradicating pound seizure from shelters, I have consistently held a high standard that those receiving my guidance will only advocate with accurate and documented facts.

When advocating in your community, state, or federal government for change, the best arguments are always based on taking the high ground and maintaining credibility. If you disseminate false or unproven information, you will lose credibility. If you do not have credibility, then no lawmaker will listen to your arguments even if they are valid. Setting this standard for accuracy in any advocacy campaign is important and becomes even more vital when pound seizure is involved because of the high financial stakes of animal research.

Do the threats, intimidation, and lawsuits occur because there are significant investments in maintaining the legitimacy of medical research involving animals? Do these scare tactics surface as a result of the dwindling existence of B dealers attempting to remain in a financially lucrative business? Or are there other factors at play? It could be all of these, or none of these. What is clear is that pound seizure campaigns can become ugly. Very quickly, you will learn who supports pound seizure and who wants it abolished. Because of the emotional nature of this issue, erratic and unreasonable behavior on both sides will surface.

What has become clear to me over the past decade is that some supporters of pound seizure have attorneys on retainer to attempt to silence any opposition. As an attorney, I have been fascinated by the power of the First Amendment that gives every U.S. citizen the right to freedom of speech. This right gives us the power to engage in discussion with political bodies to effect change. Being employed as a lobbyist is how I exercised this right on behalf of my organization and its constituents throughout the United States. Yet even when expressing speech and engaging in advocacy, some citizens have been threatened with lawsuits or intimidated into backing down. Newspapers in one Michigan county, for example, were told not to publish any information on pound seizure or they would be sued.

Why is there such a desire to keep pound seizure a secret and in practice? It could be that abolishing pound seizure could result in some of the supporters becoming obsolete. Much is at stake when someone feels like his financial existence is being marginalized or abolished.

Every pound seizure advocate should be aware of the federal Animal Enterprise Terrorism Act (AETA).[1] On November 27, 2006, President George W. Bush signed the AETA law that had been passed by the 109th Congress. The law prohibits anyone from traveling in interstate or foreign commerce, or using the mail service, for the purpose of damaging or interfering with an animal enterprise and doing one of three other acts: (1) intentionally damaging real or personal property (including animals) or the real or personal property of anyone connected to an animal enterprise; (2) intentionally placing a person connected to an animal enterprise, including immediate family, in reasonable fear of death or serious bodily injury through a course of conduct (two or more times) of threats, vandalism, property damage, criminal trespass, harassment, or intimidation; or (3) conspiring or attempting to do the prior two acts. Penalties are harsh and start with a $10,000 fine and/or one year in federal prison, or both, to life in prison if death occurs.

I have spoken with many advocates who are concerned that AETA would prevent them from advocating to stop pound seizure in their community. Are the advocacy tools outlined in this book in violation of AETA? No. AETA does not prohibit First Amendment freedom of speech or the right to speak out for change. So what does AETA actually cover? In a nutshell, AETA prohibits the extremist movement of using killing, bombings, and injuring property or people to threaten or intimidate research facilities or those associated with research facilities.

"Animal enterprise" is defined as "(A) a commercial or academic enterprise that uses or sells animals or animal products for profit, food or fiber production, agriculture, education, research, or testing; (B) a zoo, aquarium, animal shelter, pet store, breeder, furrier, circus, or rodeo, or other lawful competitive animal event; or (C) any fair or similar event intended to advance agricultural arts and sciences."[2] The AETA law specifically states that it does not "prohibit any expressive conduct (including peaceful picketing or other peaceful demonstration) protected from legal prohibition by the First Amendment to the Constitution." As long as advocates follow the advice in this book, there is no need to worry about AETA. If you know of advocates who are engaging in threatening behavior that could escalate to physical injury to person or property, it is advisable to immediately contact the police and report the situation, as well as distance yourself and your advocacy from these actions.

The remainder of this chapter will outline examples of threats, intimidation, and lawsuits, some instances which frightened citizens into silence, and other times that empowered citizens to keep advocating and shine a light on these tactics.

INTIMIDATION AND THREATS

In my first pound seizure campaign, as we ramped up the public education campaign and were advocating consistently to the county commissioners, one thing I observed was that the shelter director appeared increasingly hostile toward me and the other shelter volunteers. After the infamous rescue of Karyn the cat (featured in chapter 8), the shelter director made two strategic moves against our volunteer group. First, he approached the president and another board member of our volunteer group and made three demands: that I be removed as a board member, that the public education campaign (consisting of ads in the newspaper and flyers at pet stores) be stopped, and that the volunteers learn to "get along with shelter policies" (i.e., accept pound seizure) in order to continue helping the animals. Finally, he eventually banned the volunteers from the shelter.

In regard to the first demand, the president and board member refused to remove me as a board member, but did agree to stop parts of the public education campaign. After consulting with the remainder of the volunteer board of directors, it was determined that the agreement with the shelter director was against our bylaws and mission and should not have been made. The president and board member had been placed in a difficult situation in an effort to maintain peaceful relations with the shelter director. To avoid future situations, they agreed to step down as board members (they were still volunteers) so that the group could continue with our advocacy, and they would not be used as pawns by the director.

One Michigan advocate shares the following stories of how she has received threats during her advocacy over the years. "Since I have waged a campaign against pound seizure for several years, I and some of my associates have received several threats. In 1996 one other person and I received several letters from the dealer's attorney threatening a lawsuit if we did not retract certain statements. We ignored the letters, and no lawsuits were filed. One of my associates had a threatening note placed in her mailbox [by an unknown person]. In 1997 after speaking at [an out-of-state university], I was misquoted in [the newspaper] and received another letter from the dealer's attorney demanding a retraction of that quote. Since it was a misquote, I did write the paper and clarified my statement. I never heard anything more from the dealer's attorney, but I got threatening phone calls from members of [a national animal rights group] who preferred the misquote to my actual statement."

Another advocate shared this information about being intimidated during a pound seizure campaign. "There were several incidents but I prefer not to go into details. One incident was designed to try to stop us from winning and another was an effort at retaliation. There were no threats of violence."

This is why I recommend always working in a group so that an advocate is not going up against strong opposition alone.

LAWSUITS

The book *SLAPPs: Getting Sued for Speaking Out*[3] describes in alarming detail the experience of five concerned citizens who were advocating banning pound seizure in three Michigan shelters. This information is being provided not to frighten anyone away from pound seizure advocacy, but to make you aware of common pitfalls that can occur.

According to an opinion filed by the Michigan Court of Appeals,[4] a lawsuit was filed by a random source Michigan Class B dealer in the 1980s against a group of volunteers that had successfully banned pound seizure from three Michigan shelters. The claims made against the defendants were that they defamed the dealer and animal research in general through oral and written statements. Specifically, "the dog dealers complained that the animal advocates had falsely accused them of cruelty, 'petnapping,' 'vast profits,' 'bribes,' and conducting 'a furtive and sinister business,' in order to cause 'termination of [the kennel's] business relationship' with the governments.[5] At the time, the dealer was purchasing shelter animals from Garden City, Monroe County, and Livingston County animal shelters. One defendant was a schoolteacher who volunteered for the Michigan Humane Society and another defendant was a commercial artist who was the president of the Livingston County Humane Society.

According to *SLAPPs*, the dealers put the validity of medical research on trial, rather than the right to petition and advocate for change. In a jury trial, the defendants prevailed and received a jury verdict of $329,739 for defamation, tortuous interference with business relations, and conspiracy to defame and to tortuously interfere.[6] Three of the five defendants settled with the plaintiffs after the verdict. However, two of the defendants appealed, and in 1988 the Michigan Court of Appeals reversed the judgment and ordered a new trial, maintaining that the jury was improperly instructed on the law of defamation.

Of interest in the Court of Appeals decision is the following regarding what defamation consists of:

> A person does not have a cause of action for defamation unless it is he or she who is defamed. See Lewis v. Soule, 3 Mich. 514, 521 (1855); Curtis [*v. Evening News Ass'n*], 135 Mich. App. 101, 103, 352 N.W.2d 355. When a publication, on its face, makes no reference to a plaintiff, plaintiff must sustain the burden of pleading and proof, by way of 'colloquium,' that the defamatory meaning attached to him. When the defamatory words are directed at a group of persons rather than an individual, the plaintiff must first show that he is a

member of the class defamed. Where a statement contains not even an oblique reference to the plaintiff as an individual, the plaintiff's witnesses must show a basis for the belief that plaintiff was being attacked. *New York Times Co. v. Sullivan*, 376 U.S. 254, 288-289, 85 S.Ct. 710, 730-31, 11 L.Ed.2d 686 (1964). Additionally, the plaintiff must establish some reasonable personal application of the words to himself. Beyond that, if the words have no personal application to the plaintiff, they are not actionable by him.[7]

The court also noted that a statement is not libelous if it is substantially true. However, in 1989, the Michigan Supreme Court reversed the Court of Appeals and reinstated the jury verdict because of a technical error in the defendant's failing to preserve the issue of the improper jury instructions. Thus, the jury verdict stood, and the defendants were required to pay.

On appeal, many organizations joined forces in an amicus brief to the court in support of the defendants. Those organizations included the Animal Legal Defense Fund, the Michigan Humane Society, the Michigan Federation of Humane Societies, the Humane Society of the United States, the Animal Protection Institute of America, the Fund for Animals, and the International Primate Protection League. This case was of great interest to the national animal welfare community because of the implications it could have had to silence pound seizure advocacy.

When I first began my pound seizure advocacy in 2000, many pound seizure advocates I spoke with knew about this case. As tragic as the result was for the defendants, the lesson to be learned is clear: Always speak from fact and truth, not from emotion or belief. Consequently, I have always been overly cautious in what I say regarding pound seizure and about the players involved. It can be difficult to hold this stance, especially when dealing with the emotions involved in helping animals, but it is essential to conduct all actions this way.

So how can you legally and effectively advocate in the face of threats, potential lawsuits, and intimidation from the opposition? Just remember these simple rules. Always stick to the proven facts. Do not engage in speculation. Do not spread rumors. Do not conjure up information that is not based on verifiable evidence. Never make an allegation against anyone involved in the pound seizure campaign (the supporters or the lawmakers) unless you have documented and verifiable proof. Do not let your emotions get the best of you. And always work in a team.

If you follow these simple steps, your advocacy will be safe and effective.

CHAPTER 13

Effective Advocacy Techniques

Never doubt that a small group of thoughtfully committed citizens can change the world; indeed, it's the only thing that ever has.

—Margaret Mead

Pound seizure campaigns, as with many advocacy campaigns, can take years before success is achieved. Before starting a pound seizure campaign, it is important to lay the foundation for victory. Doing so will result in less stress and less chance of burnout for you and for other advocates, and will give your advocacy necessary credibility. Many successful techniques were featured in chapter 11. In this chapter, effective and successful techniques will be summarized. It is important to note that pound seizure advocacy can vary depending on whether it is a community, state, or national campaign. What may have worked in Des Moines may not necessarily work in Baton Rouge. Be sure to assess your community or state before creating the advocacy strategy.

Some common themes that have arisen throughout various pound seizure campaigns include resistance from the animal shelter engaging in pound seizure; opposition from the medical, veterinary, and research communities; opposition from lawmakers; and even opposition from the media. Some of the issues are a result of a lack of education on what pound seizure is and what the advocacy campaign is aiming to accomplish. The dos and don'ts of pound seizure advocacy outline various areas to consider before embarking on a campaign.

THE DOS OF POUND SEIZURE ADVOCACY

- Learn all you can about pound seizure before engaging in advocacy. This book will provide you with a solid and factual foundation. For additional reading, please visit the websites for the American Humane Association, the American Anti-Vivisection Society (Ban Pound Seizure website), Physicians Committee for Responsible Medicine, Last Chance for Animals, and the Humane Society of the United States. The more knowledgeable you can become about pound seizure, the more credibility you will have.
- Talk with other advocates who have engaged in successful pound seizure campaigns. Although many advocates were featured throughout this book, it is important to speak with those who have engaged in these campaigns and then tailor successful techniques to your community or state. I am always available to consult with any advocacy group that wishes to stop pound seizure in its community or state.
- If you are in one of the eighteen states that have a state bar association animal law section,[1] consider contacting the section to determine if an attorney is familiar with pound seizure or would be willing to provide pro bono legal advice throughout the campaign. For the other states, you can contact the American Bar Association's Animal Law Committee to seek assistance.[2]
- Establish a group of other concerned citizens who are willing to advocate collectively on the issue. It is not advisable to advocate alone on pound seizure since these can be lengthy and tiring campaigns. You will need a support system of people covering different aspects of the advocacy and providing each other much needed breaks in order to rejuvenate.
- Forming a nonprofit organization, particularly a 501(c)(3) charitable organization, will provide some protection from personal liability during your advocacy as well as allow all donations to be tax deductible. Be sure to list in your organizational bylaws that liability on behalf of organization members falls to the organization and not to the individuals personally. If you are concerned about a lawsuit to thwart your advocacy, consider purchasing insurance for your nonprofit organization's directors and volunteers.
- When working in a group, be sure to have all volunteers sign an agreement that they will work collaboratively, will only publicize factual information approved by the organization, and will not engage in

conduct that could result in legal liability for the organization. Such an agreement can be important if a rogue volunteer enters the organization and engages in conduct not condoned by the organization.

- Create a strategy of how to engage in the campaign. It is important that the strategy be based on factual and documented information and not on emotion. When advocating to lawmakers, statistics on the extent of pound seizure (from your local shelter or throughout the state) and the impact of a pound seizure ban will be the most influential.

- Depending on the scope of the campaign, ask shelters for information on how many cats and dogs have been involved in pound seizure for the past five years. If the shelter is unwilling or unable to provide you that information with a polite request, file a Freedom of Information Act letter requesting the documents. It is important to know how many shelter cats and dogs are sold to research before starting an advocacy campaign. For example, if your local shelter provides five cats and dogs per year to the local university or research facilities, the advocacy to stop that practice may be less adversarial than if 1,000 cats and dogs per year are subjected to pound seizure.

- Learn what the supporters of pound seizure say about the practice and be prepared to articulate against their position. Attempt to speak to staff at research facilities and university laboratories that obtain cats and dogs through pound seizure. Learning what happens to the cats and dogs may significantly impact your advocacy. For instance, if your local university has a veterinary school that obtains shelter cats and dogs to practice sterilization surgeries, and then returns the cats and dogs to the shelter for adoption, that is a practice that would be beneficial to continue. That particular "pound seizure" benefits the animals by making them more adoptable, benefits the shelter by providing free sterilization, reducing pet overpopulation, and benefits the future veterinarians.

- Always speak from documented facts when speaking about pound seizure (whether verbally or in writing). Doing your homework and obtaining factual information about the extent of pound seizure in your community or state will help you to craft the appropriate strategy. For instance, if shelter cats and dogs in your state are being transported across state lines to out-of-state facilities, then you might want to focus on the transportation issue; that is, if a family were looking for their lost pet, it would be more difficult to locate their pet if it was transported out of state.

- Always start from the ground and work your way up the official ladder when asking for a shelter to stop pound seizure. Do not go public with a media blitz until you have spoken personally with the shelter and staff to stop the practice. Start with the shelter staff and director to find out attitudes regarding pound seizure, and ask what can be done to move away from the practice. Approach the situation with understanding and compassion for their work, rather than with accusations and demeaning conversations. Be upfront with the shelter, and tell the staff that you want to work toward stopping pound seizure. You may learn that the shelter staff wants to end the practice too but is required by higher-ups to maintain it. Or you may learn that the shelter believes in the benefits of pound seizure. Knowing this information will greatly impact the strategy of your campaign.
- If the shelter is unwilling or unable to stop pound seizure (due to a higher mandate), speak with officials who oversee the shelter to see if they will discuss stopping the practice. Again, find out the individual and group beliefs regarding pound seizure before making your case. Prepare answers to address their beliefs supporting pound seizure. Determine what it would take to stop it. For example, if the officials simply want the shelter's euthanasia rate to remain stable, create a plan where local animal rescue groups assist the shelter with adoptions and rescues, volunteers assist the shelter with promoting adoptions, and other strategies to lower the euthanasia rate.
- If working directly with the shelter or officials overseeing the shelter fails, then create a public education campaign to engage citizens in your community or state. Start by creating a website to feature your pound seizure advocacy campaign, including easy tips of what people can do to help (i.e., donate, sign a petition, or send a pre-written letter to an official).
- Take a survey in your community or state to learn whether citizens approve or disapprove of pound seizure. Free surveys can be conducted through www.surveymonkey.com. If a majority of citizens are in favor of pound seizure, then this will affect your public education campaign. In my experience, a vast majority of citizens are against pound seizure and others simply need to be educated about the practice before they form an opinion.
- Create a brochure, flyers, and mail-in postcards that can be downloaded off your website or given to people at community events. List factual information about pound seizure in your community or

state, and why pound seizure should be stopped. Indicate who can be contacted to have the practice stopped. Always mention that phone calls and letters should be polite. Post flyers at pet stores, veterinary clinics, and send one to your local newspaper. If possible, put photos of pound seizure cats and dogs on the printed materials.

- To garner more citizen support (although some lawmakers might not appeal to this tactic), gather personal stories about shelter animals and former pets that were victims of pound seizure, or saved from pound seizure. Showing photos of animals often moves citizens to take action and get involved. Gather personal stories from shelter staff, current and former, and volunteers about how it feels to work in a pound seizure shelter. Lastly, gather stories from people who surrendered their pet, a stray, or an abused/neglected animal, and make clear that those animals were victims of pound seizure. Document how those citizens felt. This information can often be discovered in a request for records.

- Be proactive and garner support from animal rescue organizations to rescue animals from your shelter while you advocate banning pound seizure. The lower the supply of animals from the shelter that can go into pound seizure, the more impactful it might be with lawmakers to stop the practice.

- Create a petition for people to support efforts to stop pound seizure. Free online petitions can be created at www.thepetitionsite.com.

- Attend community events, and host a booth to raise awareness regarding pound seizure.

- Attend meetings of officials who will vote on whether to ban pound seizure. If there is a public comment opportunity, sign up to speak. Write out your comments ahead of time, and always make sure that you speak of proven and documented facts.

- Protect your pets by having them microchipped or tattooed, and keep your registration current.

- Take care of yourself and the other advocates. These can be lengthy campaigns, and maintaining stamina is essential.

THE DON'TS OF POUND SEIZURE ADVOCACY

- Do not fabricate stories, speculate, or publicly discuss or share rumors regarding any of the players in pound seizure. This particularly includes e-mail messages to other advocates or supporters. E-mails are public information and can be shared with anyone, even the opposition to your campaign.

- Do not let your emotions override reasonableness and common sense. Emotions can run high during a pound seizure campaign, especially if you are watching cats and dogs disappear from the shelter. It takes everyone working together to keep tempers in check so that unsupported beliefs are not spoken publicly.
- Do not say (verbal or written) anything regarding the opponents or supporters of pound seizure unless you have documentation and proof backing your statements. You may not agree with their statements, but like you, they are entitled to their opinion.
- Do not engage in illegal conduct in order to stop pound seizure. Do not threaten or harm anyone involved in pound seizure.
- Do not give up, even in the face of strong opposition. Most pound seizure campaigns take two to four years, and some longer. Yet perseverance has been successful in numerous shelters and states.

KEEPING ADVOCATES STRONG AND FOCUSED

Advocacy campaigns to improve the lives of animals are generally run by people with incredible depths of emotion and empathy. "Animal people" are among the most caring and compassionate individuals I have met. Those who volunteer to help animals are even more passionate about helping and giving a voice to those that are voiceless. However, it is these same benevolent traits that can contribute to unrealistic expectations of humans who are "not animal people," as well as strife within the advocacy group itself. In a pound seizure campaign, you will encounter people who are not "animal people," who believe that shelter animals can cure cancer and a host of other diseases, or just simply do not care about the animals. It is important to accept that not everyone feels about animals the way that you and I may.

In all my years advocating for animals, I have witnessed many scenes of caring advocates turning against each other when the stress of the campaign becomes overwhelming. Advocates who once worked well together are now bickering and distracting themselves and others from the primary goal of victory. The opposition thrives when the animal advocates have inner strife because this weakens the advocates individually and collectively.

There are a few simple methods to ensure that you and your advocacy group stay strong and determined throughout a pound seizure campaign.

First, manage expectations from the start by establishing a written mission of the group and a specific set of goals. These can often be incorporated into the bylaws for your organization. Second, write out a strategy on how to pursue a pound seizure campaign. No detail is too minute. The more specific you are about goals and expectations, the easier it will be to keep everyone on track. Third, whether or not you have formalized yourself as an organization, draft a written agreement that all advocates sign and must follow regarding appropriate and expected behavior. Fourth, assign duties according to the strengths of each advocate, and have a written description of what each duty entails. If one advocate is shy and not well-spoken publicly but enjoys computer work, assign that advocate to record keeping, the website, or other administrative work. If another advocate is well-spoken and makes a good appearance, or has an impressive career or place in the community, have that advocate be the official spokesperson of your group. By assigning specific tasks to each advocate, this will avoid duplicity in effort, as well as avoid any issues of advocates feeling like their work is being overshadowed by someone else. And lastly, choose your leader wisely. Not everyone is suited to lead a group of ardent advocates. The leader should be levelheaded, respected by other advocates, able to see both sides of the issue, able to remain calm and resilient in the face of adversity, as well as possessing an ability to motivate others to continue when the campaign runs into difficulties. A good leader will praise good deeds and prompt others to get action when needed.

If a situation arises where two or more advocates are beginning to quarrel or simply not work well together, intervene immediately in order to mediate the situation. If one advocate is simply unable to follow the goals of the group, or is too disruptive to other advocates, then consider removing that person. Having a well-written volunteer agreement will help to allow you to rely on a document that was signed by the disruptive advocate. But it is more important to resolve the situation, rather than simply remove volunteers, because a disgruntled volunteer could engage in rash and improper conduct that could harm the overall advocacy campaign.

It is important to have as many advocates as possible working collaboratively on a pound seizure campaign. The opposition may be strong in your community or state, so having a sufficiently large group will give you strength in numbers, as well as allow for assignments to be divided among the group in order to avoid burnout. If you do not have a large group to rely on, it is important to recognize the signs of burnout or compassion fatigue so that you can remain strong for the long haul.

Compassion fatigue is a type of emotional exhaustion that comes from observing suffering and trauma. It comes from a source of caring and feeling helpless when things do not go as planned. It is common for animal shelter workers and those who are involved in animal rescue to suffer from compassion fatigue at one time. Burnout, on the other hand, can result from any form of constant stress, not necessarily related to caring for others, including animals. Compassion fatigue or burnout can come from continuous stress, exposure to shelter animals being euthanized, shelter animals being victims of pound seizure, and struggles with shelter staff or lawmakers.

The following are some helpful tips to avoid burnout or compassion fatigue:

- Keep your expectations in perspective. Realize that you will not save all the animals from pound seizure immediately. Campaigns are a process, and you need to maintain a clear head in order to prevail.
- Set daily, weekly, monthly, and yearly goals for your advocacy efforts. For example, one of my goals was to ensure that every cat that entered the shelter Cat Room was safe from euthanasia or pound seizure. Each day, I would check over the list for the cat(s) that had been there the longest and then proceeded to work on securing an adoption (through placement of adoption ads in the local newspaper) or a rescue (by contacting other animal rescue organizations). I kept a list of all the cats that were saved from pound seizure and made it safely out of the shelter. At the end of each week and month, I would review the list, and it would energize me to keep going. Those assisting the shelter dogs also kept a list, and together it empowered us all, even during difficult times.
- Celebrate small victories. Those include each shelter cat and dog that is adopted or rescued from the shelter and avoided pound seizure, each new advocate who joins the cause, each donation received, each lawmaker who supports your efforts, and each media story that positively supports your goal.
- Keep a scrapbook of photos of shelter cats and dogs that were adopted or rescued as a result of your advocacy. During dark days, it is soothing to look back on the faces of all the cats and dogs that are now safe because of you and your organization. Today I still enjoy the photo albums of cats that I helped almost ten years ago.
- Take care of yourself. Animal advocacy, especially for shelter animals, can be all consuming. I know. I have been there. Be sure to have other

hobbies that do not involve animals or even your animal friends, spend time with family, go out with friends, and exercise. It is important that these outside interests not involve your work with animals. You need to take a break every now and then in order to rejuvenate. Too often I find that conversations turn toward animals during a time when I want to focus on other positive aspects of life. Be diligent in maintaining a healthy boundary so that you can be effective for the animals. One hobby that helped me keep balanced during my first pound seizure campaign was West Coast swing dancing. Several times a week, I would meet up with my dance friends, and we would dance for hours. It would instantly lift my spirit, was great exercise, and reenergized me.

- Pamper yourself. If your advocacy results in frequent visits to the animal shelter, the smells and noises at the shelter can have a toxic impact on your state of mind. Surround yourself with beauty at least once a week, if not more. Go for a walk in nature (especially if you have dogs); lie on the grass, sand, or woods in order to have direct contact with Mother Earth; burn beautiful smelling candles; take bubble baths or Epsom salts baths scented with essential oils (Epsom salt is believed to clear out negative energy); sit with and love your animals and appreciate all that they bring to your life; laugh, play, and pray. Cats and dogs know how to live in the moment and enjoy life, so consider mimicking their behavior. I often find that if I follow the lead of my cats, such as resting in a pile of fluffy blankets, cuddling, and staring off into space (to daydream), I feel better. Or with dogs, go for a walk or a run, and roll around on the ground.

- Meditate. Many people cringe when they hear the word meditate. But meditation can be very simple, and it is a healing method to calm your mind so that you can think clearly and receive inspired thoughts. Meditation can involve something as simple as spending five minutes per day sitting in silence. Sometimes this is best done as you wake in the morning. Stay in bed, sit with your back straight, and let your mind remain in that place between sleep and alertness. End the silence by setting your intentions for the day. A good intention could be to remain strong and resilient and to enjoy one success that day. Intentions should also be stated positively rather than using negative words such as "not." Gradually increase the amount of meditation time each week. A realistic goal might be to meditate for thirty minutes straight at least four times per week. Afterward, I always find that I have new ideas and strategies and feel more empowered. It helps to clear my mind of clutter, too.

- Protect yourself from the despair of others. We all know people who are negative, toxic, and always have something to complain about. If you are working with an advocate or have a friend who fits this description, make efforts to avoid or limit exposure to this person. Being around negative people can bring down your energy level. During an advocacy campaign, it is important to keep your energy uplifted. Associate with people who make you feel good and inspired, and this will spread to others.

- Read about and understand the Law of Attraction. Simply put, the Law of Attraction is a universal law where you receive what you put out. For example, if you constantly complain about situations and are negative about life, you will receive more negative things to complain about. However, if you are happy (which can be easy if you focus on the small victories each day) and truly believe that your goals will be achieved (you may not know how you will succeed, but you just know that you will), then that changes your energy, and you will receive more in line with those beliefs. Good things will start to come your way, which then increases your positivity and allows for more good events to occur. If you can remain positive, this will spread to others, and your group dynamic will benefit. The foundation for the Law of Attraction is "ask and you shall receive."

- Publicly recognize the work of yourself and others, and do so frequently. A pat on the back and some heartfelt praise can motivate everyone to keep going.

- Seek the help of a professional counselor if feelings of despair about the animals are overwhelming. It takes a courageous person to ask for help, so do not feel embarrassed to receive guidance. Or have a support system of friends and family you can talk to when the campaign becomes difficult or if you lose a beloved shelter pet to pound seizure. Do not keep your feelings bottled up inside.

- For additional information on compassion fatigue, a good resource is Charles Figley and Robert Roop, *Compassion Fatigue in the Animal Care Community*.

For most people, change can be difficult and uncomfortable. You may question and not understand why others argue so determinedly to maintain pound seizure. Change can be frightening. When pursuing a cause that you deeply believe in, let your belief be your guiding light. There will be dark days during any campaign where the opposition seems stronger and more educated than you, where shelter cats and dogs are subject to pound seizure, and where others you are advocating with start to bicker and quarrel about strategy. But there will be also be days of joy for each shelter cat and dog that is saved solely because of your advocacy, when you locate another advocate to help in the campaign, and when an unknown donor appears out of nowhere to help you fund campaign efforts. In the end, if you keep your focus on a positive result, you will be rewarded.

CHAPTER 14

Conclusion

There's More to Be Done

The world of pound seizure can be confusing and frustrating to those working to end it. Those who are determined to make a difference and get involved are to be commended. After all, the subjects of pound seizure could be any one of our family pets—pets who were not born or raised to be subjected to experimentation.

After working for the past decade to abolish pound seizure, one shelter at a time, it has become clear to me that the practice is overwhelmingly unwanted and rejected throughout the country regardless of the needs of the research community. If decisions regarding pound seizure were placed in the hands of voting citizens, knowing that more than 63 percent of American households have at least one companion animal, I have no doubt that pound seizure would immediately cease to exist in the United States. This book was written to reach as many citizens as possible in hopes that their voices as constituents and voters will be heard to convince lawmakers to end this practice in the remaining states.

After reading numerous articles and books on the use of random source cats and dogs in research and interviewing advocates and stakeholders in the business, I understand that veterinary students in particular need to conduct some hands-on training with cats and dogs. It simply makes them better at their chosen profession. However, that training can be beneficial to both the student and the animal and does not need to summarily result in the death of the animal simply because the training has concluded.

The educational and research communities continue to cling to unsupported and outdated claims regarding the use of random source cats and dogs. Tremendous scientific progress has been made in recent years. Although this book is not about ending animal research, one needs to consider whether the policies from decades ago are still relevant today. When you simply look at the growth in the technology industry, our current abilities far exceed those from even ten years ago.

Stopping pound seizure is not about stopping medical research and educational training of medical and veterinary students, it is about preventing former family pets from being used in experiments when that is not what they were raised to endure. Yet when faced with the grim realities of government and undercover investigations resulting in evidence of pet theft, the improper procurement of random source animals, and the deplorable conditions of cats and dogs at some Class B dealers' facilities, these institutions should instead work to protect the integrity of their research and grant funding rather than continue to support the speculative conduct of dealers.

The 2009 report to Congress outlining evidence and concerns regarding the random source dealers is the most up-to-date, objective, and comprehensive report on this subject and refutes many of the status quo arguments from researchers. Even the American Physiological Society, a supporter for the use of random source animals, publicly endorsed the 2009 study, which concluded that Class B dealers are no longer necessary.

The tide is changing, but there is still much more work to be done. If you have read this book and made it to this final chapter, then you have been called to action. That action can be as minimal as donating to support organizations that are working to end pound seizure, particularly animal rescue organizations that tirelessly rescue cats and dogs from pound seizure shelters, to becoming a vocal advocate yourself and launching a pound seizure campaign in your own state or community.

Malcolm Gladwell's *The Tipping Point: How Little Things Can Make a Big Difference* perfectly describes what we have seen in pound seizure advocacy over the years, and what remains to be accomplished. The tipping point is that dramatic moment when small causes drive the unexpected to become expected and propel the idea of radical change to certain acceptance. This is a function of three components: the Law of the Few (where a small percentage of people do the majority of the work to build momentum through word-of-mouth appeals); the Stickiness Factor (where the message is memorable and makes an impact); and the Power of Context (learning that humans are sensitive to their environment and that groups allow new beliefs to grow, especially small groups of fewer than 150 people being the most powerful). In the pound seizure campaigns I have been involved with, even those involving state and federal legislation, these three components have all come into play.

So what is the tipping point for pound seizure? It is banding together to stop a practice that is no longer necessary in the United States. It involves working collaboratively with others, even a small group of five people, to frame the appropriate message for your community or state, and holding steadfastly to the idea of change, even through the storm. It means making a decision to stand up for what you believe is the proper way to treat other living creatures. Finally, it is doing what is right, not what is easy. If you are privileged to have a furry companion in your home, now is your time to speak up to keep your companion, and thousands of others like him or her, safe. Now is the tipping point to stop pound seizure in America.

Appendix A

ANIMAL WELFARE ACT REGULATIONS SECTION 2.132

(a) A class "B" dealer may obtain live random source dogs and cats only from:

    (1) Other dealers who are licensed under the Act and in accordance with the regulations in part 2;

    (2) State, county, or city owned and operated animal pounds or shelters; and

    (3) A legal entity organized and operated under the laws of the State in which it is located as an animal pound or shelter, such as a humane shelter or contract pound.

(b) No person shall obtain live dogs, cats, or other animals by use of false pretenses, misrepresentation, or deception.

(c) Any dealer, exhibitor, research facility, carrier, or intermediate handler who also operates a private or contract animal pound or shelter shall comply with the following:

    (1) The animal pound or shelter shall be located on premises that are physically separated from the licensed or registered facility. The animal housing facility of the pound or shelter shall not be adjacent to the licensed or registered facility.

    (2) Accurate and complete records shall be separately maintained by the licensee or registrant and by the pound or shelter. The records shall be in accordance with Sec. Sec. 2.75 and 2.76, unless the animals are lost or stray. If the animals are lost or stray, the pound or shelter records shall provide:

        (i) An accurate description of the animal

(ii) How, where, from whom, and when the dog or cat was obtained;

(iii) How long the dog or cat was held by the pound or shelter before being transferred to the dealer; and

(iv) The date the dog or cat was transferred to the dealer.

(3) Any dealer who obtains or acquires a live dog or cat from a private or contract pound or shelter, including a pound or shelter he or she operates, shall hold the dog or cat for a period of at least 10 full days, not including the day of acquisition, excluding time in transit, after acquiring the animal, and otherwise in accordance with Sec. 2.101.

(d) No dealer or exhibitor shall knowingly obtain any dog, cat, or other animal from any person who is required to be licensed but who does not hold a current, valid, and unsuspended license. No dealer or exhibitor shall knowingly obtain any dog or cat from any person who is not licensed, other than a pound or shelter, without obtaining a certification that the animals were born and raised on that person's premises and, if the animals are for research purposes, that the person has sold fewer than 25 dogs and/or cats that year, or, if the animals are for use as pets, that the person does not maintain more than three breeding female dogs and/or cats.

ANIMAL WELFARE ACT 7 USC SECTION 2158: PROTECTION OF PETS

(a) Holding period.

(1) Requirement. In the case of each dog or cat acquired by an entity described in paragraph (2), such entity shall hold and care for such dog or cat for a period of not less than five days to enable such dog or cat to be recovered by its original owner or adopted by other individuals before such entity sells such dog or cat to a dealer.

(2) Entities described. An entity subject to paragraph (1) is—

(A) each State, county, or city owned and operated pound or shelter;

(B) each private entity established for the purpose of caring for animals, such as a humane society, or other organization that is under contract with a State, county, or city that operates as a pound or shelter and that releases animals on a voluntary basis; and

(C) each research facility licensed by the Department of Agriculture.

(b) Certification.

(1) In general. A dealer may not sell, provide, or make available to any individual or entity a random source dog or cat unless such dealer provides the recipient with a valid certification that meets the requirements of paragraph (2) and indicates compliance with subsection (a).

(2) Requirements. A valid certification shall contain—

(A) the name, address, and Department of Agriculture license or registration number (if such number exists) of the dealer;

(B) the name, address, Department of Agriculture license or registration number (if such number exists), and the signature of the recipient of the dog or cat;

(C) a description of the dog or cat being provided that shall include—

(i) the species and breed or type of such;

(ii) the sex of such;

(iii) the date of birth (if known) of such;

(iv) the color and any distinctive marking of such; and

(v) any other information that the Secretary by regulation shall determine to be appropriate;

(D) the name and address of the person, pound, or shelter from which the dog or cat was purchased or otherwise acquired by the dealer, and an assurance that such person, pound, or shelter was notified that such dog or cat may be used for research or educational purposes;

(E) the date of the purchase or acquisition referred to in subparagraph (D);

(F) a statement by the pound or shelter (if the dealer acquired the dog or cat from such) that it satisfied the requirements of subsection (a); and

(G) any other information that the Secretary of Agriculture by regulation shall determine appropriate.

(3) Records. The original certification required under paragraph (1) shall accompany the shipment of a dog or cat to be sold, provided,

or otherwise made available by the dealer, and shall be kept and maintained by the research facility for a period of at least one year for enforcement purposes. The dealer shall retain one copy of the certification provided under this paragraph for a period of at least one year for enforcement purposes.

(4) Transfers. In instances where one research facility transfers animals to another research facility a copy of the certificate must accompany such transfer.

(5) Modification. Certification requirements may be modified to reflect technological advances in identification techniques, such as microchip technology, if the Secretary determines that adequate information such as described in this section, will be collected, transferred, and maintained through such technology.

(c) Enforcement.

(1) In general. Dealers who fail to act according to the requirements of this section or who include false information in the certification required under subsection (b), shall be subject to the penalties provided for under section 19.

(2) Subsequent violations. Any dealer who violates this section more than one time shall be subject to a fine of $5,000 per dog or cat acquired or sold in violation of this section.

(3) Permanent revocations. Any dealer who violates this section three or more times shall have such dealers license permanently revoked.

(d) Regulation. Not later than 180 days after the date of enactment of this section [enacted Nov. 28, 1990], the Secretary shall promulgate regulations to carry out this section.

ANIMAL WELFARE ACT 7 USC SECTION 2135: TIME PERIOD FOR DISPOSAL OF DOGS OR CATS BY DEALERS OR EXHIBITORS

No dealer or exhibitor shall sell or otherwise dispose of any dog or cat within a period of five business days after the acquisition of such animal or within such other period as may be specified by the Secretary: Provided, That operators of auction sales subject to Section 12 [7 USC 2142] of this Act shall not be required to comply with the provisions of this section.

Appendix B

PET SAFETY AND PROTECTION ACT OF 2009 (S 1834/HR 3907)

To amend the Animal Welfare Act to ensure that all dogs and cats used by research facilities are obtained legally.

Be it enacted by the Senate and House of Representatives of the United States of America in Congress assembled,

SECTION 1. SHORT TITLE

This Act may be cited as the 'Pet Safety and Protection Act of 2009'.

SEC. 2. PROTECTION OF PETS

(a) Research Facilities: Section 7 of the Animal Welfare Act (7 U.S.C. 2137) is amended to read as follows:

SEC. 7. SOURCES OF DOGS AND CATS FOR RESEARCH FACILITIES

(a) Definition of Person: In this section, the term "person" means any individual, partnership, firm, joint stock company, corporation, association, trust, estate, pound, shelter, or other legal entity.

(b) Use of Dogs and Cats: No research facility or Federal research facility may use a dog or cat for research or educational purposes if the dog or cat was obtained from a person other than a person described in subsection (d).

(c) Selling, Donating, or Offering Dogs and Cats: No person, other than a person described in subsection (d), may sell, donate, or offer a dog or cat to any research facility or Federal research facility.

(d) Permissible Sources: A person from whom a research facility or a Federal research facility may obtain a dog or cat for research or educational purposes under subsection (b), and a person who may sell, donate, or offer a dog or cat to a research facility or a Federal research facility under subsection (c), shall be—

   (1) a dealer licensed under section 3 that has bred and raised the dog or cat;

   (2) a publicly owned and operated pound or shelter that—

      (A) is registered with the Secretary;

      (B) is in compliance with section 28(a)(1) and with the requirements for dealers in subsections (b) and (c) of section 28; and

      (C) obtained the dog or cat from its legal owner, other than a pound or shelter;

   (3) a person that is donating the dog or cat and that—

      (A) bred and raised the dog or cat; or

      (B) owned the dog or cat for not less than 1 year immediately preceding the donation;

   (4) a research facility licensed by the Secretary; and

   (5) a Federal research facility licensed by the Secretary.

(e) Penalties:

   (1) IN GENERAL: A person that violates this section shall be fined $1,000 for each violation.

   (2) ADDITIONAL PENALTY: A penalty under this subsection shall be in addition to any other applicable penalty.

(f) No Required Sale or Donation: Nothing in this section requires a pound or shelter to sell, donate, or offer a dog or cat to a research facility or Federal research facility.

(b) Federal Research Facilities- Section 8 of the Animal Welfare Act (7 U.S.C. 2138) is amended—

   (1) by striking "Sec. 8. No department" and inserting the following:

SEC. 8. FEDERAL RESEARCH FACILITIES

Except as provided in section 7, no department;

(2) by striking "research or experimentation" or; and

(3) by striking "such purposes" and inserting "that purpose"

(c) Certification: Section 28(b)(1) of the Animal Welfare Act (7 U.S.C. 2158(b)(1)) is amended by striking "individual or entity" and inserting "research facility or Federal research facility"

SEC. 3. EFFECTIVE DATE

The amendments made by section 2 take effect on the date that is 90 days after the date of enactment of this Act.

Michigan House Bill 4663 (Note: The bold text is the new legislative language whereas the text that is stricken is language to be removed) March 19, 2009, Introduced by Reps. Espinoza, Huckleberry, Mayes, and Terry Brown and referred to the Committee on Agriculture.

A bill to amend 1969 PA 224, entitled "An act to license and regulate dealers in and research facilities using dogs and cats for research purposes; and to repeal certain acts and parts of acts," by amending sections 1, 8, and 9 (MCL 287.381, 287.388, and 287.389); and to repeal acts and parts of acts.

THE PEOPLE OF THE STATE OF MICHIGAN ENACT:

Sec. 1. ~~When~~ **AS** used in this act:

~~(a) "Person" includes any individual, partnership, association, or corporation.~~

~~(b) "Director" means the director of the department of agriculture.~~

(A) **"ANIMAL BLOOD BANKING" MEANS THE PROVISION OF VETERINARY TRANSFUSION PRODUCTS THROUGH SPECIES-SPECIFIC DONATION THAT DOES NOT RESULT IN HARM TO THE DONOR.**

(B) **"ANIMAL CONTROL SHELTER" MEANS THAT TERM AS DEFINED IN SECTION 1 OF 1969 PA 287, MCL 287.331, AND THAT IS LICENSED UNDER THAT ACT.**

(C) **"ANIMAL PROTECTION SHELTER" MEANS THAT TERM AS DEFINED IN SECTION 1 OF 1969 PA 287, MCL 287.331, AND THAT IS LICENSED UNDER THAT ACT.**

(D) (c) "Cat" means any live domestic cat (~~felis~~ **OF THE SPECIES FELIS** catus.) ~~for use or intended to be used for research, tests or experiments at research facilities.~~

(E) **"DEALER" MEANS A PERSON WHO FOR COMPENSA-TION OR PROFIT DELIVERS FOR TRANSPORTATION, TRANSPORTS, BOARDS, BUYS, OR SELLS DOGS OR CATS FOR RESEARCH PURPOSES AND DOES NOT IN-CLUDE A PERSON WHO BREEDS OR RAISES DOGS OR CATS ON HIS OR HER PREMISES FOR SALE TO A RE-SEARCH FACILITY.**

(F) **"DIRECTOR" MEANS THE DIRECTOR OF THE DEPART-MENT OF AGRICULTURE.**

(G) (d) "Dog" means any live dog of the species ~~canis~~ **CANIS** familia-ris. ~~for use or intended to be used for research tests or experiments at research facilities.~~

(H) **"PERSON" INCLUDES ANY INDIVIDUAL, LIMITED LI-ABILITY COMPANY, PARTNERSHIP, ASSOCIATION OR CORPORATION.**

(I) **"PREEXISTING MEDICAL CONDITION" MEANS AN ILL-NESS, DISEASE, OR OTHER CONDITION THAT REQUIRES IMMEDIATE MEDICAL ATTENTION IN ORDER TO PRE-VENT FURTHER PHYSICAL HARM OR DEATH.**

(J) **"RANDOM SOURCE ANIMAL" MEANS A DOG OR CAT OBTAINED FROM A PERSON WHO DID NOT BREED AND RAISE THE DOG OR CAT ON HIS OR HER PREM-ISES, AN AUCTION SALE, OR AN ANIMAL SHELTER, OR A STRAY OR LOST ANIMAL.**

(K) (e) "Research facility" means any school, hospital, laboratory, insti-tution, organization, or person that uses or intends to use dogs or cats in research, ~~tests~~ **TESTING,** or experiments, and that ~~(1) purchases~~ **DOES 1 OR MORE OF THE FOLLOWING:**

(i) **PURCHASES, RECEIVES,** or transports ~~such animals, or (2) receives~~ **DOGS OR CATS.**

(ii) **RECEIVES** any funds from ~~the~~ **THIS** state or **A** local government or any agency or instrumentality thereof to finance its operations by means of grants, loans, or otherwise.

(f) ~~"Dealer" means any person who for compensation or profit deliv-ers for transportation, transports, boards, buys or sells dogs or cats~~

~~for research purposes and does not mean a person who breeds or raises dogs or cats for sale to a research facility.~~

Sec. 8. **(1)** A dealer ~~,~~ **OR** a county, city, village, or township operating a dog pound or animal **CONTROL SHELTER OR ANIMAL PROTECTION** shelter shall not sell or otherwise dispose of a dog or cat within 4 days after its acquisition. If the dog or cat has a collar, license, or other evidence of ownership, the operator of the pound or **ANIMAL CONTROL SHELTER OR ANIMAL PROTECTION** shelter shall notify the owner in writing and disposition of the animal shall not be made within 7 days from the date of mailing the notice. Each operator of a pound or **ANIMAL CONTROL SHELTER OR ANIMAL PROTECTION** shelter shall be required to maintain a record on each identifiable dog or cat acquired, indicating a basic description of the animal, the date it was acquired, and ~~under what~~ **THE** circumstances **UNDER WHICH IT WAS ACQUIRED**. The record shall also indicate the date of notice sent to the owner of an animal and subsequent disposition. This ~~section~~ **SUBSECTION** does not apply to animals ~~which~~ **THAT** are sick or injured to the extent that the holding period ~~would~~ **IS LIKELY TO** cause undue suffering, or to animals whose owners request immediate disposal.

(2) REGARDLESS OF WHETHER THE PERSON IS LICENSED TO PURCHASE, OBTAIN, OR RESELL RANDOM SOURCE ANIMALS BY THE UNITED STATES DEPARTMENT OF AGRICULTURE AND SUBJECT TO SUBSECTION (3), A PERSON SHALL NOT DO ANY OF THE FOLLOWING:

(A) PURCHASE OR OTHERWISE ACQUIRE A RANDOM SOURCE ANIMAL FOR THE PURPOSE OF RESALE FOR EXPERIMENTATION.

(B) SELL OR OTHERWISE MAKE AVAILABLE A RANDOM SOURCE ANIMAL FOR THE PURPOSE OF EXPERIMENTATION.

(3) SUBSECTION (2) DOES NOT APPLY TO ANY OF THE FOLLOWING:

(A) A RESEARCH FACILITY THAT RECEIVES A CAT OR DOG FROM AN ANIMAL CONTROL SHELTER OR ANIMAL PROTECTION SHELTER FOR THE SOLE PURPOSE OF PERFORMING A PROCEDURE TO CORRECT A PREEXISTING MEDICAL CONDITION.

(B) A RESEARCH FACILITY THAT CONDUCTS A NO-COST OR SUBSIDIZED STERILIZATION PROGRAM OF SHELTER CATS AND DOGS UNDER THE FOLLOWING CONDITIONS:

(i) THE PROGRAM IS PART OF A VETERINARY UNIVERSITY TRAINING PROGRAM THAT IS SUPERVISED BY A LICENSED VETERINARIAN.

(ii) CATS AND DOGS PARTICIPATING IN THE STERILIZATION PROGRAM ARE RETURNED TO THE ANIMAL CONTROL SHELTER OR ANIMAL PROTECTION SHELTER FOR ADOPTION OR PLACEMENT IN A SUITABLE HOME BY THE PROGRAM UNLESS THE ANIMAL IS FOUND TO BE SUFFERING FROM A PREEXISTING MEDICAL CONDITION THAT REQUIRES HUMANE EUTHANASIA TO AVOID IMMINENT PAIN AND SUFFERING.

(iii) CATS AND DOGS IN NEED OF OTHER VETERINARY CARE FOR A PREEXISTING MEDICAL CONDITION ARE GIVEN TREATMENT BY A LICENSED VETERINARIAN.

(iv) CATS AND DOGS ARE ACCEPTED INTO THE STERILIZATION TRAINING PROGRAM SOLELY FOR THE PURPOSE OF TRAINING STUDENTS IN SPAY/NEUTER SURGERY TECHNIQUES.

(C) A FACILITY ENGAGED IN ANIMAL BLOOD BANKING THAT OBTAINS A RANDOM SOURCE ANIMAL SOLELY FOR THE PURPOSE OF THE DONATION OF BLOOD FOR VETERINARY USE SO LONG AS THE PROCEDURE IS PERFORMED BY, OR UNDER THE SUPERVISION OF, A LICENSED VETERINARIAN AND THE CAT OR DOG IS THEREAFTER PLACED IN A SUITABLE HOME UNLESS IT SUFFERS FROM A PREEXISTING MEDICAL CONDITION REQUIRING EUTHANASIA IN ORDER TO AVOID IMMINENT PAIN OR SUFFERING.

Sec. 9. **(1)** ~~Dogs and cats shall not be offered for sale or sold~~ **A PERSON SHALL NOT SELL OR OFFER TO SELL A DOG OR CAT** to a research facility at public auction or by weight. ~~; or purchased by a research facility at public auction or by weight.~~

(2) A research facility shall not purchase any dogs or cats except from a licensed dealer ~~, public dog pound, humane society,~~ or from a person who breeds or raises dogs or cats for sale. ~~Any county, city, village or township operating a dog pound or animal shelter may sell for an amount not to exceed $10.00 per animal or otherwise dispose of unclaimed or unwanted dogs and cats to a Michigan research facility.~~

(3) **A RESEARCH FACILITY OR DEALER SHALL ONLY OBTAIN A DOG OR CAT FROM AN ANIMAL CONTROL SHELTER OR ANIMAL PROTECTION SHELTER UNDER THE CIRCUMSTANCES DESCRIBED UNDER SECTION 8(3).**

Enacting section 1. Section 15 of 1969 PA 224, MCL 287.395, is repealed.

Appendix C

LIVE ANIMAL USE FOR ADVANCED TRAUMA LIFE SUPPORT COURSES IN U.S. AND CANADIAN PROGRAMS: AN ONGOING SURVEY UPDATED: JANUARY 25, 2010

Programs Using Live Animals for ATLS Courses (10)

Baystate Medical Center—Springfield, MA
Elvis Presley Memorial Trauma Center/University of Tennessee Health Science Center—Memphis, TN
Hartford Hospital—Hartford, CT
Massachusetts General Hospital—Boston, MA
MeritCare Hospital/North Dakota State University—Fargo, ND
Ottawa Hospital—Ottawa, ON
Tulane Life Support—New Orleans, LA
University of Massachusetts Medical School—Worcester, MA
University of Texas Medical Branch—Galveston, TX
Vanderbilt University—Nashville, TN

Programs Using Non-animal Models for ATLS Courses (198)

Akron City Hospital—Akron, OH
Albany Medical College—Albany, NY
Allegheny General Hospital—Pittsburgh, PA
Altoona Hospital—Altoona, PA
AtlantiCare Regional Medical Center—Atlantic City, NJ
Barnes-Jewish Hospital—St. Louis, MO
Baylor University Medical Center—Dallas, TX

Bellevue Hospital—New York, NY
Berkshire Medical Center—Pittsfield, MA
Beth Israel Deaconess Medical Center—Boston, MA
Bethesda North Hospital—Cincinnati, OH
Borgess Medical Center—Kalamazoo, MI
Boston University School of Medicine—Boston, MA
Brigham and Women's Hospital—Boston, MA
Bristol Regional Medical Center—Bristol, TN
Brody School of Medicine at East Carolina University—Greenville, NC
Bronson Methodist Hospital—Kalamazoo, MI
CAMC Life Support Training Center—Charleston, WV
Carle Foundation Hospital—Urbana, IL
Carolina's Medical Center—Charlotte, NC
Cedars Sinai Medical Center—Los Angeles, CA
Central Ohio Trauma System—Columbus, OH
Christ Hospital and Medical Center—Chicago, IL
Christiana Hospital—Newark, DE
Cincinnati Children's Hospital Medical Center—Cincinnati, OH
Cooper Hospital—Camden, NJ
Cowichan District Hospital—Duncan, BC
Dartmouth-Hitchcock Medical Center—Lebanon, NH
Deaconess Hospital—Evansville, IN
Deaconess Medical Center—Spokane, WA
Denver Health Medical Center—Denver, CO
Detroit Receiving Hospital—Detroit, MI
Duluth Clinic—Duluth, MN
East Texas Medical Center—Tyler, TX
Eastern Maine Medical Center—Bangor, ME
Emmanuel Hospital—Portland, OR
Emory University—Atlanta, GA
Erlanger Hospital—Chattanooga, TN
Flagstaff Medical Center—Flagstaff, AZ
Geisinger Medical Center—Danville, PA
George E. Moerkirk Emergency Medicine Center at Lehigh Valley Hospital Center—Allentown, PA
Good Samaritan Hospital—Downers Grove, IL
Good Samaritan Hospital—Kearney, NE
Grand Rapids Medical Education and Research Center—Grand Rapids, MI

Greenville Hospital—Greenville, SC
Gundersen Lutheran Medical Center—La Crosse, WI
Hahnemann Medical College at Drexel University—Philadelphia, PA
Hamot Medical Center—Erie, PA
Harborview Medical Center—Seattle, WA
Harlem Hospital—New York, NY
Harris Methodist Fort Worth Hospital—Fort Worth, TX
Hays Medical Center—Hays, KS
Hennepin County Medical Center—Minneapolis, MN
Henry Ford Hospital—Detroit, MI
Hermann Hospital—Houston, TX
Hershey Medical Center—Hershey, PA
Hilltop Church—Sioux Falls, SD
Holston Valley Hospital—Kingsport, TN
Hospital of the University of Pennsylvania—Philadelphia, PA
Hotel Dieu Hospital/Queen's University—Kingston, ON
Huntsville Hospital—Huntsville, AL
Hurley Medical Center—Flint, MI
Idaho State University—Boise, ID
Idaho State University—Pocatello, ID
Illinois Masonic Medical Center—Chicago, IL
Intermountain Medical Center—Murray, UT
Iowa Health—Des Moines, IA
Iowa Methodist Medical Center—Des Moines, IA
Jacobi Hospital Center—Bronx, NY
Jamaica Hospital Center—Jamaica, NY
John C. Lincoln Hospital—Dunlap, AZ
John H. Stroger Hospital of Cook County—Chicago, IL
Johnson City Medical Center—Johnson City, TN
JPS Health Network—Fort Worth, TX
Kern Medical Center—Bakersfield, CA
Kings County Hospital Center—Brooklyn, NY
Labette County Medical Center—Parsons, KS
LDS Hospital—Salt Lake City, UT
Lincoln Hospital—Bronx, NY
Loma Linda University Medical Center—Loma Linda, CA
Loyola University—Chicago, IL
Maine Medical Center—Portland, ME

Maricopa Medical Center—Phoenix, AZ
Marquette General Hospital—Marquette, MI
Marshfield Clinic—Marshfield, WI
Mary I. Bassett Hospital—Cooperstown, NY
Medical Center of Central Georgia—Macon, GA
Medical Center of the Rockies—Loveland, CO
Medical College of Georgia—Augusta, GA
Medical College of Ohio—Toledo, OH
Medical College of Virginia—Richmond, VA
Memorial Hospital and Health System—South Bend, IN
Memorial Medical Center—Savannah, GA
Memorial Regional Hospital—Hollywood, FL
Mercy Hospital Medical Center—Des Moines, IA
Mercy Medical Center—Sioux City, IA
Methodist Hospital—Indianapolis, IN
MetroHealth Medical Center—Cleveland, OH
Miami Valley Hospital—Dayton, OH
Middletown Regional Hospital—Middletown, OH
Mission Hospital—Asheville, NC
Morristown Memorial Hospital—Morristown, NJ
Moses Cone Hospital Health System—Greensboro, NC
Mount Sinai Medical Center—Chicago, IL
Nassau County Medical Center—East Meadow, NY
New York Hospital—New York, NY
New York Presbyterian Hospital—New York, NY
North Memorial Medical Center—Robbinsdale, MN
North Mississippi Medical Center—Tupelo, MS
Poudre Valley Hospital—Fort Collins, CO
Providence Alaska Medical Center—Anchorage, AK
Queen Elizabeth II Health Center—Halifax, NS
R. Adams Cowley Shock Trauma Center—Baltimore, MD
R. E. Thomason Hospital—El Paso, TX
Regional West Medical Center—Scottsbluff, NE
Regions Hospital—St. Paul, MN
Renown Health—Reno, NV
Rhode Island Hospital—Providence, RI
Richland Memorial Hospital—Columbia, SC
Robert Wood Johnson University Hospital—New Brunswick, NJ

Rush-Presbyterian-St. Luke's Medical Center—Chicago, IL
Saint Louis University Medical Center—St. Louis, MO
Saint Mary's Hospital—Rochester, MN
Salem Hospital—Salem, OR
San Francisco General Hospital—San Francisco, CA
Santa Barbara Cottage Hospital—Santa Barbara, CA
Scott and White Hospital and Clinic—Temple, TX
Scottsdale Healthcare—Scottsdale, AZ
Southern Illinois University School of Medicine—Springfield, IL
St. Alexius Medical Center—Bismarck, ND
St. Anthony's Hospital—Denver, CO
St. Charles Medical Center—Bend, OR
St. Cloud Hospital—St. Cloud, MN
St. Elizabeth Health Center—Youngstown, OH
St. Francis Hospital—Peoria, IL
St. Francis Hospital—Tulsa, OK
St. John Medical Center—Tulsa, OK
St. John's Mercy Medical Center—St. Louis, MO
St. John's Mercy Regional Health Center—Springfield, MO
St. Joseph's Hospital and Medical Center—Phoenix, AZ
St. Lawrence Hospital—Lansing, MI
St. Luke's Hospital—Bethlehem, PA
St. Mary's Hospital—Grand Junction, CO
St. Mary's Medical Center—Huntington, WV
Stony Brook University Hospital—Stony Brook, NY
Sunnybrook Health Science Center—Toronto, ON
SUNY Upstate Medical University—Syracuse, NY
Tampa General Hospital—Tampa, FL
Temple University Hospital—Philadelphia, PA
Texas Tech University—Lubbock, TX
Tidewater Center for Life Support—Norfolk, VA
Truman Medical Center—Kansas City, MO
United Health Services at Wilson Hospital—Johnson City, NY
University of Buffalo—Buffalo, NY
University Hospital—Cincinnati, OH
University Hospitals—Cleveland, OH
University Medical Center—Fresno, CA
University Medical Center—Las Vegas, NV

University Medical Center—Tucson, AZ
University of Arkansas—Little Rock, AR
University of California Davis Medical Center—Sacramento, CA
University of California Irvine Medical Center—Orange, CA
University of Chicago—Chicago, IL
University of Florida—Gainesville, FL
University of Iowa Hospitals and Clinics—Iowa City, IA
University of Kansas Medical Center—Kansas City, KS
University of Kentucky Medical Center—Lexington, KY
University of Louisville Hospital—Louisville, KY
University of Medicine and Dentistry of New Jersey University Hospital—
    Newark, NJ
University of Michigan—Ann Arbor, MI
University of Minnesota Medical School—Duluth, MN
University of Mississippi School of Medicine—Jackson, MS
University of Missouri Health Sciences Center—Columbia, MO
University of Oklahoma Medical Center—Oklahoma City, OK
University of Pittsburgh Medical Center—Pittsburgh, PA
University of Rochester—Rochester, NY
University of Saskatchewan/Saskatoon ATLS—Saskatoon, SK
University of South Alabama—Mobile, AL
University of Tennessee Medical Center—Knoxville, TN
University of Texas, Southwestern Medical Center—Dallas, TX
University of Toledo Medical Center—Toledo, OH
University of Utah Hospital—Salt Lake City, UT
University of Vermont College of Medicine—Burlington, VT
University of Victoria—Victoria, BC
University of Virginia Health System—Charlottesville, VA
University of Wisconsin Hospital—Madison, WI
Valley Baptist Medical Center—Harlingen, TX
Via Christi Regional Medical Center—Wichita, KS
WakeMed—Raleigh, NC
Washington Hospital Center—Washington, DC
Wesley Medical Center—Wichita, KS
West Virginia University Center for Rural Emergency Medicine—
    Morgantown, WV
Westchester County Medical Center—Valhalla, NY
Winthrop-University Hospital—Mineola, NY

Wishard Memorial Hospital—Indianapolis, IN
Wyoming Family Practice Center—Casper, WY
Yale University School of Medicine—New Haven, CT
York Hospital—York, PA

Information provided by Physicians Committee for Responsible Medicine.

LIVE ANIMAL LABORATORIES IN U.S. ALLOPATHIC AND OSTEOPATHIC (*) MEDICAL SCHOOLS
UPDATED: NOVEMBER 10, 2009

Schools with Live Animal Use in Medical School Curricula (8 Allopathic)

Johns Hopkins University School of Medicine
Medical College of Wisconsin
Oregon Health and Science University School of Medicine
Uniformed Services University of the Health Sciences F. Edward Hébert
  School of Medicine
University of Mississippi School of Medicine
University of Tennessee College of Medicine (Chattanooga campus only)
University of Virginia School of Medicine
University of Wisconsin School of Medicine and Public Health

Schools with No Live Animal Use in Medical School Curricula (123 Allopathic; 28 Osteopathic)

*A.T. Still University Kirksville College of Osteopathic Medicine
*A.T. Still University School of Osteopathic Medicine in Arizona
Albany Medical College
Albert Einstein College of Medicine of Yeshiva University
*Arizona College of Osteopathic Medicine of Midwestern University
Baylor College of Medicine
Boston University School of Medicine
Brody School of Medicine at East Carolina University
Brown University School of Medicine
Case Western Reserve University School of Medicine
*Chicago College of Osteopathic Medicine of Midwestern University
Columbia University College of Physicians and Surgeons
The Commonwealth Medical College

Creighton University School of Medicine
Dartmouth Medical School
*Des Moines University College of Osteopathic Medicine
Drexel University College of Medicine
Duke University School of Medicine
East Tennessee State University James H. Quillen College of Medicine
Eastern Virginia Medical School
*Edward Via Virginia College of Osteopathic Medicine
Emory University School of Medicine
Florida International University College of Medicine
Florida State University College of Medicine
George Washington University School of Medicine and Health Sciences
Georgetown University School of Medicine
Harvard Medical School
Howard University College of Medicine
Indiana University School of Medicine
Jefferson Medical College of Thomas Jefferson University
Joan C. Edwards School of Medicine at Marshall University
*Kansas City University of Medicine and Biosciences College of Osteo-
    pathic Medicine
Keck School of Medicine of the University of Southern California
*Lake Erie College of Osteopathic Medicine
*Lake Erie College of Osteopathic Medicine—Bradenton Campus
*Lincoln Memorial University, DeBusk College of Osteopathic Medicine
Loma Linda University School of Medicine
Louisiana State University School of Medicine in New Orleans
Louisiana State University School of Medicine in Shreveport
Loyola University of Chicago Stritch School of Medicine
Mayo Medical School
Medical College of Georgia School of Medicine
Medical College of Northeastern Pennsylvania
Medical University of South Carolina College of Medicine
Meharry Medical College, School of Medicine
Mercer University School of Medicine
Michigan State University College of Human Medicine
*Michigan State University, College of Osteopathic Medicine
Morehouse School of Medicine
Mount Sinai School of Medicine

*New York College of Osteopathic Medicine of the New York Institute of Technology
New York Medical College
New York University School of Medicine
Northeastern Ohio University College of Medicine
Northwestern University Medical School
*Nova Southeastern University, College of Osteopathic Medicine
Ohio State University College of Medicine
*Ohio University College of Osteopathic Medicine
*Oklahoma State University Center for Health Sciences College of Osteopathic Medicine
*Pacific Northwest University of Health Sciences College of Osteopathic Medicine
Pennsylvania State University College of Medicine
*Philadelphia College of Osteopathic Medicine
*Philadelphia College of Osteopathic Medicine—Georgia Campus
*Pikeville College School of Osteopathic Medicine
Ponce School of Medicine
*Rocky Vista University College of Osteopathic Medicine
Rosalind Franklin University of Medicine and Science
Rush Medical College of Rush University
Saint Louis University School of Medicine
San Juan Bautista School of Medicine
Southern Illinois University School of Medicine
Stanford University School of Medicine
State University of New York Downstate Medical Center College of Medicine
State University of New York Upstate Medical University
Stony Brook University Health Sciences Center School of Medicine
Temple University School of Medicine
Texas A&M Health Science Center College of Medicine
Texas Tech University Health Sciences Center Paul L. Foster School of Medicine (El Paso)
Texas Tech University Health Sciences Center School of Medicine
*Touro College of Osteopathic Medicine—New York
*Touro University College of Osteopathic Medicine—California
*Touro University College of Osteopathic Medicine—Nevada
Tufts University School of Medicine

Tulane University School of Medicine
Universidad Central del Caribe School of Medicine
University of Alabama School of Medicine
University of Arizona College of Medicine
University of Arkansas College of Medicine
University at Buffalo School of Medicine and Biomedical Sciences
University of California, Davis School of Medicine
University of California, Irvine School of Medicine
University of California, Los Angeles David Geffen School of Medicine
University of California, San Diego School of Medicine
University of California, San Francisco School of Medicine
University of Central Florida College of Medicine
University of Chicago Pritzker School of Medicine
University of Cincinnati College of Medicine
University of Colorado School of Medicine
University of Connecticut School of Medicine
University of Florida College of Medicine
University of Hawaii John A. Burns School of Medicine
University of Illinois
University of Iowa College of Medicine
University of Kansas School of Medicine
University of Kentucky College of Medicine
University of Louisville School of Medicine
University of Maryland School of Medicine
University of Massachusetts Medical School
University of Medicine and Dentistry of New Jersey—New Jersey Medical School
University of Medicine and Dentistry of New Jersey—Robert Wood Johnson Medical School
*University of Medicine and Dentistry of New Jersey—School of Osteopathic Medicine
University of Miami School of Medicine
University of Michigan Medical School
University of Minnesota Medical School
University of Missouri—Columbia School of Medicine
University of Missouri—Kansas City School of Medicine
University of Nebraska College of Medicine
University of Nevada School of Medicine

*University of New England College of Osteopathic Medicine
University of New Mexico School of Medicine
University of North Carolina at Chapel Hill School of Medicine
University of North Dakota School of Medicine and Health Sciences
*University of North Texas Health Science Center Texas College of Osteopathic Medicine
University of Oklahoma College of Medicine
University of Pennsylvania School of Medicine
University of Pittsburgh School of Medicine
University of Puerto Rico School of Medicine
University of Rochester School of Medicine and Dentistry
University of South Alabama College of Medicine
University of South Carolina School of Medicine
University of South Dakota School of Medicine
University of South Florida College of Medicine
University of Texas Medical Branch School of Medicine
University of Texas Medical School at Houston
University of Texas School of Medicine at San Antonio
University of Texas Southwestern Medical School
University of Toledo College of Medicine
University of Utah School of Medicine
University of Vermont College of Medicine
University of Washington School of Medicine
Vanderbilt University School of Medicine
Virginia Commonwealth University, School of Medicine
Wake Forest University School of Medicine
Washington University in St. Louis School of Medicine
Wayne State University School of Medicine
Weill Cornell Medical College
*West Virginia School of Osteopathic Medicine
West Virginia University School of Medicine
*Western University of Health Sciences College of Osteopathic Medicine of the Pacific
Wright State University School of Medicine
Yale University School of Medicine

Information provided by Physicians Committee for Responsible Medicine.

Notes

CHAPTER 2: WHAT IS POUND SEIZURE?

1. The Humane Society of the United States, "HSUS Pet Overpopulation Estimates," www.hsus.org/pets/issues_affecting_our_pets/pet_overpopulation_and_ownership_statistics/hsus_pet_overpopulation_estimates.html (accessed 7 July 2008).

2. www.petfinder.com (accessed 10 August 2009).

3. American Humane Association, www.americanhumane.org/about-us/newsroom/fact-sheets/animal-shelter-euthanasia/html. See also No Kill Advocacy Center, www.nokilladvocacycenter.org/ (accessed 20 August 2009).

4. USDA, www.aphis.usda.gov/animal_welfare/efoia/downloads/reports/B_cert_holders.txt (accessed 10 September 2009).

5. Written statement to Michigan's Montcalm County Commissioners, 26 January 2009.

6. United States Department of Agriculture, Animal and Plant Health Inspection Service, Application for License, 25 February 2008.

7. United States Department of Agriculture, Animal and Plant Health Inspection Service, Application for License, 9 February 2007.

8. United States Department of Agriculture, Animal and Plant Health Inspection Service, Fiscal Year 2007 Animal Care Annual Report of Activities, www.aphis/usda.gov/publications/animal_welfare/content/printable_version/2007_AC_Report.pdf (accessed September 2008).

9. USDA 2007 Fiscal Year Report, 38.

10. USDA 2007 Fiscal Year Report, 46.

11. USDA 2007 Fiscal Year Report, 45.

12. Michigan Department of Agriculture, 2004 Individual Michigan Animal Shelter Reports.

13. Michigan Department of Agriculture, 2008 Individual Michigan Animal Shelter Reports, michigan.gov/documents/mda/2008_Shelter_Report_274392_7.pdf. (accessed 10 September 2009).

CHAPTER 3: LAWS AND LEGISLATION ON POUND SEIZURE

1. Daniel Engber, "Where's Pepper?" *Slate*, www.slate.com/id/2219224/ (accessed 1 June 2009).

2. Engber, "Where's Pepper?"

3. Daniel Engber, "Pepper Goes to Washington," *Slate*, www.slate.com/id/2219226 (accessed 3 June 2009).

4. Engber, "Pepper Goes to Washington."

5. Stan Wayman, "Concentration Camps for Dogs," *Life*, 4 February 1966.

6. American Anti-Vivisection Society, www.aavs.org/research/Animals.html (accessed 10 June 2009).

7. R. Greek and N. Shanks, *FAQs about the Use of Animals in Science* (Lanham, MD: University Press of America, Inc., 2009), 11. Citing, APHIS: Rats/Mice/and Birds Database: Researchers, Breeders, Transporters, and Exhibitors. A Database Prepared by the Federal Research Division, Library of Congress under an Interagency Agreement with the United States Department of Agriculture's Animal Plant Health Inspection Service (USDA ed., Washington, DC: 2000).

8. "Scientific and Humane Issues in the Use of Random Source Dogs and Cats," Institute for Laboratory Animal Research Division on Earth and Life Studies," National Research Council of the National Academies of Science, www.nap.edu/catalog/12641 .html (The National Academies Press, 29 May 2009), 1.

9. USDA 2007 Fiscal Year Report, 7.

10. National Research Council, 2003. *Guidelines for the Care and Use of Mammals in Neuroscience and Behavioral Research*. Washington, DC: National Academies Press, 10.

11. "Scientific and Humane Issues," 137.

12. "Scientific and Humane Issues," 18.

13. "Scientific and Humane Issues," 23.

14. Personal interview with Dr. Robert Willems, 13 November 2009.

15. "Mass Ban Sale of Pets for Research," *Detroit Free Press*, 28 December 1983, 5A.

16. Personal interview with Amy Draeger, 24 June 2009.

17. "Middlebrook Offers New Plan for Buying Dogs," *Minnesota Daily*, 30 January 1940, 1.

18. Personal e-mail communication from Amy Draeger, 9 November 2009.

19. St. Paul, Minnesota, shelter fees, www.ci.stpaul.mn.us/index.aspx?NID=1612 (accessed 29 December 2009).

20. Personal interview with Cynthia Armstrong, 24 June 2009.

21. Madeleine Pickens's personal website, www.madeleine pickens.com/%20/that's-barbaric/ (accessed 26 November 2009).

22. Monique Headle, "Replacing, Refining, and Reducing," *Stillwater News Press*, 17 April 2009, www.stillwater-newspress.com/archivesearch/local_story_108002441.html (accessed 26 November 2009).

23. Headle, "Replacing."

24. Colorado State University College of Veterinary Medicine and Biomedical Sciences, Shelter Derived Animal Use Guidance Statements Prohibition Against Use of Shelter-Derived Animals for Research or Teaching. Revised March 2006, www.cvmbs .colostate.edu/cvmbs/ShelterAnimalUse.htm (accessed 25 November 2009).

25. Association of American Veterinary Medical Colleges, www/aavmc.org/students_ admissions/vet_schools.htm (accessed 22 November 2009).

26. Personal e-mail communication, 5 May 2009.

27. American Veterinary Medical Association position statement on the Use of Random-Source Dogs and Cats for Research, Testing, and Education, approved by the AVMA Executive Board, 1983; revised June 1991, April 2000, November 2007, www.avma .org/issues/policy/animal_welfare/random.asp (accessed 26 November 2009).

28. AVMA Resolution 2-2009, "Revise Policy on Use of Random-Source Dogs and Cats for Research, Testing, and Education."

29. AVMA Resolution 2-2009.

30. AVMA Resolution, "Use of Random-Source Dogs and Cats for Research, Testing, and Education," www.avma.org/issues/policy/animal_welfare/random.asp (accessed 15 January 2010).

CHAPTER 4: BETRAYAL OF TRUST

1. "Scientific and Humane Issues in the Use of Random Source Dogs and Cats," Institute for Laboratory Animal Research Division on Earth and Life Studies, National Research Council of the National Academies of Science, www.nap.edu/catalog/12641 .html (The National Academies Press, 29 May 2009), 68–71.

2. Personal interview with Dr. Robert Willems, 13 November 2009.

3. Crystal Miller-Spiegel, "Dirty Deeds (Done Dirt Cheap): Random Source Dog and Cat Dealers Selling Former Pets," *AV Magazine* (Spring–Summer 2009): 7.

4. American Humane Stop Pound Seizure, www.americanhumane.org/stop-pound-seizure.html (accessed 15 January 2010).

5. Personal interview with Dr. Robert Willems, 13 November 2009.

6. Laura Ducceschi and Nicole Green, *Dying to Learn: Exposing the Supply and Use of Dogs and Cats in Higher Education* (Animalearn, the education division of the American Anti-Vivisection Society, 2009): 11.

7. Personal e-mail with USDA/ASPHIS, 30 April 2009.

8. Personal communication with Tattoo-a-Pet, 13 October 2008.

9. Excerpts from Last Chance for Animals' undercover investigator's journal, September 2002 to January 2003.

10. Amylou Wilson and Susan Porter, "Why Is This Dog Smiling?" *Fayetteville Weekly*, 20 October 2005.

11. *Snyder, et al. v. Seidelman, et al.*, 1995 U.S. Dist. LEXIS 19302, Opinion, Defendants' Motion for Summary Judgment, 1 November 1995.

12. National Academies of Science, meeting January 2009, notes taken by author.

13. American Humane Stop Pound Seizure, www.americanhumane.org/stop-pound-seizure.html (accessed 15 January 2010).

14. Written statement to the Montcalm (Michigan) County Commissioners, 26 January 2009.

15. Jackson County Volunteers against Pound Seizure, www.s275870067.onlinehome.us/conan.html (accessed 3 October 2009).

16. Excerpts from Last Chance for Animals' undercover investigator's journal, September 2002 to January 2003.

17. Jackson County Volunteers against Pound Seizure, www.s275870067.onlinehome.us/ (accessed 3 October 2009).

18. Jackson County Volunteers against Pound Seizure, www.s275870067.onlinehome.us/chance.html (accessed 3 October 2009).

CHAPTER 5: EXPOSING DEALERS WHO VIOLATE THE LAW

1. Last Chance for Animals, Field Notes from Undercover Investigator, "Pete," www.lcanimal.org/org/cmpgn/cmpgn_dog_pete_notes.htm (accessed 6 December 2001 through 5 January 2002).

2. Christina Gillham, "Bought to Be Sold: A New Documentary Investigates a Dealer's Maltreatment of Dogs Intended for Medical Research." *Newsweek*, www.newsweek.com/id/57139 (accessed 1 February 2006).

3. Gillham, "Bought to Be Sold," *Newsweek*.

4. "Scientific and Humane Issues," 76.

5. "Scientific and Humane Issues," 77.

6. *The Case against "B" Dealers*, produced by Last Chance for Animals.

7. *The Case against "B" Dealers*.

8. *The Case against "B" Dealers*.

9. *The Case against "B" Dealers*.

10. *The Case against "B" Dealers*.

11. *The Case against "B" Dealers*.

12. Personal interview with Dr. Robert Willems, 13 November 2009.

13. Personal interview with Dr. Robert Willems, 13 November 2009.

14. United States Department of Agriculture, Animal Welfare Report, 2007 Fiscal Year, 8. www.aphis.usda.gov/publications/animal_welfare/content/printable_version/2007AC_Report.pdf (accessed 15 September 2009).

15. United States Department of Agriculture, Animal and Plant Health Inspection Services, Report of Class B dealer licensees, www.aphis.usda.gov/animal_welfare/efoia/downloads/reports/B_cert_holders.txt (accessed 15 September 2009).

16. United States Department of Agriculture, Animal Welfare Inspection Reports, www.aphis/usda/gov/animal_welfare/inspection_list.shtml (accessed 15 September 2009).

17. USDA 2007 Fiscal Report, 9.

18. Personal interview with Dr. Robert Willems, 13 November 2009.

19. "Scientific and Humane Issues," 78.

20. Animal Legal Defense Fund, http://org2.democracyinaction.org/5154/t/6225/campaign.jsp?campaign_KEY=1614 (accessed 3 October 2009).

21. *Dying to Learn*, 27, citing footnotes 270 and 271.

CHAPTER 6: EXPERIMENTS CONDUCTED ON SHELTER CATS AND DOGS

1. Patricia Collier, "Scientists 'Discover' Emotions in Animals," *Animal New Center*, 8 August 2003.

2. J. P. Balcombe, N. D. Barnard, and C. Sandusky (2004). "Laboratory Routines Cause Animal Stress," *Contemporary Topics in Laboratory Animal Science* 43(6): 42–51. www.ncbi.nlm.nih.gov/pubmed/15669134?dopt=Abstract (accessed 26 November 2009).

3. "Scientific and Humane Issues in the Use of Random Source Dogs and Cats," Institute for Laboratory Animal Research Division on Earth and Life Studies, National Research Council of the National Academies of Science, www.nap.edu/catalog/12641 .html (The National Academies Press, 29 May 2009), 45.

4. "Scientific and Humane Issues," 54.

5. See Consolidated Appropriations Act, 2008, P.L. 110–61, signed 26 December 2007.

6. "Scientific and Humane Issues," 3.

7. "Scientific and Humane Issues," 3.

8. "Scientific and Humane Issues," 4.

9. "Scientific and Humane Issues," 4–5.

10. "Scientific and Humane Issues," 5.

11. "Scientific and Humane Issues," 8.

12. "Scientific and Humane Issues," 1.

13. "Scientific and Humane Issues," 56.

14. "Scientific and Humane Issues," 6.

15. "Scientific and Humane Issues," 12.

16. "Scientific and Humane Issues," 4.

17. "Scientific and Humane Issues," 68–71.

18. "Scientific and Humane Issues," 74.

19. "Scientific and Humane Issues," 56.

20. "Scientific and Humane Issues," 33.

21. "Scientific and Humane Issues," 29 (emphasis added), citing H. Herzog, A. Rowan, and D. Kossow, "Epidemiologic Study of Cats and Dogs Affected by the 1999 Oakland Fire," *Journal of the American Veterinary Medical Association*, 212(4): 504–11 (1998).

22. "Scientific and Humane Issues," 46, citing R. E. Parsons, M. L. Martin, F. J. Veith, L. A. Sanchez, R. T. Lyon, W. D. Suggs, P. L. Fairies, and M. L. Schwartz, "Fluoroscopically Assisted Thromboembolectomy: An Improve Method for Treating Acute Arterial Occlusions," Annals of Vascular Surgery 10(3): 201–10; and T. Sasajima, V. Bhattacharya, M. H. Wu, O. Shi, N. Hayashida, and L. R. Sauvage, "Morphology and Histology of Human and Canine Internal Thoracic Arteries," *Annals of Thoracic Surgery* 68(1): 143–48 (1999).

23. "Scientific and Humane Issues," 46, citing J. A. Serpell and J. A. Jagoe, "Early Experience and the Development of Behaviour," in *The Domestic Dog: Its Evolution, Behaviour, and Interactions with People*, J. A. Serpell, ed. (Cambridge: Cambridge University Press, 1995, 80–102; and D. C. Turner, "The Human-Cat Relationship," in *The Domestic Cat: The Biology of Its Behaviour*, 2nd ed., D. C. Turner and P. P. G. Bateson, eds. (Cambridge: Cambridge University Press), 2000, 194–206.

24. "Scientific and Humane Issues," 59.

25. "Scientific and Humane Issues," 59.

26. R. Greek and N. Shanks, *FAQs about the Use of Animals in Science* (Lanham, MD: University Press of America, 2009), 2.

27. Greek and Shanks, *FAQs*, 2.

28. Greek and Shanks, *FAQs*, 3.

29. Greek and Shanks, *FAQs*, 3

30. Greek and Shanks, *FAQs*, 4.

31. Greek and Shanks, *FAQs*, 4.

32. Greek and Shanks, *FAQs*, 4.

33. Greek and Shanks, *FAQs*, 1.

34. Greek and Shanks, *FAQs*, 1.

35. Greek and Shanks, *FAQs*, 132–33.

36. Greek and Shanks, *FAQs*, 8, citing N. Shanks, R. Greek, J. Greek, "Are Animal Models Predictive for Humans?" *Philos Ethics Humanit Med* (2009): 4:2.

37. Greek and Shanks, *FAQs*, 9.

38. Greek and Shanks, *FAQs*, 22.

39. Greek and Shanks, *FAQs*, 54, 55.

40. Greek and Shanks, *FAQs*, 62.

41. Greek and Shanks, *FAQs*, 57. Citing F. Coulston, "Final Discussion." In *Human Epidemiology and Animal Laboratory Correlations in Chemical Carcinogenisis*. Edited by F. Coulston, P. Shubick (Norwood, NJ: Ablex, 1980), 407.

42. Greek and Shanks, *FAQs*, 63.

43. Greek and Shanks, *FAQs*, 72.

44. Greek and Shanks, *FAQs*, 100, citing FDA Issues Advice to Make Earliest Stages of Clinical Drug Development More Efficient, www.fda.gov/bbs/topics/news/2006/NEW01296.html.

45. Greek and Shanks, *FAQs*, 133.

46. Greek and Shanks, *FAQs*, 133.

47. Physicians Committee for Responsible Medicine, "Point-Counterpoint on Medical School Laboratories," 111.pcrm.org/resch/meded/ethics_med_point.html (accessed 26 November 2009).

48. R. J. Wall, M. Shani (2008), "Are Animal Models as Good as We Think?" *Theriogenology*, 69:2–9.

49. S. H. Curry, "Why Have So Many Drugs with Stellar Results in Laboratory Stroke Models Failed in Clinical Trials? A Theory Based on Allometric Relationships," *Annals of the New York Academy of Sciences* 2003, 993:69–74.

50. Greek and Shanks, *FAQs*, 137.

51. Greek and Shanks, *FAQs*, 138.

52. Laura Ducceschi and Nicole Green, *Dying to Learn: Exposing the Supply and Use of Dogs and Cats in Higher Education* (Animalearn, the education division of the American Anti-Vivisection Society, 2009).

53. *Dying to Learn*, 7.

54. *Dying to Learn*, 4–5, citing UGA AUP #A2006-10224.

55. *Dying to Learn*, 5.

56. *Dying to Learn*, 8.

57. *Dying to Learn*, 11.

58. *Dying to Learn*, 13, citing footnote 94: "Four hundred and sixteen dogs were acquired from Lehman Animal Shelter in Giddings, TX; 28 dogs were from Fayette County Animal Shelter in LaGrange, TX; 25 dogs were from Bastrop County Animal Shelter in Bastrop, TX; and 5 from Brenham Pound in Brenham, TX."

59. Telephone conversation with Lehman Animal Shelter chief animal control officer, 5 January 2010.

60. *Dying to Learn*, 14, citing footnote 98: "Between 2005–2007, Colorado State University received 210 dog cadavers from the Larimer County Humane Society in Fort Collins, CO."

61. *Dying to Learn*, 15, citing footnote 99: "In 2006, Stephens County Animal Country (SCAC) donated 26 live dogs to the University of Georgia. In 2007, SCAC donated 65 live dogs; and as of July 2008, SCAC had donated 33 live dogs. . . . In 2007, University of Georgia, Athens received 31 dog cadavers and three cat cadavers as donations from Athens Clarke County Animal Control. In 2007, 23 dogs and nine cat cadavers were donated from Madison Oglethorpe Animal Shelter."

62. *Dying to Learn*, 14, citing footnote 100: "In 2005, Michigan State University purchased three live dogs and two live cats from Jackson County Animal Control (Jackson, MI) for use in education. In 2007, MSU purchased six live dogs from Eaton County Animal Shelter (Charlotte, MI)."

63. *Dying to Learn*, 14, citing footnote 101: "In 2005, Iowa State University bought six live dogs and two live cats from the Des Moines Animal Shelter for use in education. Between 2005 and 2006, two local animal pounds donated live cats and dogs to Iowa State: the Perry City Dog Pound (Perry, IA) and the Jefferson City Dog Pound (Jefferson City, IA). Perry City donated 46 live cats and kittens and 22 dogs. Almost all of the cats and kittens were euthanized. Jefferson City donated 31 live dogs and 18 live cats, and most of the cats were euthanized."

64. *Dying to Learn*, 14, citing footnote 101: "In 2005, University of Minnesota used 798 live dogs and 424 live cats who were obtained from animal shelters, students, or clients and returned. Similarly, in 2006, the University used 748 dogs and 480 cats, and in 2007, it used 572 dogs and 361 cats. The University did not specify how the animals were used, from which shelters they were acquired, or if they were used specifically in education. Minnesota state law (Minn. Stat. § 35.71 (2002) requires pound seizure. It is unclear whether all of these animals were returned to the shelter." However, Amy Draeger indicated that the animals obtained by the university were for the veterinary spay-neuter training clinic, and the animals were then placed for adoption. *Dying to Learn*, 13–14.

65. *Dying to Learn*, 26.

66. "Be a Hero to Animals in Labs," www.stopanimaltests.com/Whistleblower.asp (accessed 26 November 2009).

67. Douglass Starr, "A Dog's Life," *Boston Globe*, www.boston.com/news/globe/magazine/articles/2004/04/18/a_dogs_life (accessed 27 November 2009).

68. Starr, "A Dog's Life."

69. Starr, "A Dog's Life."

70. Starr, "A Dog's Life."

71. www.stopanimaltests.com (accessed 26 November 2009).

72. www.lcanimal.org (accessed 26 November 2009).

73. "People for the Ethical Treatment of Animals, All in a Day's Work: Confinement, Torment, Killing in University Labs," blog.peta.org/archives/2009/11/university_of_utah .php (accessed 26 November 2009).

74. "People for the Ethical Treatment of Animals, Robert's Story," www.peta.org/FeatureUtahLabsRobert.asp (accessed 26 November 2009).

75. "People for the Ethical Treatment of Animals, Live Cats Used in Cruel Training Courses at Texas Tech," http://secure.peta.org/site/Advocacy?cmd=display&page=UserAction&id=2081 (accessed 26 November 2009). In a personal e-mail communication with the American Academy of Pediatrics verifying its position on the use of animals in research, AAP provided the following statement: "The Neonatal Resuscitation Program (NRP) recommends resuscitation mannequins for skills training and practice. The NRP Steering Committee is supportive of continued industry efforts to develop, refine, and provide more realistic and cost effective anatomical models for hands-on practice that allow individuals to learn the necessary skills for effective resuscitation. While the NRP encourages the use of mannequins and simulators, the committee leaves the decision to local institutions to determine the most effective method(s) for teaching the curriculum and skills to their constituents." E-mail communication, 20 November 2009.

76. "New Human-Based Study Refutes Past March of Dimes' Finding on Visual Deprivation in Kittens," *Good Medicine Magazine*, www.pcrm.org/magazine/gm07spring .blindness.html (accessed 8 October 2009).

77. Crystal Miller-Spiegel, "Dirty Deeds (Done Dirt Cheap): Random Source Dog and Cat Dealers Selling Former Pets," *AV Magazine* (Spring–Summer 2009): 9.

78. "This Is No Dummy: With Advanced Human Simulators for Medical Training, Why Harm Animals?" *Good Medicine Magazine*, www.pcrm.org/magazine/gm08autumn/no-dummy.html (accessed 8 October 2009).

79. "University of Michigan Ends Live Dog Lab," *Good Medicine Magazine*, www .pcrm.org/magazine/gm09spring.michigan.html (accessed 8 October 2009).

CHAPTER 7: ALTERNATIVES TO ANIMAL RESEARCH

1. R. Greek and N. Shanks, *FAQs about the Use of Animals in Science* (Lanham, MD: University Press of America, 2009), 8.

2. Elizabeth Weise, "Three U.S. Agencies Aim to End Animal Testing," *USA Today*, www.usatoday.com/tech/science/2008-02-14-animal-tests_N.htm?POE=click-refer (accessed 1 November 2009).

3. Greek and Shanks, *FAQ*s, 9, citing http://yosemite.epa.gov/opa/admpress.nsf/bd43 79a92ceceeac8525735900400c2735995a22ceb67467852573f0006559de!OpenDocument (accessed 26 November 2009).

4. Greek and Shanks, *FAQ*s, 49.

5. Greek and Shanks, *FAQ*s, 56.

6. "Replacing Animals in Medical Education," *Good Medicine Magazine*, www.pcrm .org/magazine/gm08spring.replacing_animals.html (accessed 8 October 2009).

7. Physicians Committee for Responsible Medicine, "Live Animal Laboratories in U.S. Allopathic and Osteopathic Medical Schools, Updated: November 10, 2009."

8. Physicians Committee for Responsible Medicine, "Live Animal Use for Advanced Trauma Life Support Courses in U.S. and Canadian Programs: An Ongoing Survey, Updated, October 30, 2009."

9. "PCRM, Wisconsin Humane Society Push for End to Dog Labs at Medical College of Wisconsin," *Good Medicine Magazine*, www.pcrm.org/magazine/gm07winter/mcw .html (accessed 26 November 2009).

10. "Medical Schools' Dog Days Nearing Their End? PCRM Helps Schools Switch from Animal Labs to Human-Focused Alternatives in 2006," *Good Medicine Magazine*, (Winter 2007) www.pcrm.org/magazine/gm07winter/dogday.html (accessed 8 October 2009).

11. "Dog Days."

12. Physicians Committee for Responsible Medicine. Sources: American Association of Medical Colleges: www.aamc.org; American Osteopathic Association: www/ osteopathic.org; Physicians Committee for Responsible Medicine (data on file); S. W. Ammons, "Use of Live Animals in the Curricula of U.S. Medical Schools in 1994," *Academic Medicine* 1995, 70:740–73; Roberta Hershenson, "Live Animal Use Spurs Protests," *New York Times*, March 24, 1996; L. A. Hansen, G. R. Boss, "Use of Live Animals in the Curricula of U.S. Medical Schools: Survey Results 2001," *Academic Medicine* 2002, 77:1147–49.

13. Laura Ducceschi and Nicole Green, *Dying to Learn: Exposing the Supply and Use of Dogs and Cats in Higher Education* (Animalearn, the education division of the American Anti-Vivisection Society, 2009), 35, citing Animal Welfare Information Center (AWIC). "Alternatives in Education." United States Department of Agriculture, 7 August 2008. USDA, 19 March 2009. www.awic.nal.usda.gov/nal_display/index.php?info_center=3&tax_level=2&tax_subject=183&level3_id=0&level4_ id=0%level5_id=0&topic_id=1093&&pplacement_default=0 (accessed 26 November 2009).

14. *Dying to Learn*, 2.

15. *Dying to Learn*, B–2, B–16.

CHAPTER 8: THE VICTIMS AND SURVIVORS OF POUND SEIZURE AND PET THEFT

1. Crystal Miller-Spiegel, "Dirty Deeds (Done Dirt Cheap): Random Source Dog and Cat Dealers Selling Former Pets," *AV Magazine* (Spring–Summer 2009): 7.

CHAPTER 9: THE VOICES OF THE RESEARCH AND EDUCATIONAL COMMUNITIES ON RANDOM SOURCE CATS AND DOGS

1. "Scientific and Humane Issues in the Use of Random Source Dogs and Cats," Institute for Laboratory Animal Research Division on Earth and Life Studies," National Research Council of the National Academies of Science, www.nap.edu/catalog/12641 .html (The National Academies Press, 29 May 2009).

2. "Scientific and Humane Issues," 78.

3. "Scientific and Humane Issues," 78.

4. "Scientific and Humane Issues," 78.

5. "Scientific and Humane Issues," 75.

6. "Scientific and Humane Issues," 74.

7. "Scientific and Humane Issues," Report in Brief: 3.

8. "Scientific and Humane Issues," 81.

9. "Scientific and Humane Issues," 82–83.

10. Robert Whitney, letter to U.S. House of Representatives, 27 July 2007.

11. Interview with Dr. James Serpell, 29 October 2009.

12. Publications involving Dr. Serpell's studies on shelter dogs include R. C. Hubrecht, J. A. Serpell, and T. B. Poole (1992). "Correlate of Pen Size and Housing on the Behaviour of Kenneled Dogs," *Applied Animal Behaviour Science*, 34:365–83; S. A. Segurson, J. A. Serpell, and B. L. Hart (2005). "Evaluation of a Behavioral Assessment Questionnaire for Use in the Characterization of Behavioral Problems of Dogs Relinquished to Animal Shelters," *Journal of the American Veterinary Medical Association*, 227(11): 1755–61; and R. P. Timmins, K. D. Cliff, C. T. Day, B. L. Hart, L. A. Hart, R. C. Hubrecht, K. F. Hurley, C. J. C. Phillips, J. S. Rand, I. Rochlitz, J. A. Serpell, and S. L. Zawistowski (2007). "Enhancing Quality of Life for Dogs and Cats in Confined Situations," *Animal Welfare*, 16(S): 83–88.

13. Interview with Dr. James Serpell, 29 October 2009.

14. Interview with Dr. James Serpell, 29 October 2009.

15. Interview with Dr. James Serpell, 29 October 2009.

16. Crystal Miller-Spiegel, "Dirty Deeds (Done Dirt Cheap): Random Source Dog and Cat Dealers Selling Former Pets," *AV Magazine* (Spring–Summer 2009): 7.

17. Unit for Laboratory Animal Medicine, University of Michigan Medical School, Ann Arbor (undated). Canine Receiving, Quarantine, and Conditional Protocol, www .ulam.umich.edu/sops/Quarantine%20Dogs%208-05.pdf (accessed 10 October 2009).

18. Miller-Spiegel, "Dirty Deeds," 7.

19. Michigan Society for Medical Research, "The Use of Pound Animals in Medical Research," www.mismr.org/educational/pound.html (accessed 10 October 2009).

20. MSMR, "Pound Animals."

21. MSMR, "Pound Animals."

22. MSMR, "Pound Animals."

23. Physicians Committee for Responsible Medicine, Live Animal Laboratories in U.S. Allopathic and Osteopathic Medical Schools (10 November 2009).

24. MSMR, "Pound Animals."

25. MSMR, "Pound Animals."

26. American Physiological Society, www.the-aps.org/pa/resources/policyStmnts/pa-PolicyStmnts_dogscats.htm (accessed 27 November 2009).

27. Foundation for Biomedical Research, www.fbresearch.org/survivors/truth.htm (accessed 27 November 2009).

CHAPTER 10: SHELTERS AND POUND SEIZURE

1. Thank you to Tracy Coppola, legislative analyst for American Humane, for her perseverance in working on the national survey.

2. 2007 Michigan Animal Shelter Report, www.michigan.gov/documents/mda/ANI-MAL_SHELTER_ACTIVITY_REPORT_2007_236804_7.pdf; 2008 Michigan Animal Shelter Reports, www.michigan.gov/documents/mda/2008_Shelter_Report_274392_7.pdf (accessed 27 December 2009).

3. Michigan Animal Shelter Report, www.michigan.gov/documents/mda/ANIMAL_SHELTER_ACTIVITY_REPORT_2007_236804_7.pdf; 2008 Michigan Animal Shelter Reports, www.michigan.gov/documents/mda/2008_Shelter_Report_274392_7.pdf (accessed 27 December 2009).

4. "Scientific and Humane Issues in the Use of Random Source Dogs and Cats," Institute for Laboratory Animal Research Division on Earth and Life Studies," National Research Council of the National Academies of Science, www.nap.edu/catalog/12641 .html (The National Academies Press, 29 May 2009), 68–71.

CHAPTER 11: VOICES OF THE ADVOCATES TO STOP POUND SEIZURE

1. Personal interview with Dr. John Pippin, 15 December 2009.

2. "Dogs, Cats Used in Experiment," www.humanesociety.org/news/press_releases/2009/11/experiments_on_pets_111709.html (accessed 20 November 2009).

3. Personal interview with Amy Draeger, 24 June 2009.

4. Personal interview with Anne Davis, 14 December 2009.

5. "Investigation Exposes Animal Suffering at University of Utah Labs," People for the Ethical Treatment of Animals, www.peta.org/FeatureUtahLabs.asp (accessed 23 December 2009).

6. Personal interview with Holly Sauvé, 22 October 2009.

7. Personal interview with Mike Severino, 18 December 2009.

8. Personal interview with Judy Dynnik, 9 August 2009.

9. Personal interview with Judy Oisten, 22 August 2009.

10. Personal interview with Sandy Carlton, 6 November 2009.

11. Personal interview with Frances Schuleit, 22 November 2009.

CHAPTER 12: LAWSUITS, THREATS, AND INTIMIDATION

1. Animal Enterprise Terrorism Act, http://thomas.loc.gov/cgi-bin/query/D?c109:5: .temp/~c1099LkHXk: (accessed 30 December 2009).

2. 18 USC 43.

3. George W. Pring and Penelope Canan, *SLAPPs: Getting Sued for Speaking Out* (Philadelphia: Temple University Press, 1996).

4. *Hodgins Kennels, Inc. v. Durbin and Blight*, 429 N.W. 2d 189; 170 Mich. App. 474 (1988).

5. Pring and Canan, *SLAPPs*, 102.

6. Pring and Canan, *SLAPPs*, 103; Buddy Moorehouse, "Howell Kennel Owners Win Suit," Livingston County Press, 21 November 1984, 3A.

7. *Hodgins v. Durbin*, 429 N.W. 2d at 193.

CHAPTER 13: EFFECTIVE ADVOCACY TECHNIQUES

1. Arizona, Connecticut, Florida, Georgia, Indiana, Illinois, Louisiana, Massachusetts, Maryland, Michigan, Minnesota, Missouri, New Jersey, New York, Oregon, Pennsylvania, Texas, and Washington.

2. American Bar Association Tort Trial and Insurance Practice Section, Animal Law Committee, www.abanet.org/tips/animal (accessed 30 December 2009).

Bibliography

American Anti-Vivisection Society. www.aavs.org/researchAnimals.html.

American Association of Medical Colleges. www.aamc.org.

American Bar Association Tort Trial and Insurance Practice Section, Animal Law Committee. www.abanet.org/tips/animal/.

American Humane Association. www.americanhumane.org/about-us/newsroom/fact-sheets/animal-shelter-euthanasia.html.

American Humane Association Stop Pound Seizure. www.americanhumane.org/stop-pound-seizure.html.

American Osteopathic Association. www.osteopathic.org.

American Physiological Society. "Random Source Dogs and Cats in Medical Research." www.the-aps.org/pa/resources/policyStmnts/paPolicyStmnts_dogscats.htm.

American Veterinary Medical Association. Resolution 2–2009. "Revise Policy on Use of Random-Source Dogs and Cats for Research, Testing, and Education."

American Veterinary Medical Association. "Use of Random-Source Dogs and Cats for Research, Testing, and Education." www.avma.org/issues/policy/animal_welfare/random.asp.

American Veterinary Medical Association. Resolution, "Use of Random-Source Dogs and Cats for Research, Testing, and Education (Amended)." www.avma.org/issues/policy/animal_welfare/random.asp.

Ammons, S. W. "Use of Live Animals in the Curricula of U.S. Medical Schools in 1994." *Academic Medicine* 1995, 70:740–43.

Animal Enterprise Terrorism Act. thomas.loc.gov/cgi-bin/query/D?c109:5:./temp/~c1099LkHXk:.

Animal Legal Defense Fund. org2.democracyinaction.org/o/5154/t/6225/campaign.jsp?campaign_KEY=1614.

Animal Welfare Information Center (AWIC). "Alternatives in Education." United States Department of Agriculture. 7 August 2008. USDA, 19 March 2009. awic.nal.usda.gov/nal_display/index.php?info_center=3&tax_level=2&tax_subject=183&level3_id=0&level4_id=0&level5_id=0&topic_id=1093&&placement_default=0.

APHIS: RATS/MICE/and BIRDS DATABASE: RESEARCHERS, BREEDERS, TRANSPORTERS, AND EXHIBITERS. A Database Prepared by the Federal Research Division, Library of Congress under an Interagency Agreement with the United States Department of Agriculture's Animal Plant Health Inspection Service. (Washington, DC: USDA ed., 2000).

Association of American Veterinary Medical Colleges. www.aavmc.org/students_admissions/vet_schools.htm.

Balcombe, J. P., N. D. Barnard, and C. Sandusky. (2004). "Laboratory Routines Cause Animal Stress." *Contemporary Topics in Laboratory Animal Science*, 43(6), 42–51. www.ncbi.nlm.nih.gov/pubmed/15669134?dopt=Abstract.

Collier, Patricia. "Scientists 'Discover' Emotions in Animals." *Animal New Center*, 8 August 2003.

Colorado State University College of Veterinary Medicine and Biomedical Sciences. *Shelter Derived Animal Use Guidance Statements Prohibition Against Use of Shelter-Derived Animals for Research or Teaching*. Revised March 2006. www.cvmbs.colostate.edu/cvmbs/ShelterAnimalUse.htm.

Consolidated Appropriations Act, 2008, P.L. 110–161, signed 26 December 2007.

Coulston, F. "Final Discussion." In *Human Epidemiology and Animal Laboratory Correlations in Chemical Carcinogenisis*. Edited by F. Coulston and P. Shubick. Norwood, NJ: Ablex, 1980, 407.

Detroit Free Press. "Massachusetts Bans Sale of Pets for Research." 28 December 1983, 5A.

Ducceschi, Laura, and Nicole Green. *Dying to Learn: Exposing the Supply and Use of Dogs and Cats in Higher Education* (Animalearn, the education division of the American Anti-Vivisection Society, 2009).

Engber, Daniel. "Where's Pepper?" *Slate*. www.slate.com/id/2219224/.

Engber, Daniel. "Pepper Goes to Washington." *Slate*. www.slate.com/id/2219226.

Foundation for Biomedical Research. www.fbresearch.org/survivors/truth.htm.

Gillham, Christina. "Bought to Be Sold: A New Documentary Investigates a Dealer's Maltreatment of Dogs Intended for Medical Research." *Newsweek*. www.newsweek.com/id/57139.

Gladwell, Malcolm. *The Tipping Point: How Little Things Can Make a Big Difference*. Boston: Little, Brown and Company, 2000.

Greek, R., and N. Shanks. *FAQs about the Use of Animals in Science*. Lanham, MD: University Press of America, 2009.

Hansen, L. A, and G. R. Boss. "Use of Live Animals in the Curricula of U.S. Medical Schools: Survey Results from 2001." *Academic Medicine* 2002, 77:1147–149.

Headle, Monique. "Replacing, Refining and Reducing," *Stillwater News Press,* 17 April 2009, www.stillwater-newspress.com/archivesearch/local_story_108002441.html.

Hershenson, Roberta. "Live Animal Use Spurs Protests." *New York Times*, 24 March 1996.

Herzog, H., A. Rowan, and D. Kossow. "Epidemiologic Study of Cats and Dogs Affected by the 1991 Oakland Fire," *Journal of the American Veterinary Medical Association*, 212(4): 504–11 (1998).

Hodgins Kennels, Inc. v. Durbin and Blight, 429 N.W. 2d 189; 170 Mich. App. 474 (1988).

Hubrecht, R. C., J. A. Serpell, and T. B. Poole. (1992). "Correlates of Pen Size and Housing on the Behaviour of Kenneled Dogs." *Applied Animal Behaviour Science*, 34: 365–83.

The Humane Society of the United States. "Dogs, Cats Used in Experiment." www .humanesociety.org/news/press_releases/2009/11/experiments_on_pets_111709.html.

The Humane Society of the United States, "HSUS Pet Overpopulation Estimates." www .hsus.org/pets/issues_affecting_our_pets/pet_overpopulation_and_ownership_statistics/hsus_pet_overpopulation_estimates.html.

Institute for Laboratory Animal Research Division on Earth and Life Studies, National Research Council of the National Academies of Science. "Scientific and Humane Issues in the Use of Random Source Dogs and Cats." www.nap.edu/catalog/12641.html (The National Academies Press, 29 May 2009).

Jackson County Volunteers against Pound Seizure. www.s275870067.onlinehome.us/ conan.html.

Jackson County Volunteers against Pound Seizure. www.s275870067.onlinehome.us/.

Jackson County Volunteers against Pound Seizure. www.s275870067.onlinehome.us/ chance.html.

Last Chance for Animals. www.lcanimal.org/.

Last Chance for Animals. *"The Case Against 'B' Dealers."*

Last Chance for Animals. Excerpts from Undercover Investigator's Journal, September 2002 to January 2003.

Last Chance for Animals, Field Notes from Undercover Investigator "Pete." www.lcanimal.org/cmpgn/cmpgn_dog_pete_notes.htm.

Madeleine Pickens' personal website. www.madeleinepickens.com/%20/thats-barbaric/.

Michigan Department of Agriculture. 2004 Individual Michigan Animal Shelter Reports.

Michigan Department of Agriculture. 2007 Michigan Animal Shelter Report www .michigan.gov/documents/mda/ANIMAL_SHELTER_ACTIVITY_REPORT_2007_ 236804_7.pdf.

Michigan Department of Agriculture. 2008 Individual Michigan Animal Shelter Reports. www.michigan.gov/documents/mda/2008_Shelter_Report_274392_7.pdf.

Michigan Society for Medical Research. "The Use of Pound Animals in Medical Research." www.mismr.org/educational/pound.html.

Miller-Spiegel, Crystal. "Dirty Deeds (Done Dirt Cheap): Random Source Dog and Cat Dealers Selling Former Pets." *AV Magazine* (Spring–Summer 2009).

Minnesota Daily. "Middlebrook Offers New Plan for Buying Dogs," 30 January 1940, 1.

Moorehouse, Buddy. "Howell Kennel Owners Win Suit." *Livingston County Press*, 21 November 1984, 3A.

National Research Council. 2003. *Guidelines for the Care and Use of Mammals in Neuroscience and Behavioral Research*. Washington, DC: National Academies Press, 10.

No Kill Advocacy Center. www.nokilladvocacycenter.org/.

Parsons, R. E., M. L. Marin, F. J. Veith, L. A. Sanchez, R. T. Lyon, W. D. Suggs, P. L. Faries, and M. L. Schwartz. "Fluoroscopically Assisted Thromboembolectomy: An Improved Method for Treating Acute Arterial Occlusions," *Annals of Vascular Surgery*,

10(3): 210–10; and T. Sasajima, V. Bhattacharya, M. H. Wu, Q. Shi, N. Hayashida, and L. R. Sauvage, "Morphology and Histology of Human and Canine Internal Thoracic Arteries," *Annals of Thoracic Surgery* 68(1): 143–48 (1999).

People for the Ethical Treatment of Animals. www.stopanimaltests.com/.

People for the Ethical Treatment of Animals. "All in a Day's Work: Confinement, Torment, Killing in University Labs." blog.peta.org/archives/2009/11/university_of_utah.php.

People for the Ethical Treatment of Animals. "Be a Hero to Animals in Labs." www.stopanimaltests.com/Whistleblower.asp (accessed 26 November 2009).

People for the Ethical Treatment of Animals. "Investigation Exposes Animal Suffering at University of Utah Labs," People for the Ethical Treatment of Animals." www.peta.org/FeatureUtahLabs.asp.

People for the Ethical Treatment of Animals. "Live Cats Used in Cruel Training Courses at Texas Tech." http://secure.peta.org/site/Advocacy?cmd=display&page=UserAction&id=2081.

People for the Ethical Treatment of Animals. "Robert's Story." www.peta.org/FeatureUtahLabsRobert.asp.

Personal interview with Cynthia Armstrong, 24 June 2009.

Personal interview with Sandy Carlton, 6 November 2009.

Personal interview with Anne Davis, 14 December 2009.

Personal interview with Amy Draeger, 24 June 2009.

Personal e-mail communication with Amy Draeger, 9 November 2009.

Personal interview with Judy Dynnik, 9 August 2009.

Personal e-mail communication with Humane Society Veterinary Medical Association, 5 May 2009.

Personal interview with Judy Oisten, 22 August 2009.

Personal interview with Dr. John Pippin, 15 December 2009.

Personal interview with Holly Sauvé, 22 October 2009.

Personal interview with Dr. James Serpell, 29 October 2009.

Personal interview with Frances Schuleit, 22 November 2009.

Personal interview with Mike Severino, 18 December 2009.

Personal e-mail communication with Tattoo-A-Pet, 13 October 2008.

Personal e-mail communication with USDA/APHIS, 30 April 2009.

Personal interview with Dr. Robert Willems, 13 November 2009.

Petfinder. www.petfinder.com.

Physicians Committee for Responsible Medicine. "Live Animal Laboratories in U.S. Allopathic and Osteopathic Medical Schools, Updated: November 10, 2009."

Physicians Committee for Responsible Medicine. "Live Animal Use for Advanced Trauma Life Support Courses in U.S. and Canadian Programs: An Ongoing Survey, Updated, October 30, 2009."

Physicians Committee for Responsible Medicine. "Medical Schools' Dog Days Nearing Their End? PCRM Helps Schools Switch from Animal Labs to Human-Focused Alternatives in 2006." *Good Medicine Magazine* (Winter 2007), www.pcrm.org/magazine/gm07winter/dogdays.html.

Physicians Committee for Responsible Medicine. "New Human-Based Study Refutes Past March of Dimes' Findings on Visual Deprivation in Kittens." *Good Medicine Magazine.* www.pcrm.org/magazine/gm07spring.blindness.html.

Physicians Committee for Responsible Medicine. "PCRM, Wisconsin Humane Society Push for End to Dog Labs at Medical College of Wisconsin." *Good Medicine Magazine.* www.pcrm.org/magazine/gm07winter/mcw.html.

Physicians Committee for Responsible Medicine. "Point-Counterpoint on Medical School Laboratories." www.pcrm.org/resch/meded/ethics_med_point.html.

Physicians Committee for Responsible Medicine. "Replacing Animals in Medical Education." *Good Medicine Magazine,* www.pcrm.org/magazine/gm08spring/replacing_animals.html.

Physicians Committee for Responsible Medicine. "This Is No Dummy: With Advanced Human Simulators for Medical Training, Why Harm Animals?" *Good Medicine Magazine.* www.pcrm.org/magazine/gm08autumn/no-dummy.html.

Physicians Committee for Responsible Medicine. "University of Michigan Ends Live Dog Lab," *Good Medicine Magazine.* www.pcrm.org/magazine/gm09spring.michigan.html.

Pring, George W., and Penelope Canan. *SLAPPs: Getting Sued for Speaking Out.* Philadelphia: Temple University Press, 1996.

Saint Paul, Minnesota, shelter fees. www.ci.stpaul.mn.us/index.aspx?NID=1612.

Segurson, S. A., J. A. Serpell, and B. L. Hart. (2005). "Evaluation of a Behavioral Assessment Questionnaire for Use in the Characterization of Behavioral Problems of Dogs Relinquished to Animal Shelters." *Journal of the American Veterinary Medical Association,* 227(11): 1755–61.

Serpell, J. A., and J. A. Jagoe. "Early Experience and the Development of Behaviour." *The Domestic Dog: Its Evolution, Behaviour, and Interactions with People,* J. A. Serpell (ed.), pp. 80–102. Cambridge: Cambridge University Press, 1995; and D. C. Turner. "The Human-Cat Relationship." In *The Domestic Cat: The Biology of Its Behaviour,* 2nd ed., D. C. Turner and P. P. G. Bateson (eds.), pp. 194–206. Cambridge: Cambridge University Press, 2000.

Shanks, N., R. Greek, and J. Greek. "Are Animal Models Predictive for Humans?" *Philosophy Ethics Humanity Medicine* 2009, 4:2.

Snyder, et al. v. Seidelman, et al., 1995 U.S. Dist. LEXIS 19302, Opinion, Defendants' Motion for Summary Judgment, 1 November 1995.

Starr, Douglass. "A Dog's Life." *The Boston Globe.* www.boston.com/news/globe/magazine/articles/2004/04/18/a_dogs_life/.

Timmins, R. P., K. D. Cliff, C. T. Day, B. L. Hart, L. A. Hart, R. C. Hubrecht,, K. F. Hurley, C. J. C. Phillips, J. S. Rand, I. Rochlitz, J. A. Serpell, and S. L. Zawistowski. (2007). "Enhancing Quality of Life for Dogs and Cats in Confined Situations." *Animal Welfare,* 16(S): 83–88.

UGA AUP #A2006-10224.

Unit for Laboratory Animal Medicine, University of Michigan Medical School, Ann Arbor. (Undated). Canine Receiving, Quarantine, and Conditional Protocol. www.ulam.umich.edu/sops/Quarantine%20Dogs%208-05.pdf.

United States Code, 18 USC 43.

United States Department of Agriculture, Animal and Plant Health Inspection Service, Application for License.

United States Department of Agriculture, Animal and Plant Health Inspection Service, Fiscal Year 2007 Animal Care Annual Report of Activities. www.aphis.usda.gov/publications/animal_welfare/content/printable_version/2007_AC_Report.pdf.

United States Department of Agriculture, Animal and Plant Health Inspection Service, Report of Class B Dealer Licensees. www.aphis.usda.gov/animal_welfare/efoia/downloads/reports/B_cert_holders.txt.

United States Department of Agriculture, Animal Welfare Inspection Reports. www.aphis.usda.gov/animal_welfare/inspection_list.shtml.

United States Environmental Protection Agency. "NIH Collaborates with EPA to Improve the Safety Testing of Chemicals—New Strategy Aims to Reduce Reliance on Animal Testing." http://yosemite.epa.gov/opa/admpress.nsf/bd4379a92ceceeac8525735900400c27/35995a22ceb67467852573f0006559de!OpenDocument.

United States Food and Drug Administration. "FDA Issues Advice to Make Earliest Stages of Clinical Drug Development More Efficient." www.fda.gov/bbs/topics/news/2006/NEW01296.html.

Wall, R. J., and M. Shani. (2008). "Are Animal Models as Good as We Think?" *Theriogenology*, 69:2–9.

Wayman, Stan. "Concentration Camps for Dogs." *Life*, 4 February 1966.

Weise, Elizabeth. "Three U.S. Agencies Aim to End Animal Testing," *USA Today*. www.usatoday.com/tech/science/2008-02-14-animal-tests_N.htm?POE=click-refer (accessed 1 November 2009).

Wilson, Amylou, and Susan Porter. "Why Is This Dog Smiling?" *Fayetteville Weekly*, 20 October 2005.

Written statement to the Montcalm (Michigan) County Commissioners, 26 January 2009.

Index

About the Author

Allie Phillips is an attorney licensed in Michigan and Maryland and has dedicated her career to helping victims of crime, particularly animals and children. She currently works for the American Humane Association (www.americanhumane.org) as the vice president of human-animal strategic initiatives, and previously as vice president of public policy. She has drafted and analyzed federal and state legislation to protect animals and children, including being the author of the 2009–2010 legislative bill to ban pound seizure in Michigan. Allie is now in charge of special initiatives related to human-animal interactions, including overseeing the Pets and Women's Shelters (PAWS)® Program which she created and nationally launched in 2008. The PAWS Program assists domestic violence shelters to create on-site housing for family pets so that families in crisis do not have to be separated from their pets or leave them behind in an abusive home. Allie appeared on The Today Show in March 2009 where the PAWS Program was featured and her work has been featured in *USA Today*, the *Washington Post*, and *Chatelaine Magazine* in Canada. She also oversees the Therapy Animals Supporting Kids (TASK)™ Program that she cocreated. The TASK Program sets forth guidelines on how to effectively incorporate therapy animals with abused children, especially children going through the court process. In her work, she will create new programs that celebrate the human-animal bond.

Allie was previously employed as an assistant prosecuting attorney in Michigan for more than eight years and then as a senior attorney with the National District Attorneys Association's National Center for

Prosecution of Child Abuse and National Child Protection Training Center in Alexandria, Virginia. She specialized in the investigation and prosecution of child abuse, created a training program on The Link® between animal cruelty and human violence, authored numerous professional articles, and traveled the country training prosecutors, law enforcement, and child protection professionals.

Allie is a nationally recognized trainer, author, and media commentator on issues involving child abuse and animal cruelty, The Link, human-animal interactions, pound seizure, and pets caught in the recession crisis. She is a graduate of Michigan State University and received her Juris Doctorate *cum laude* from the University of Detroit Mercy School of Law. She is an active member of the Michigan State Bar Animal Law Section, vice president of No Paws Left Behind, and a member of the Association of Prosecuting Attorneys Animal Cruelty Advisory Committee.

Allie volunteers with King Street Cat Rescue in Alexandria, Virginia, a free-roaming no-kill cat orphanage, where she manages the website, photographs the cats, assists with publicity and marketing, and fosters cats and kittens. She also assists the St. Croix Animal Welfare Center Pets from Paradise Program by having shelter cats flown from St. Croix to Virginia so that they can be adopted into loving homes. Since visiting the island of St. Croix in January 2009 and seeing the need that the shelter has for mainland transfers and adoptions, she has helped numerous St. Croix cats travel to Virginia to be adopted through King Street Cats. She is also trained in energy healing as a Usui Reiki Master Practitioner, Advanced Integrated Energy Therapy Practitioner, and is a Certified Law of Attraction Counselor. Allie enjoys providing energy healing to abandoned and abused cats, as well as ballroom/ swing dancing, gardening, yoga, and practicing healthy eating and lifestyles.

You can do more at www.alliephillips.com.